W9-CFJ-919

The Oats, Peas, Beans
& Barley Cookbook

To the men and women whose long years
of painstaking research
have made this work possible
and
to the homemakers in whose hands
it may help to produce
the values which are above price,
this book is dedicated.

The Oats, Peas, Beans & Barley Cookbook

By Edith Young Cottrell

Research Nutritionist

Loma Linda University • Loma Linda, California

Published by

Woodbridge Press
®

Santa Barbara, California 93111

Published by
Woodbridge Press Publishing Company
Post Office Box 6189
Santa Barbara, California 93111

Copyright © 1974 by Edyth Young Cottrell

World Rights Reserved

All rights reserved. No part of this
publication may be reproduced, stored in
a retrieval system, or transmitted, in any form
or by any means, electronic, mechanical,
photocopying, recording, or otherwise, without
the prior written permission of the publisher.

Printed in the United States of America
Published Simultaneously in Canada

International Standard Book Numbers:
Cloth 0-912800-08-9
Soft Cover 0-912800-07-0
Loose Leaf 0-912800-06-2
Library of Congress Catalog Card Number: 73-77411

Third Printing, 1974

Acknowledgements

To express my gratitude for all the help I have received in the preparation of this book would require a volume in itself. It would cover an expanse of thirty years and include a host of helpers, many of whom I have never met. The first I wish to honor is Margie Bsharah Hill whose generosity enabled me to continue with my studies at the University of Washington.

The second is the late Dr. Clive McCay, formerly of Cornell University. My interest in improving the quality of foods by applying principles developed through nutrition research was a result of Doctor McCay's urgent appeal for the nutritional improvement of bakery products and cereal foods. He generously gave of his time in reading articles, evaluating visual materials, and writing letters of encouragement.

It is impossible to name all to whom I am indebted. In my heart is deep gratitude to each one whether names are mentioned or not.

Among those who have been of special help to me are A. J. Gordon and Don Spillman; my nephew Bill Dopp; his wife Francie and sister Marilyn. Esther and Ernest Mackie, Mrs. J. M. Rowland, Emma Loop, Helen Smith, the Luvene Hilde family, Kay Dower, Don and Melinda Vollmer, Dr. H. W. Vollmer — and Marion W. Vollmer who was of immense help in reading, consulting and in making many valuable suggestions.

My thanks to Dr. U. D. Register, Dr. Irma Vyhmeister, Dr. Claude Thurston, and Loma Linda Foods for their assistance in the animal growth studies which indicated the high nutritive quality of Soy-Oat Waffles.

To Dr. A. D. Butterfield for a financial grant for nutrition research which made possible the development of many of the recipes in this book.

To Loma Linda Foods, the Lassen Foundation, and the Pacific Union Conference for additional grants to carry on the program.

To Dr. Alan Magie, School of Environmental Health, Loma Linda University, and Dr. Malcolm Bourne, Cornell University, for assistance with the Cornell method of making soy milk.

To Cornell University for the generous gift of this method to the public.

To Dr. James Blankenship for his help in developing other formulas in the Soybean section.

To Dr. Register for reading the manuscript and giving valuable suggestions.

To Dr. Mervyn G. Hardinge, Lydia Sonnenberg, and Dr. Albert Sanchez for reading sections of the manuscript and for their helpful suggestions.

To Dr. Walter Roberts for his diligent help in preparing the section, *Your Health . . . Chance or Your Choice?*

To Drs. Bernell and Marjorie Baldwin for valuable help and guidance.

To Dr. Paul Y. Yakiku for his assistance in evaluating the quality of protein in various recipes.

To George W. Cummings and Jerry Crispin for invaluable assistance with the computer.

To Shirley Hustler, my statistician who has done most ably under adverse circumstances.

To Audrey Otto, Shirley Newell, Dena Schwartz, and Virginia Madruga for their faithful help with the typing of the manuscript.

To Elwyn Spaulding and Health Education Media for use of pictures as illustrations for the book.

To my large and wonderful family and to my friends who have tested recipes and have helped in determining acceptability.

Edith Young Cottrell

Contents

More of Everything
With Basic Foods

"Oats, peas, beans, and barley grow; oats, peas, beans, and barley grow . . ." are lines from an old-time song that accompanied an old-time fun game for children. Simple times; simple fun.

A review of the past discloses many things of intrinsic value, some of which we might do well to emulate. For one thing, simplicity: simplicity of diet, simplicity of living. Such, in their time, produced a hardy, healthy people.

"Simplicity is the keynote of good taste and saves a lot of time," someone said; an apt observation that applies as truly to foods as it does in other areas of life and we might well add, "often saves a lot of money."

Observation of the patterns of diet that have emerged through the ages and around the world disclose common, basic principles of good nutrition. These principles, developed unknowingly and through necessity can readily be explained by the newer knowledge of nutrition.

From the available and often scanty direct food crops many delicious recipes have evolved, providing an invaluable heritage from the past. It has been the purpose of the author to glean the best from these timeless favorites, apply them according to good principles of nutrition, and with the advantage of modern technology to present the modern housewife with recipes that are superior and, as often as possible, timesaving.

Why oats, peas, beans, and barley . . . and other such simple foods?
1. Because they are direct food crops — not secondary foods of animal origin, or processed, "fractioned" foods.
2. Because they are foods which, eaten together, give improved nutritive value.
3. Because, as direct food crops, they best utilize the land, producing the highest yield per acre of high-quality proteins, minerals, vitamins, and essential calories.
4. Because they are generally economical even though their nutritive quality is high.
5. Because many of them can be grown in the home garden, or even a small area in the back yard or in a flower border.
6. Because of the delicious goodness of these foods.
7. Just because . . . !

These direct products of nature offer **much, much more for your money,** not only in quantity and quality of foods but also in other values which are above price.

Plain, wholesome food prepared with simplicity is delicious and when eaten in moderation will promote health of body and mind. "Oats, peas, beans, and barley" may be said to symbolize all unrefined, direct food crops used in these recipes.

"Grains, fruits, nuts and vegetables constitute the diet chosen for us by our Creator. These foods prepared in as simple and natural a manner as possible are the most healthful and nourishing. They impart a strength, a power of endurance, and a vigor of intellect that are not afforded by a more complex and stimulating diet. . . . Daniel's clearness of mind and firmness of purpose, his strength of intellect in acquiring knowledge, were due in a great degree to the plainness of his diet, in connection with his life of prayer."[1] "The erect form, the firm, elastic step, the fair countenance, the undimmed senses, the untainted breath — all were so many certificates of good habits, insignia of the nobility with which nature honors those who are obedient to her laws."[2]

Simple, natural products of the earth provide the best nutrition.

My years of experience in teaching food preparation have brought the consciousness of the need for recipes using simple, basic, high-quality foodstuffs and for methods of preparation to enhance and retain their nutritive value.

Much work in nutrition research and food technology has helped to determine the nutritional effect on food values of supplementation or combining of vegetable proteins — as well as the effects of various methods of cookery. Adapting experimental evidence to food preparation makes it possible to retain the highest nutritive quality and, better yet, through protein supplementation, to substantially increase some values.

In the recipes contained in this book a sincere effort has been made to secure much more for your money by obtaining maximum nutritive quality through adapting the invaluable findings of nutrition research.

1. Ellen G. White, *Counsels on Diet and Foods* (Washington, D.C.: Review and Herald Publishing Association, 1946), pp. 81-82.
2. *Ibid.*, p. 28.

11

10 Objectives
of This Book

1. **Simplicity** — Use of simple, basic, available foodstuffs to prepare wholesome, appealing dishes. Use of few ingredients in a recipe and moderate variety in each meal.

"The use of direct food crops (grain crops, vegetables, and fruits) when whole-heartedly put to full use according to the knowledge of today, carries us further than we formerly supposed toward a food supply of optimal nutritional value."[1]

Limited use has been made of some foods that are not direct food crops such as milk and eggs, as well as some "convenience foods."

Special attention has been given to improvement of nutritive quality in recipes in which "fractioned" foods (such as gluten) are used by addition of some of the parts removed in processing.

2. **Variety** — Use of a wide variety of foodstuffs to meet a variety of needs arising from special health problems such as allergies, blood sugar abnormalities, low-cholesterol diets, and others.

3. **Low cholesterol** — Use of vegetable ingredients with polyunsaturated oils to prepare acceptable, adequate-protein foods; "sour cream," whipped topping, and other items on the restricted list to provide the interesting, satisfying, low-cholesterol diet "the doctor ordered."

4. **Limited use of sugar** — Use fresh or dried fruits and unsweetened fruit juices to prepare an interesting variety of delightful desserts.

12

5. **Improved quality of vegetable proteins** — Use of combinations of foodstuffs of vegetable origin to prepare foods with protein values comparable to those found in animal proteins. "Properly supplemented vegetable proteins cannot be distinguished nutritionally from those of animal origin."[2]

6. **Ample mineral and vitamin content** — Use of unrefined grains, nuts, fruits, and vegetables to supply an adequate store of minerals and vitamins in a balance provided by an all-wise Creator. Use of dark-green, leafy vegetables or fortified soy milk as sources of calcium, riboflavin, and vitamin A (fortified soy milk or brewers yeast for B_{12}) in case milk is restricted in the diet.

7. **Low cost** — Production of foods with acceptable tastes, textures, and satisfying qualities, often at a cost that is only a fraction of that for foods comparable in nutritive value. To make every food of the highest value possible at reasonable cost.[3]

8. **Time saving** — Use of simple methods and time-saving suggestions for the benefit of the busy mother and the homemaker with outside employment.

9. **Meal planning** — Use of a simple pattern as a quick guide in selecting the variety and amounts of foods necessary for good nutrition. Use of nutritional analyses as a check for those with special dietary problems.

10. **Optimal health** — The best possible use of the ability placed in our hands through scientific research "to deal with the values which are above price; for the health, happiness, and efficiency, and for the enhanced duration and dignity of human life."[4]

It has been demonstrated experimentally that improved diet gives improved mental development, alertness, general progress in studies, and the rate of learning specific things in children; and improvement in performance and efficiency in adults.

There is also clinical evidence that people living more largely on fruits, vegetables, and milk show less evidence of senility or degenerative diseases at a given age. There is evidence that the life cycle becomes longer when life has been lived on a higher health level throughout — that the prime of life may be lengthened as much as ten years.

1. Henry C. Sherman, "The Nutritional Improvement of Life," *Journal of the American Dietetic Association* 22:579. July, 1946.

2. R. Bressani and M. Behar, *Proceedings of the Sixth International Congress on Nutrition* (Edinburgh: E. and S. Livingston, 1964).

3. C.M. McCay, "Increasing the Use of Plant Proteins," *Federation Proceedings* 4:128. June, 1944.

4. Sherman, *op. cit.*, pp. 578, 579.

Mathematics
of a Good Diet

For the best diet, start with the best food: legumes, nuts, unrefined flour, cereal products or grains, and fresh fruits and vegetables whenever possible. Home gardens, even in the back yard or in a flower border of the city lot, provide healthful exercise and help to reduce the food budget. They may supply an abundance of fruits and vegetables, garden-fresh, at the very peak of their nutritional value.

ADD to the value of high quality foodstuffs by using a variety of foods together to furnish a good assortment of minerals and vitamins, and mutually supplementary values to improve protein quality and to provide adequate calories.

Avoid FRACTIONS, foods from which part of the natural nutrition value has been removed or lost in processing or handling. Use care in cleaning, storage, preparation, and cooking in order to retain the maximum values. Foods which lose part of their value through processing or through careless methods of handling and cooking are FRACTIONS.

BALANCE is essential and assured through selection of a variety of **unrefined foods** with their **natural balance** provided by an all-wise Creator. Empty calories supplied by sugary drinks, large use of sugar, refined flour and breakfast cereals, oils, and the like produce IMBALANCE.

"The deficient food products — chiefly exemplified by foods containing a great deal of refined sugar, syrups, bleached white bread and cake flour, heat-processed, sweetened cereals, and the popular cooking fats — are the 'empty calorie' foods that we should reduce to a minimum in our diets. Factory additions of vitamins to an inherently deficient food, such as bleached and chemically 'matured' flour, do not make a good food out of a poor one; moreover, one cannot balance a poorly chosen diet by taking vitamin and mineral dietary supplements."[1]

Do not SUBTRACT from the value by discarding peelings, valuable tops and outer leaves, liquids in which foods have been cooked, or by careless methods of handling or cooking.

MULTIPLY the value you receive by DIVIDING with the poor. "Is it not to deal thy bread to the hungry, and that thou bring the poor that are cast out to thy house? . . . Then shall thy light break forth as the morning, **and thine health shall spring forth speedily.**"Isaiah 58:7,8.

The Saviour taught us to pray: Give us this day our daily bread — not just "me and my children." Us includes our brothers and sisters around the circle of the globe. We may divide with the poor not alone by giving him food. There are three ways of "dealing bread to the hungry":

1. "We help a hungry man by giving him food,
2. . . . but to truly help him we must teach him to help himself." — Orville Freeman, former U.S. secretary of agriculture.
3. We also give when we eat in moderation of the direct food crops such as the grains, legumes, nuts, fruits, and vegetables which are quickly produced — making it possible to obtain larger yields of calories, proteins, vitamins, and minerals per acre to supply the world's food needs.

One acre of wheat will supply 27 times as many **calories,** 13 times as much **protein,** and 17 times as many **vitamins** as beef produced on one acre. The ratio per acre of soybeans to beef is: **calories,** 34 to 1; **protein,** 49 to 1; **vitamins,** 33 to 1. The ratio per acre of peanuts to beef is: **calories,** 28 to 1; **protein,** 16.6 to 1; **vitamins,** 11 to 1.[2]

Combinations of cereals and legumes have prevented or cured protein deficiency diseases in children. Dark-green, leafy vegetables contain a protein of growth-promoting

value as well as an abundant supply of minerals and vitamins. Since these foods can be produced in greater abundance and in much less time than meat proteins, a reduction
of one-third in the consumption of meat would increase the
world food supply very materially.

The number of additional people that could be fed if the
whole population of the United States were willing to ex-
change a third of their protein from meat and milk for that
from soybeans would run from ten to thirty millions.[3]

"As the world supply of complete animal proteins becomes
increasingly short, the economic significance of this concept
is evident. In developing countries, where protein deficiencies are endemic,... a well-planned vegetarian diet based
on the concept of mutual supplementation would appear to
be one logical solution to the protein problem."[4]

"If men today were simple in their habits, living in har-
mony with nature's laws ... there would be an abundant
supply for the needs of the human family. . . . But selfishness
and indulgence of unnatural taste have brought sin and
misery into the world, from excess on the one hand and from
want on the other."[5]

Instruction in better methods of raising food crops is
essential in the developing countries. Equally important in
preparing simple, well-balanced meals that combine foods
with mutual supplementary values to insure protein that is
adequate for child growth and pregnant women.

Both of these programs are being developed concurrently
at the present time.

Each of us can help "deal bread to the hungry" by eating
more simply, by using more of the direct food crops and by
sharing our knowledge with others. Each, in turn, will have
a more wholesome diet and, other things being equal, may
experience improved health, longer years of usefulness, and
greater satisfaction of living. Thus in DIVIDING with the
world's needy we are MULTIPLYING to ourselves blessing.
This is the consummation of "the mathematics of a good
diet."

1. U.S. Department of Agriculture, *Consumer Bulletin* (Washington, D.C.: Government Printing Office, February, 1961), p. 10.

2. U.S. Army Medical Service Graduate School, *Notes: Medical Basic Sciences Course* (Washington, D.C.: Government Printing Office, 1950-1953) II.

3. C.M. McCay, "Increasing the Use of Plant Proteins," *Federation Proceedings* 4:128. June, 1944.

4. Michael G. Wohl, *Modern Nutrition in Health and Disease – Dietotherapy* (Philadelphia: Lea and Febiger, 1968), pp. 113, 114.

5. Ellen G. White, *The Desire of Ages* (Mountain View, Calif.: Pacific Press Publishing Association, 1949), p. 346.

Entrées

The meal planning pattern has long been built around a protein-rich food — the "entrée."

The first recommended daily allowance for protein was high — approximately 120 grams per day, a standard derived from the amount eaten by German workers.

However, experimental studies have indicated that:

a. Body needs can be satisfied by much smaller quantities of protein.

Several food researchers "found that men could exist without apparent harm on intakes of protein from vegetable foods at a level of 30 to 40 g. a day; or 25 to 35 g. daily if one-third of the protein is supplied by animal foods."[1]

Garbanzo-Soy Patties provide superior-quality protein with a satisfying, meaty texture and taste – for pennies a serving!

b. Excessive protein in the diet is wasteful and may be injurious due to the extra work required of the liver and kidneys to break down protein to a fuel food and excrete the wastes.

"Each protein has an upper limit for utilization. Feeding more than that amount is inefficient and may put an excess burden on the organism to form and excrete organic compounds containing waste nitrogen."[2]

"What are we really doing to our bodies by giving them nutrients well beyond their needs as a result of our great fear of nutritional deficiencies? . . . To get rid of the additional protein means more work for the liver and the kidney, and these organs gradually hypertrophy to take care of the load."[3]

c. Protein adequate in quality and quantity may readily be supplied by a mixed vegetarian diet made up largely of direct food crops (non-animal, unrefined) prepared to retain their maximum nutrients.

"African children suffering from protein deficiency disease responded as quickly when fed a combination of corn and beans (their native foods) as when given milk."[4]

Here is a review of body needs and the improvement of protein quality through good combination in which one food supplements another in protein kind and quality.

Protein needs. Protein is a basic part of most of the body tissues and fluids. It is necessary for growth, body repair and maintenance, good blood, resistance to disease, and healing — in case of broken bones, burns, or other injuries.

Protein sources and structure. Protein is found in all growing things, both animal and vegetable. All proteins are composed of nitrogen containing building blocks called **amino acids.** The amino acids from vegetable sources are equal in value to those of animal origin.

The body is able to produce some of the amino acids necessary for growth and body maintenance from other nitrogen substances in the food. The amino acids that cannot be synthesized by the body are called **essential amino acids.**

The assortment and amount of essential amino acids in a food determines the quality rating of the protein. When all essential amino acids are present in sufficient quantity to meet the body needs, we rate the protein as "top quality."

Protein evaluation. Protein evaluation, based upon the essential amino acid content is called the **Essential Amino Acid Index** or the **Biological Value** of the protein and is computed on a percentage basis. The "passing grade" of protein for child growth is 70 percent; for adult maintenance, 60 percent. Higher ratings indicate superior quality.

Supplementation. Many foods contain proteins that are **limited** in one or more of the essential amino acids. (See following table.) This lack may be supplied by combining such foods with foods that are high in the **limited** amino acids.

This process is called **supplementation** and is just as simple as this example: bread is **low** in certain essential amino acids; pinto beans are **high** in the same amino acids; bread and beans together contain all the essential amino acids in good amounts; together they provide a protein of **good quality.** One slice of whole wheat bread with one-half cup cooked pinto beans has a protein rating of 78 — very good in growth-promoting value.

The same supplementary principle holds true for the proteins of a wide variety of cereal grains which may be supplemented (or improved) by combining with peas, soybeans, beans, lentils, garbanzos or any of a variety of legumes, nuts, dark-green, leafy vegetables, or milk.

Meeting protein needs. Proteins adequate in quantity and quality may be readily supplied by a mixed diet made up largely of direct food crops prepared to retain their maximum nutrients.

"From a nutritional point of view animal or vegetable proteins should not be differentiated. It is known today that the relative concentration of the amino acids, particularly of the essential ones, is the most important factor determining the biological value of a protein. . . . By combining different proteins in appropriate ways, vegetable proteins cannot be distinguished nutritionally from those of animal origin. The amino acids and not the proteins should be considered as the nutritional units."[5]

It is entirely unlikely that a normal, healthy adult obtaining all the calories necessary from a mixed diet of fruits, grains, nuts, and vegetables would develop a protein shortage.

"Bayliss said: 'Take care of the calories and the proteins will take care of themselves' because if dietaries are studied it is found that when the value of a mixed diet is adequate it generally contains 100 g. protein or even more."[6]

"The physician practicing in the United States is rarely confronted with a case of protein deficiency. In fact, most American adults are subsisting on diets providing two to five times the minimal requirements for protein."[7]

While it seems to be an established fact that adults who obtain sufficient calories from a mixed diet are assured of an ample protein supply, more careful consideration should be given to providing for the protein needs of children. The biological value required for child growth is higher than for adult maintenance. A meal may be so planned that the total protein is of excellent growth-promoting quality but if the child declines to eat some food that is served he may fail to receive adequate protein. For this reason each food prepared should be of the highest value possible at reasonable cost. It may be as simple as a bean sandwich or split pea chowder served over a slice of whole wheat bread.

Excessive use of sweets, sugary drinks, sugary cereals, snacks, empty calories of a wide variety pose the greatest problem as far as children are concerned.

The child who eats a simple, varied diet of unrefined foods of vegetable origin has little danger of shortages of protein, minerals, or vitamins.

"It is now known that suitable mixtures of vegetable proteins can replace satisfactorily the animal protein in the diet of the young child."[8]

Pregnant women and other persons in stress situations may similarly be assured of high-quality protein.

Adequate protein of good quality is also important in a reducing diet.

"There is little evidence, however, that even in children protein shortage is common in America, as is claimed by some authors. Probably the only large groups in danger of being deficient in protein, as well as in calories, and various nutrients, are young women and adolescent girls who place themselves on faddish reducing diets and attempt to lose weight without much justification and at an excessive rate."[9]

1. L. Jean Bogert, *Nutrition and Physical Fitness,* 8th ed. (Philadelphia: Saunders, 1966), pp. 106, 107.

2. M.L. Anson and John T. Edsall, "Advances in Protein Chemistry," *Biological Evaluation of Proteins,* ed. by J.B. Allison (New York: New York Academic Press, 1949), p. 115.

3. L.E. Holt, "Nutrition in a Changing World," *American Journal of Clinical Nutrition* 11:543. November, 1962.

4. Albert S. Whiting, Report on treatment of kwashiorkor victims, Muganeroe Hospital, Kibuye, Rwanda, Africa, 1973.

5. C.F. Mills and R. Passmore, *Proceedings of the Sixth International Congress on Nutrition* (Edinburgh: E. and S. Livingston, 1964), p. 182.

6. Samson Wright, *Applied Physiology* (London: Oxford University Press, 1965), p. 418.

7. Jean Mayer, "Amino Acid Requirements of Man," *Post graduate Medicine* 26:252. August, 1959.

8. Stanley Davidson, *et al., Human Nutrition and Dietetics* (Baltimore: Williams and Wilkins, 1959), p. 732.

9. Mayer, *Ibid.*

Biological Values of Food Proteins

The biological values* of many selected food proteins exceed the recommended protein quality of 60 for adults or 70 for infants when fed as the only source of protein.

Foods	Biological Values	Foods	Biological Values
Cereals		**Meat and poultry**	
Barley	64	Beef and veal	74
Buckwheat	77	Chicken	74
Oats	65	Fish	76
Rice, whole	73	Pork	74
polished	64		
Rye, whole	73	**Eggs, chicken**	94
milled	63		
Wheat, whole	65	**Milk and products**	
germ	74	Casein	72
gluten	40	Cheese, cheddar	72
		Milk (cow)	85
Legumes			
Chick peas	68	**Vegetables**	
Lima beans	67	Kale	64
Peas	64	Maize, sweet	73
Soybeans	73	Mustard (greens)	74
		Potato	73
Nuts and seeds		Sweet potato	72
Cashews	72		
Coconut	69	**Yeast and fungi**	
Cottonseed meal	67	Brewer's yeast	67
Pecans	60	Mushrooms	80
Pumpkin seed	63		
Sesame	62	**Recommended as**	
Sunflower	70	**adequate protein quality**	
Watermelon seeds	73	Adults	60
		Children	70

* Biological value is a measure of the proportion of the absorbed protein (nitrogen) that is retained by the body. For adequate nutrition the U.S. Food and Nutrition Board recommends 60 or above for adults and similarly 70 for infants and children.

— Courtesy of Albert Sanchez, Dr.P.H.

Cooking Beans
(Pilot Recipe)

2¼ cups dry beans (1 lb.)　　　2 teaspoons salt
7 cups boiling water

Method I
Sort beans carefully. **Wash** with cold water. **Add** beans to boiling water in large kettle. **Bring** to full boil. **Turn** off heat.

Let stand for an hour or more. **Bring** to boiling and let boil until tender (about an hour). **Add** salt and simmer until well done.

Note: There is some evidence that beans cooked by this method cause less flatulence (gas). **Yield: 6 servings.**

Method II
Soak beans overnight. **Drain. Add** drained beans to rapidly boiling water. **Heat** to boiling point. Boil gently until tender. **Add** salt. **Simmer** until well-done.

Note: Grease inside top edge of kettle to avoid boiling over.

Variation
Add one cup chopped onions to beans.

Baked Beans

2½ cups (1 lb.) dried beans　　¼ cup brown sugar
7 cups boiling water　　　　　2 tablespoons molasses
3½ cups tomatoes　　　　　　2 tablespoons oil
2 teaspoons salt　　　　　　　1 large, whole onion
½ cup tomato paste　　　　　1 teaspoon sweet basil

Follow general method in **Pilot Recipe** for cooking beans. **Add** all ingredients except onion and sweet basil. **Mix** well. **Put** in bean pot. **Place** whole, peeled onion in center.

Bake covered for 1 hour. **Remove** cover. **Add** sweet basil. **Stir** in with fork. **Bake** uncovered until liquid is thickened. **Yield: 6 servings.**

Beans with Bread

4 slices whole wheat bread
(homemade if possible,
¹/₂″ thick)

2 tablespoons margarine
2 cups beans with liquid

Follow method in **Pilot Recipe** for cooking beans. **Serve** hot beans over slices of bread spread with margarine. **Yield: 4 servings.**

Variation
Use whole wheat burger buns cut in half instead of bread.

Even simple foods like beans on a slice of whole wheat bread provide a fully-balanced protein equal in quality to beef.

Granddaughter's Favorite Patties

1½ cups cooked brown
   beans (soupy)
¼ cup bean liquid or
   vegetable broth
1 cup rolled oats
2 tablespoons food yeast

¼ cup chopped Brazil nuts
½ cup sautéed onions
½ teaspoon sage (fresh if
   possible)
salt – to taste

Follow general method in **Pilot Recipe** for cooking beans. **Measure** beans, add liquid. **Mash** beans, add other ingredients and mix well.

Drop from tablespoon or scoop into oiled baking dish or lightly oiled skillet.

Cover. Bake 10 minutes at 350°F. **Turn** and cover. **Let cook** an additional 15 minutes.

Serve with Soy Sour Cream (see recipe) or sauce of your choice. **Yield: 8 patties.**

Burritos

6 tortillas or lefse

3 cups mashed beans

Follow general method in **Pilot Recipe** for cooking beans. **Steam** tortillas or sprinkle lightly with water, place in pan, cover with foil. **Heat** in oven at 350°F., 10-15 minutes. **Cook** beans with onion and a little tomato purée if desired. Simmer until thick. Season with 1 tablespoon margarine. **Mash.**

Spread hot, mashed beans on hot tortillas. **Roll. Put** into oven until ready to serve. Or spread cold beans on cold tortillas, roll, freeze. **Heat** by baking just before serving. **Yield: 6 servings.**

Variations
1. Use lentils in place of mashed beans.
2. Mash garbanzos with mushroom sauce. Use in place of mashed beans.

Chili with Beans

2¹/₄ cups pinto beans
7 cups boiling water
3¹/₂ cups cooked tomatoes
¹/₂ cup tomato paste
1 cup sautéed onions
2 tablespoons oil
1 tablespoon sugar
¹/₂ tablespoon salt
¹/₄ teaspoon oregano

1 cup cooked wheat,
   commercial "vegemeat"
   such as Vegeburger or
   soaked, textured vegetable
   protein (TVP) granules
¹/₄ teaspoon cumin
¹/₂ teaspoon sweet basil
¹/₄ teaspoon garlic powder

Follow general method in **Pilot Recipe** for preparing beans. When tender add salt, sugar, onion, tomatoes, cooked wheat, oil, and tomato paste. **Let simmer** until liquid is evaporated to a thick consistency. **Add** herbs and garlic powder. **Let simmer** 20 minutes. **Serve** with crackers or zwieback. **Yield: 5 1-cup servings.**

Chili with beans, using wheat instead of ground beef or gluten – a delightful treat and pleasing variation!

Cuban Black Beans with Rice

The Beans

1½ cups black beans
4½ cups water
1 bay leaf
1 cup sautéed onions

1 cup chopped green
  peppers
2 tablespoons oil
1 teaspoon salt

Follow general method in **Pilot Recipe** for cooking beans, cooking until tender. **Sautée** onion in oil in skillet over low heat. Do not brown. **Add** chopped peppers and simmer 10 or 15 minutes. Add bay leaf and salt. **Add** to beans and let simmer until most of the water is absorbed and the flavor is well blended.

The Rice

1 cup brown rice
3½ cups water
1 cup cut green onions

1 teaspoon salt
1 tablespoon oil

Do not wash rice. **Examine** rice and remove any dark kernels. **Bring** salted water to rapid boil in top of double boiler or sauce pan. **Add** rice, stir. **Bring** to full boil.

Cook over boiling water **or** put in baking dish, cover, and bake at 350°F for 45 to 60 minutes. All water should be absorbed. Do not drain.

Serve in mounds on plate, topped with black beans. **Garnish** with green onions, tops and all, cut in even lengths. **Yield: 4 servings.**

Garbanzos (Chick Peas)

Garbanzos or Chick Peas are widely used in the Middle East. They are often combined in about equal portions with bulgar or "parched wheat," providing a protein of good quality. In some areas this garbanzo-wheat combination has, for centuries, provided the major part of the protein intake for a rugged people.

Whole garbanzos are somewhat difficult to cook to a soft texture without a pressure cooker. Soaking, freezing, and adding to rapidly boiling water helps to shorten the cooking time. Best results are secured when soft water is used.

Cooked, whole garbanzos may be used in a variety of interesting, tasty, nutritious entrées, and make a pleasing addition to salads.

Ground or blended garbanzos cook very quickly, have a very good "binding" value and may be widely used in combination with cereals and other legumes to prepare foods with a protein of high quality. Some of the recipes used have their background in Israel, Lebanon, and other eastern countries.

Garbanzos
(Pilot Recipe)

Method to soak and freeze: Use 2¼ cups garbanzos (1 lb.), examining carefully for husks, little stones, or dirt. Wash thoroughly. Soak overnight in 7 cups water. Use soft water for soaking and cooking to reduce the length of cooking time. Drain off water and rinse well. Garbanzos need careful washing and rinsing because the dirt tends to cling to the little creases.

Put garbanzos to drain on several thicknesses of paper towels. Place loosely on tray and freeze with garbanzos remaining separate. Store in cartons in freezer.

To cook: Use 2 cups frozen garbanzos, 2 cups rapidly boiling water, and 1 teaspoon salt. **Bring** water to boil in a kettle large enough to prevent boiling over. **Add** slowly the partly frozen garbanzos. If water stops boiling, **cover** kettle and let return to a boil. **Add** a few more at a time until all have been added.

Cover. Let boil quite briskly for an hour. **Add** salt. **Let boil** gently until of desired texture. **Season** as desired.

Garbanzo Burgers

2 cups soaked garbanzos
3/4 cup water
2 tablespoons soy sauce
1 small onion or 1/2 tea-
 spoon onion powder
1 1/2 cups soaked soybeans

1 teaspoon beef-like
 seasoning
sprinkle garlic powder
salt if necessary
1/2 cup water

Combine soaked garbanzos, water, onion (quartered) and other seasonings. **Blend** until medium-fine. **Pour** into bowl. **Grind** soybeans medium-fine. **Add** to garbanzo mixture.

Heat skillet to medium (325°F). **Oil** with 1 tablespoon oil or less.

Dip mixture with half-cup scoop or measuring cup, and flatten as much as desired to fit buns.

Cover, let cook 10 minutes or until nicely browned. **Turn,** cover, let cook for 10 minutes. **Reduce** heat, let cook for an additional 10 minutes. **Yield: 8 servings.**

Variations
1. Chicken-like seasoning may be used instead of beef-like seasoning.
2. May be baked as a loaf or in casserole.

Bulgar Chick Patties

1/2 cup bulgar wheat
1 cup boiling water
1/2 cup sautéed onions
2 tablespoons oil
1/2 teaspoon salt

1 teaspoon chicken-like
 seasoning
1/8 teaspoon garlic powder
1 cup soaked garbanzos
1/2 cup cold water

Stir bulgar wheat into boiling water in a heavy saucepan. **Stir** until evenly moistened, place on low heat. **Add** onions, oil, and seasonings. **Stir** with fork to mix. **Blend** soaked garbanzos with cold water until fine. **Add** to bulgar wheat. **Mix** well. **Drop** from tablespoon or scoop on lightly oiled skillet or baking dish.

Cover, bake at 350°F, 10 minutes. **Turn. Cover. Reduce** heat. **Cook** 15 minutes.

Serve with chopped parsley and Tahini Sauce (see recipe). **Yield: 6 servings.**

Garbanzo-Pimiento Cheese

2 cups soaked garbanzos (1 cup dry)	$1/2$ teaspoon onion powder
$1/3$ cup Brazil nuts	$1/8$ teaspoon garlic powder
$1/4$ cup food yeast with B_{12}	$1/4$ cup lemon juice
4-oz. jar pimientos	1 to $1/2$ cup water
	1 teaspoon salt

Soak garbanzos 24 hours in 3 cups water. **Drain** off soaking water. **Scrape** off brown husk from Brazil nuts and cut into medium-size pieces. **Combine** all the ingredients in blender. **Blend** until very fine.

Place in double boiler over boiling water. **Cook** covered 25-30 minutes or longer. **Stir** occasionally.

Mold in two small bread pans rinsed with cold water. Chill, unmold, slice and serve. **Yield: 2 pounds; 16 2-ounce servings.**

Variation
Garbanzo-Herb Cheese: Substitute fresh chives and sage or other herbs of your choice for pimientos.

Gluten Roast, Page 63

Soy-Oat Patties with Tomato Sauce, Page 53

Savory Roll'ems, Page 51

Burger Buns and Pizza Rolls (See Page 31)

Garbanzo-Gluten Roast with Vegetables, Page 37

Cuban Black Beans with Rice, Page 29

Soya Curd and Tofu, Pages 54, 55 (See Soybean Magic, Page 121)

Rice with Tofu, Pages 56, 57

Falafels

2 cups soaked garbanzos
1/2 cup cold water
1 clove garlic
2 tablespoons parsley

1/4 teaspoon cumin
1 teaspoon salt
1 cup savory crumbs
 (see recipe)

Wash garbanzos carefully and soak overnight in cold water sufficient to keep covered.

Grind 1 1/3 cup soaked garbanzos through a food chopper, using a medium blade. Or chop in blender if possible without water. **Blend** 2/3 cup soaked garbanzos with 1/2 cup cold water until very fine. **Add** minced parsley, chopped garlic, cumin, and salt. **Add** to ground gabanzos. **Mix.**

Dip with a dessert spoon, drop into bowl of savory crumbs. **Roll** and coat on all sides with crumbs. **Shape** with fingers if necessary. Approximately 1" x 1 1/2".

Place on ungreased baking pan. **Cover** with foil. Bake at 350°F covered 15 minutes. **Turn. Bake** uncovered 10 minutes.

Serve hot in Pita (falafel) buns with Tahini Sauce (see recipes), pieces of cucumber, tomato, lettuce, and green onion. **Yield: 8 servings; 24 3-falafel servings.**

Savory Crumbs

1/2 cup whole wheat bread
 crumbs (dry)
1/4 cup brewers flake yeast

1 tablespoon oil
2 drops butter flavoring

Combine and mix well.

Tahini Sauce

1 cup sesame seeds
 (not refined)
2 tablespoons oil

1/2 cup water
1 teaspoon salt
1/4 cup lemon juice

Blend seeds, oil, and water until seeds are fine. **Add** salt and lemon juice, and more water if necessary.

Falafels - Complete

1 pita (falafel bun) slit at top

Fill with: 3 falafels (garbanzo "meat balls"), diced cucumbers, tomatoes, green onions, and lettuce. Spoon over contents, 2 tablespoons of Tahini Sauce (see recipe).

Garbanzo Chicken-Style

2 cups soaked garbanzos
1 cup bran water
1 cup "do pep" (gluten flour)
1/4 cup wheat germ

1/4 cup flake yeast
2 teaspoons chicken-like
    seasoning
1 teaspoon salt

Blend garbanzos in Bran Water (see recipe). **Combine** remaining ingredients and mix. **Add** mixture to garbanzos. **Blend** at low speed to develop gluten. **Pour** into greased, flat baking dish. **Cover. Bake** at 350°F, 45 to 60 minutes.

Green Rice

2 cups cooked brown rice
1 cup grated garbanzo
    cheese – pimiento or herb
    (see recipe)
1 cup chopped chives

1 1/2 cups whipped,
    uncooked soybean
    concentrate (see recipe)
1 cup chopped parsley
salt if necessary

Combine rice, cheese, and Whipped Soybean Concentrate. **Bake in** covered baking dish 30 minutes.

Stir in chopped chives and parsley and salt if needed. **Bake** an additional 5 minutes. **Yield: 6 servings.**

Garbanzo-Gluten Roast

2 cups soaked garbanzos
or 1 cup dried
1½ cups bran water
(see recipe)
2 tablespoons soy sauce
1 teaspoon salt
⅛ teaspoon garlic powder

½ cup "do pep" (gluten
flour, 75% gluten)
1 cup sautéed onions
1 cup chopped celery
⅔ cup chopped Brazil nuts
2 tablespoons wheat germ

Follow generally method in **Pilot Recipe** for soaking the garbanzos. **Combine** 2 cups soaked garbanzos, oil, 1 cup water, soy sauce, and seasonings in blender. **Blend** at high speed until fine. **Pour** into bowl. **Rinse** blender with ½ cup water and add to mixture. (Or, **grind** in food chopper, put into bowl and add water).

Add chopped celery, nuts, and wheat germ. **Mix. Stir** in gluten flour and mix until well-blended and gluten is developed.

Shape in long roll. **Put** into well-greased oval baking dish

A Garbanzo-Gluten Roast, surrounded by colorful vegetables makes a "company dinner" main dish with high nutritional value.

or a bread pan. **Cover** with foil for first 45 minutes. **Bake** 1 hour at 350°F. **Yield: 1³/₄ pound; 8 3¹/₂-ounce servings.**

　1. Surround with vegetables (see following recipe).
　2. Bake with dressing.

Vegetables for Garbanzo-Gluten Roast

2 medium potatoes
8 carrots
¹/₂ cup water
20 small boiling onions, or
　5 medium onions quartered

1 teaspoon salt
2 tablespoons oil
1 teaspoon beef-like
　seasoning

Quarter potatoes. **Peel** onion, leaving whole. **Steam-boil** onions 15 minutes before putting into baking dish. **Cut** carrots into 3″ wedges.

Follow instructions of recipe for Garbanzo Gluten Roast.

Shape half of mixture into loaf in center of large, greased baking dish. Arrange vegetables around loaf. **Add** oil and seasoning to water and beat with fork to emulsify and spoon half over vegetables and roast. **Sprinkle** with salt.

Bake covered at 400°F, 45 minutes. **Uncover,** baste with remaining liquid and bake 15 minutes longer, to brown. **Yield: 4 servings.**

Garbanzo-Rice Patties

1¹/₂ cups soaked garbanzos
³/₄ cup water
1¹/₂ cups cooked rice
3 tablespoons brewers
　flake yeast
¹/₃ cup chopped Brazil nuts

¹/₂ teaspoon onion powder
1 teaspoon chicken-like
　seasoning
1 teaspoon salt
¹/₈ teaspoon garlic powder

Blend garbanzos in water until fine. **Put** in bowl. **Add** other ingredients and mix. **Drop** from tablespoon or scoop onto lightly oiled skillet or a baking dish that has been brushed lighty with oil. **Cover. Bake** at 350°F for 10 minutes. **Turn** and cover. **Bake** 10 minutes, reduce heat and let cook an additional 5 minutes.

Serve plain or with Soy Sour Cream (see recipe) or tomato sauce. **Yield: 4 2-patty servings.**

Garbanzo-Soy-Oat Patties
with Brazil Nuts

2 cups soaked garbanzos
1 cup soaked soybeans
1 1/2 cups water
1 cup rolled oats

1/3 cup chopped Brazil nuts
1 tablespoon oil
1 tablespoon salt
1/2 tablespoon onion powder

Follow generally method in recipe for Soy-Oat Patties, and add chopped Brazil nuts just before cooking. **Yield: 10 servings.**

Garbanzo-Wheat Roast or Patties

2 cups soaked garbanzos
1 cup cold water
2 cups cooked, unground
  wheat*
1/2 teaspoon sage

1 teaspoon salt
  (approximately)
2 teaspoons chicken-like
  seasoning or 2 teaspoons
  beef-like seasoning

Blend garbanzos in cold water until very fine. **Combine** with cooked wheat. **Add** seasonings and mix.

Bake in oiled covered pan for 30 minutes. **Uncover. Bake** an additional 15 minutes. Or drop from tablespoon on lightly oiled skillet or baking dish. **Bake** at 350°F for 10 minutes, covered. **Turn. Cover** and bake 10 minutes. **Reduce** heat and let cook an additional 10 minutes.

Serve plain or with tomato sauce or mushroom sauce. **Yield: 8 servings.**

*Follow method in recipe for cooking unground wheat.

Garbanzos with Onions
(Pilot Recipe)

2 cups soaked, frozen
　garbanzos
2 cups water
1 teaspoon salt
1 cup sautéed onions

1 tablespoon oil
2 tablespoons brewers
　flake yeast with B$_{12}$
　(optional)

Follow generally the method in **Pilot Recipe** instructions for preparing and cooking garbanzos until soft. **Add** onion, salt, oil, and brewers yeast. **Simmer** a half hour or until juice is thickened and flavor is absorbed by garbanzos.

Variation
1 can condensed mushroom soup may be added.

Garbanzos and Onions with Bulgar Wheat

3 cups garbanzos with
　onions
2 cups boiling water
1 tablespoon oil

$1/2$ teaspoon salt
1 teaspoon chicken-like
　seasoning
1 cup bulgar wheat

Follow generally the method in **Pilot Recipe** for Garbanzos with Onions. **Bring** water to boil in heavy sauce pan. **Add** oil, salt, and chicken-like seasoning.

Stir in bulgar wheat and let cook at low temperature for 15 minutes or until well-done. **Serve** topped with garbanzos and onions.

Garbanzos with Onions and Rice

The Garbanzos

2 cups cooked garbanzos with onions

Follow generally method in **Pilot Recipe** for Garbanzos with Onions.

The Rice

²/₃ cups brown rice	1 teaspoon salt
1 cup boiling water	1 tablespoon oil

Look rice over and remove any dark kernels. **Add** to rapidly boiling water in top of double boiler or sauce pan. **Stir. Cook** in double boiler over boiling water or in covered baking dish in oven at 350°F for 1 hour, or until water is absorbed. **Serve** in mounds on plate topped with garbanzos. **Garnish** with parsley. **Yield: 4 servings.**

Garbanzos with Onions and Whole Wheat Noodles

2 cups boiling water	1 cup whole wheat noodles,
¹/₄ teaspoon salt or to taste	dry (see recipe)
1 teaspoon chicken-like	2 cups cooked garbanzos
seasoning (optional)	with onions
1 tablespoon oil	parsley or green onions

Follow generally **Pilot Recipe** for Garbanzos with Onions. **Add** noodles to rapidly boiling, seasoned water. **Boil** gently for 15 minutes. or until tender. **Add** oil. **Stir** with fork. **Serve** in mounds on plate. **Top** with garbanzos and onions. **Garnish** with parsley or chopped green onions. Or garbanzos may be combined with noodles before serving.

Variations

1. Enriched noodles may be substituted with the same proportion and method.

2. 1 can condensed mushroom sauce may be added.

Whole Wheat Noodles

1 cup fine whole wheat flour	²/₃ cup cold water
¹/₃ cup soy flour	2 tablespoons oil
¹/₃ cup pure gluten flour	¹/₂ teaspoon salt

Combine dry ingredients in a medium-size bowl. **Mix** well with a fork. **Measure** water and oil together in cup. **Beat** with fork to emulsify. **Add** slowly to dry mixture, stirring flour with fork to moisten as evenly as possible.

Gather into a ball and knead thoroughly to develop the gluten, at least 5 minutes. The dough should be firm but pliable and not sticky.

Divide into two equal parts. Roll paper-thin on well-floured board. **Let dry** until surface is not sticky. **Turn** over. **Dry** other side.

Cut into 2$^1/_2$" strips. **Stack** 5 or 3 strips and cut into fine shreds with a sharp knife.

Spread out on clean tea towel to dry. These will keep well when thoroughly dried.

Cook until tender in boiling broth. (They may be cooked without drying if desired.)

Garbanzos for Thickening

1 cup soaked garbanzos $^2/_3$ cup water

Blend until fine.

6 level tablespoons thicken 1 cup water to soft custard consistency when cold.

9 level tablespoons thicken 1 cup water to regular custard consistency when cold.

12 level tablespoons thicken 1 cup water to very firm custard consistency when cold.

Lentils

1 cup lentils   3 cups boiling water
1 cup onions, sautéed   1$^1/_2$ teaspoons salt

Examine lentils carefully. **Wash. Add** to rapidly boiling water. **Boil gently 30 minutes. Add** salt and **cook** until tender. **Yield: 6 $^1/_2$-cup servings.**

Variations

1. **For quicker cooking:** Put 1 cup lentils to soak in 3 cups water, 6-8 hours. Drain water into a sauce pan and bring to boil. Add lentils. Boil gently 10 minutes. Add salt, oil, and other seasonings. Simmer briefly. Serve plain or over rice or whole wheat bread.

2. **For quickest cooking:** Soak lentils 24 hours. Drain in colander. Cover with damp paper towels (white). Let stand at room temperature until sprouted, rinse two or three times. When sprouted, cook 3-5 minutes in $1/4$ cup (or less) boiling water. Season and serve over rice, with soy sauce.

Lentil Roast

2 cups cooked lentils	$1/2$ cup Brazil nuts, chopped
1 cup cooked rice	$1^1/3$ teaspoons torula yeast
1 cup soaked garbanzos	1 teaspoon salt, or to taste
$1/2$ cup water	$1/2$ teaspoon sage

Cook lentils according to **Pilot Recipe** for lentils. **Measure** lentils into a bowl. **Add** rice. **Blend** garbanzos with water until fine and add to lentils and rice. **Add** chopped Brazil nuts and seasonings.

Bake in oiled baking dish or casserole 350°F, 45 minutes. **(Covered** for first 30 minutes, **uncovered** for last 15 minutes.)

Garnish with parsley and strips of pimiento or red bell pepper and serve. **Yield: 6 servings.**

Mary Lou's Lentil Tostados

2 cups chopped lettuce	3 cups cooked lentils
$1/2$ cup chopped green onions	$1/2$ cup salad dressing
$1/2$ cup sliced cucumbers	$1/2$ cup soy cream (see recipe) or evaporated milk
6 slices tomatoes	1 tablespoon lemon juice
6 slices whole wheat bread	$1/8$ teaspoon garlic powder

Arrange salad greens on platter or oval serving bowl with chopped lettuce in center. **Place** a row of sliced tomatoes on both sides, chopped green onions (with tops) on one end and sliced cucumbers on the other end. Or serve on individual salad plates.

Toast bread on cookie sheet under broiler, stack and bring to table the last minute, or toast at table as desired.

Heat lentils that have been cooked with onions and seasoned with margarine and cooked until thick. **Serve** in large bowl.

Put salad dressing in bowl, add Soy Cream or evaporated milk gradually while beating with a fork. **Add** lemon juice and garlic powder. **Spread** dressing over toast.

Spoon lentils on top. **Cover** with chopped salad greens. **Top** with slices of tomato. **Drizzle** salad dressing over all. **Eat** with fork. May be served buffet style. **Yield: 6 servings.**

Variations
1. May be served in lefse or tortilla as a tostado.
2. May be served in a pita bun in place of falafels.

Quick Lentil Roast

2 cups cooked lentils (soupy)	1/3 cup chopped celery
1/2 cup sautéed onion	1/3 cup chopped Brazil nuts
2/3 cup brown rice	1 teaspoon rubbed sage
(quick cooking)	2/3 teaspoon salt

Follow Pilot Recipe for cooking lentils. **Place** lentils in saucepan and bring to the boiling point. **Add** sautéed onions and rice and let boil gently while chopping celery and nuts. **Add** seasonings and, last of all, chopped celery and nuts. **Mix** well and place in a greased baking dish.

Bake at 350°F, 25 to 30 minutes. **Garnish** with parsley and strips of pimiento or red and green peppers. **Yield: 6 servings.**

Stew with Lentils

1 large onion
1 tablespoon oil
1 cup sliced carrots
1 cup celery, sliced
   diagonally
2 cups diced potatoes

$^1/_2$ cup dry lentils
$1^1/_2$ cups water
1 teaspoon salt
1 teaspoon beef-like
   flavoring

Follow generally method in **Pilot Recipe** for Stew with Tenderbits, except add lentils which have been soaked 3 hours or longer, in $1^1/_2$ cups water to simmered onions. **Bring** to boiling and add remaining ingredients as directed. **Yield: 4 servings.**

Macaroni and Cashew Nut Cheese

1 cup macaroni, enriched
1 qt. boiling water

$^1/_2$ teaspoon salt
1 tablespoon oil

Cheese Sauce

$^1/_2$ cup cashew nuts, raw
2 oz. pimientos (2 medium)
$^1/_4$ cup lemon juice
3 tablespoons brewers
   flake yeast with B_{12}

1 teaspoon salt
$^1/_4$ teaspoon onion powder
speck of garlic powder
$1^1/_2$ cups water

Crumbs

$^1/_4$ cup whole wheat crumbs
1 tablespoon brewers flake
   yeast with B_{12}

1 tablespoon oil
few drops of butter
   flavoring

Add macaroni to rapidly boiling, salted water in large kettle. **Let cook** uncovered 15 minutes. **Add** 1 tablespoon oil to cooked macaroni. **Mix** lightly.

While macaroni is cooking, combine cheese sauce in-gredients and blend until very fine. **Add** to macaroni. **Salt** to taste.

Put in casserole, **Cover. Bake** at 350°F, 30 minutes. **Sprinkle** with buttered crumbs, and bake uncovered 15 min-utes. Or omit putting in casserole. **Cook** 15 minutes on low heat after adding cheese mixture.

Serve with crumbs sprinkled over top. **Yield: 4 servings.**

Variations:

Use same amounts, methods, and ingredients as for above recipe except in place of cashew nuts:

1. Macaroni and Almond Cheese: substitute ¹/₂ cup raw almonds.

2. Macaroni and Peanut Cheese: substitute ¹/₂ cup raw peanuts which have been heated in oven 250°F for 20 minutes.

3. Macaroni and Soy Cheese: substitute 1 cup soaked soybeans.

4. Macaroni and Soya Cheese: substitute ³/₄ cup soy flour.

Note: These substitutes are suggested to make possible the selection of a supplement that may be easily obtained in the area, or one that is most suitable for the restricted diets.

Onion Pie

2 cups small boiling onions	1 teaspoon salt
or wedges of large onions	2 cups soy cream, raw
¹/₂ cup water	(see recipe)
1 tablespoon oil	¹/₂ cup cashew nuts

Simmer onions briefly in oil at low temperature. **Add** ¹/₂ cup water and salt. **Bring** to boiling point and boil gently until tender. **Add** Soy Cream to onions. **Add** cashew nuts.

Heat until thickened. **Fill** pastry shell and garnish.

Variation

Cooked garbanzos, chicken-like soya-meat, or other pro-tein food with texture may be used.

Rice Pastry for Onion and Other Savory Pies

²/₃ cups whipped soybean
concentrate raw
(see recipe)

2 cups cooked brown rice

Put cooked rice in bowl. **Mash** partially with fork. **Add** Soybean Concentrate. **Mix** with fork to blend thoroughly. **Grease** individual 5″ foil pans (deep pans are best).

Spoon mixture into pans and press into shape with fork; will fill six pans. **Set** in deep broiler pan and cover with cookie sheet.

Bake at 350°F, 25 minutes. **Fill** with onion or other savory filling. **Garnish** with parsley.

Variation

Rice Muffins: Use an additional one-half cup of rice and follow the method for Rice Pastry. Drop in oiled muffin pans. Make the size desired for finished muffins. Raisins may be added.

Peanut Butter-Carrot Loaf

¹/₃ cup peanut butter
¹/₃ cup tomato purée
¹/₂ teaspoon onion powder
2 teaspoons brown sugar
1 teaspoon salt

¹/₂ teaspoon garlic powder
¹/₂ teaspoon sweet basil
1 cup shredded carrots
1¹/₂ cups dry bread crumbs

Combine peanut butter and tomato purée and seasonings. **Beat** with fork to mix. Add shredded carrots and crumbs. **Mix. Put** into greased baking dish.

Cover with foil. **Bake** at 350°F, 30 to 40 minutes, **covered** until nicely browned. **Garnish** with parsley and serve. **Yield: 8 servings.**

Peanut-Carrot Roast

1 cup peanuts
1 cup soaked garbanzos
1 cup water
2 cups cooked rice

2 cups shredded carrots, raw
1 cup sautéed onions
1 teaspoon salt, or to taste
speck garlic powder

Place peanuts, garbanzos, and water in blender, and **chop** fine. **Combine** all ingredients. **Mix** well.

Bake in greased dish, 8″x 12″, at 350°F, 45 minutes (**covered** first 30 minutes, **uncovered** last 15 minutes), **garnish** with parsley. **Yield: 12 3-ounce servings.**

Esau's Pottage

1/3 cup rice
4 cups water
1 teaspoon salt

1 cup sautéed onions
2 tablespoons oil
1 cup lentils

Add rice to boiling salted water. **Cover** and let cook 15 minutes. **Add** onions, oil, and lentils. **Boil** until lentils are tender. Should be the consistency of mush.

Garnish with parsley and slices of red bell pepper or pimiento. **Serve** piping hot. **Yield: 6 servings.**

Golden Rice

1 1/2 cups cooked brown rice
2 1/2 cups finely grated carrots
1 1/2 cups soy sour cream
    concentrate (see recipe)

1/2 cup sautéed onions
1 teaspoon salt
1 tablespoon margarine

Combine ingredients, except 1/2 cup of carrots. **Pour** into a 1 1/2-quart baking dish or casserole. **Sprinkle** 1/2 cup grated carrots over top. **Cover.**

Let bake at 350° F, 20 minutes. **Remove** cover. **Bake** 15 minutes longer. **Dot** with margarine. **Yield: 6 servings.**

Variation

Add ½ cup peanut butter.

Golden Nuggets

2 cups soaked, yellow split peas	½ teaspoon onion powder
¾ cup water	¼ teaspoon sweet basil
½ teaspoon salt	⅛ teaspoon garlic powder
	1½ cups savory crumbs

Measure 1½ cups soaked peas, combine with water and seasonings and blend until very fine. Add remaining ½ cup of soaked peas whole or chop or grind medium-coarse before adding.

Dip with tablespoon and drop in bowl of crumbs, making one "nugget" at a time. **Roll** over to coat on all sides.

Bake in medium-hot (350°F) ungreased, covered skillet or baking dish — 10 minutes. **Turn. Bake** 10 minutes more, reduce heat and let cook 5 or 10 additional minutes. **Yield: 6 servings.**

Hurry-up Hearty Hash

2 cups cooked brown rice	2 tablespoons oil
½ cup sautéed onions	½ teaspoon salt
½ cup chopped celery	⅛ teaspoon garlic powder
½ cup chopped Brazil nuts	2 tablespoons soy sauce
¼ cup brewers flake yeast (with B$_{12}$)	2 cups shredded raw potatoes

Measure and combine all ingredients except potatoes. **Wash** potatoes, scrubbing off only part of skin with plastic or steel scouring pad. **Cut** out spots. **Shred** potatoes and add. **Mix.**

Spoon in thin layers into unoiled skillet or baking dish. Medium-hot, 350°F. **Cover. Let cook** 10 minutes. **Turn. Stir. Cover. Cook** 10 or 15 minutes longer. **Yield: 6 servings.**

Variations

1. Breadnut Hearty Hash. 1 cup stale whole wheat bread crumbs, instead of rice; $^1/_2$ cup Brazil nuts, or walnuts. (Other ingredients same as above.)

2. Walnut-Oat Patties. 2 cups shredded raw potatoes, 1 cup rolled oats, $^1/_2$ cup walnuts. (Other ingredients same as above.)

3. May be cooked as patties.

Tamale Pie

1 cup cornmeal (not degerminated)	1 cup ripe olives, pitted and sliced
$^3/_4$ cup boiling water	2 tablespoons oil
1 cup soaked garbanzos	$^1/_4$ cup chopped bell pepper, red and green
$^1/_2$ cup water	
1 cup whole-kernel corn	1 teaspoon salt
1$^3/_4$ cups tomatoes, cut in small pieces	$^1/_4$ teaspoon oregano
	$^1/_2$ teaspoon sweet basil
$^1/_2$ cup sautéed onions	

Pour boiling water over cornmeal and mix. **Blend** soaked garbanzos with water until chopped fine. **Add** to cornmeal mixture.

Combine other ingredients reserving slices of olives and 2 tablespoons of chopped peppers to garnish top. **Mix** well.

Put into flat, greased baking dish. **Decorate** top with slices of olives and bits of red and green peppers.

Cover with foil and bake at 375°F for 25 minutes. **Remove** foil. **Bake** 20 minutes longer or until firm and well done. **Yield: 12 servings.**

Savory Roll'ems

1 cup shredded potato (raw)
1 cup rolled oats
$1/2$ cup chopped Brazil nuts
2 tablespoons oil
$1/4$ cup brewers flake yeast
   (with B_{12})
$1/2$ teaspoon onion powder

6 6-inch wheat lefse or
   tortillas
$1/2$ teaspoon salt
$1/2$ teaspoon beef or
   chicken-like seasoning
1 can mushroom soup

Follow general method in **Pilot Recipe** for making Hurry-up Hearty Hash. **Mix** ingredients well, except mushroom soup. **Boil** undiluted mushroom soup. (Add 2 tablespoons of soup to mixture if needed for moisture.) **Place** large spoonful of mixture in center of each lefse or tortilla and roll.

Place in baking dish. **Cover** partially with mushroom soup. Bake at 350°F for 10 minutes, or may be served without additional heating. **Yield: 6 servings.**

Soybeans — Prairie Gold
(Pilot Recipe)

Soybeans are difficult to cook tender without a pressure cooker. Freezing the soaked soybeans helps to shorten the cooking time.

Method to soak and freeze: Look soybeans over for foreign particles. Wash in colander or strainer. Soak overnight, using more than three times as much water as beans. (Use of soft, or spring water in soaking and cooking helps to reduce cooking time.) Drain. Dry partially on several thicknesses of paper towels.

Spread in single layer on large cookie sheets and freeze. The beans should freeze separately. They may be cooked at once or stored in cartons in the freezer. It is well to have a store of soaked, frozen soybeans and garbanzos on hand for immediate use in case of emergency.

To cook: Use equal amounts of frozen beans and boiling

Soybeans, double in volume when soaked, are the basis of many healthful entrées as well as products to replace eggs and milk.

water with ½ teaspoon salt to each cup of beans. (Do not add salt until beans have cooked at least an hour.) Add frozen beans gradually to the rapidly boiling water, a few at a time so the water will not stop boiling. Boil gently for 1½ hours, or until tender.

Baked Soybeans

2⅛ cups soybeans (dry)	¼ cup brown sugar
3½ cups tomatoes	(packed)
(1 No. 2½ can)	2 teaspoons salt
1 cup sautéed onions	¼ cup lemon juice
¼ cup oil	1 teaspoon sweet basil
6½ cups water	½ cup tomato paste

52

Follow general method in **Pilot Recipe** for cooking soybeans. **Drain** juice from No. $2^1/2$ can of tomatoes and add to sautéed onions in a heavy skillet. **Simmer. Cut** tomatoes in small pieces and add to juice. **Add** brown sugar, oil, and salt. **Mix. Add** to cooked soybeans.

Bake at 350°F until juice is thickened. **Add** lemon juice and sweet basil. **Add** $^1/2$ can plain tomato paste. **Season** to taste. **Serve. Yield: 8 servings.**

Soy-Oat Patties with Tomato Sauce

The Patties

1 cup soaked soybeans	1 tablespoon oil
$^1/2$ cup water	$^1/4$ teaspoon onion powder
2 tablespoons flake yeast or	speck garlic powder
1 tablespoon powdered	1 teaspoon Italian seasoning
yeast	$^1/2$ teaspoon salt (or to taste)
1 tablespoon soy sauce	$^5/8$ cups rolled oats, regular

Combine all ingredients except rolled oats in blender and chop fine; or, beans may be ground in a food chopper and combined with other ingredients. **Place** in bowl. **Add** rolled oats and let stand 10 minutes to absorb moisture.

Drop from tablespoon or half-cup scoop on oiled baking pan or electric skillet. **Cover.**

Bake at 350°F for 10 minutes until nicely browned. **Turn. Cover** and bake additional 10 minutes. **Reduce heat** and cook 10 minutes more. **Serve** with tomato sauce. **Yield: 4 2-patty servings.**

The Tomato Sauce

2 cups cooked tomatoes	1 tablespoon oil
$^1/2$ cup sautéed onions	1 tablespoon sugar
$^1/2$ cup chopped green	$^1/2$ teaspoon salt
pepper	1 teaspoon sweet basil

Add sautéed onions and chopped pepper to juice of tomatoes in sauce pan and bring to boil. **Let simmer** until reduced about half in volume. **Cut** tomatoes in small pieces or mash and add with seasoning to juice. **Let simmer** briefly. (Should be quite thick.) **Serve** over patties.

Variation

Crumble patties into tomato sauce. Add $1/4$ teaspoon each cumin and oregano. May be served on crisp lefse or as pizza filling.

Tofu

6 cups soaked soybeans	$1^1/2$ to 2 tablespoons
9 cups boiling water	calcium lactate or
3 teaspoons oil	calcium carbonate
1 tablet Vitamin B_{12}	1 tablespoon or more
	lemon juice

Follow recipe for Soy Milk. **Blend** 2 cups of soaked beans in 2 cups boiling water until very fine. **Strain. Squeeze** out as much liquid as possible.

Blend briefly with 1 teaspoon oil and $1/3$ of the seasoning. **Place** in top of double boiler over boiling water. **Repeat** process until all beans are blended and all liquid in double boiler.

Cook for 20 minutes over rapidly boiling water. **Remove** from heat. **Add** dissolved B_{12} tablet.

Dissolve calcium salt in 1 cup of boiling water. **Add** 3 cups boiling water to hot soy milk and check temperature with thermometer. Temperature should be 180°F when dissolved calcium is added. **Stir** gently to mix.

Add lemon juice, stirring gently until precipitation is complete, indicated by the formation of a clear yellowish liquid and the separation of a solid white precipitate.

Allow to stand for a few minutes to enable curd to form into a large mass which gradually sinks to the bottom of the container.

(The liquid which accumulates on the top is whey, which contains soluble proteins, minerals, and vitamins, and may be used in many ways to prepare delicious foods.)

Drain off whey, measure a quart into a flat container and chill.

Put curd into a strainer, colander, or press lined with cheesecloth. **Fold** cloth over top. **Place** plate on top and set weight on top to press out extra liquid. **Let stand** for few minutes until very firm.

Put tofu into a large bowl and cover with chilled, seasoned whey. **Cover. Let stand** in refrigerator until seasoning permeates the mass.

Variations

Several seasonings may be used: coconut flavoring, pimiento, beef-like, chicken-like.

Soya Curd: Follow method for Tofu, except do not strain the blended soybeans. Put pulp and all into top of double boiler and proceed as for tofu. This will provide a more crumbly cheese that has many uses.

Creamed Curd Cheese
(May Be Used as Cottage Cheese)

2 cups soya curd (see recipe)   1 cup soy sour cream
½ teaspoon salt

Mash soya curd. **Add** salt and mix well. **Add** Soy Sour Cream. **Mix. Chill. Serve. Yield: 6 ½-cup servings.**

Variations
1. Add ½ cup chopped chives.
2. Add drained, chilled pineapple tid bits.
3. Add ¼ cup chopped walnuts, Brazil nuts, or almonds.
4. Serve in peach, pear, or cantaloupe halves.
5. Serve a scoop in potato soup, or other vegetable or legume soup.

Scrambled Tofu

1 cup uncooked soybean concentrate (see recipe)	1/4 teaspoon tumeric
1/2 teaspoon salt	2 tablespoon oil
1/2 teaspoon chicken-like seasoning	1/2 teaspoon lecithin
	2 cups mashed tofu (see recipe)

Combine concentrate and seasonings. **Blend** until smooth and light. **Add** oil gradually. **Add** lecithin. **Fold** into Tofu.

Coat skillet with small amount of lecithin. **Heat** to 350°F. **Add** tofu mixture. **Cover. Cook** 5 minutes. Stir from bottom and fold over. **Cover. Reduce** heat. **Cook** 10 minutes.

Variations

1. With Green Onions: Add 1/2 cup sautéed green onions before putting into skillet.

2. With "Baco Chips": Add 1/4 cup Baco Chips (textured soy protein).

3. Omelet: Follow method in recipe for Scrambled Tofu, except mash tofu very fine before folding into whipped concentrate. Spread out evenly in hot skillet. Cover. Let cook for 10 minutes. Crease center lightly. Fold over. Cover. Turn off heat. Cook an additional 5 minutes. Serve plain or with cream or tomato sauce. Creamed filling may be added before folding over.

4. With Soy Sauce: Add 2 tablespoons soy sauce and 1 cup oatmeal.

Rice with Tofu — Chicken Style

Preparing the Rice

1 cup brown rice	1 teaspoon chicken-like seasoning (optional)
3 cups whey from tofu	
1/2 teaspoon salt	

Put rice in flat dish. **Sort** out any dark kernels, weed seed, or foreign particles. **Bring** whey to rapid boil in top of double boiler with tight-fitting cover. **Add** rice.

Cover. Bring to boil. **Place** over boiling water and keep boiling gently for one hour. Water should all be absorbed and kernels should be separate and fluffy.

Preparing the Tofu

2 cups cubed tofu (see recipe)	1/2 cup savory crumbs

Leave tofu cubes in whey until ready to use. **Roll** wet cubes in Savory Crumbs to coat well on all sides.

Place in oven at 350°F for 20 minutes before serving time.

Preparing the Sauce

2 cups whey	1/4 cup flour which has been
1 teaspoon chicken-like seasoning	treated in oven
1 teaspoon salt, or to taste	1 tablespoon oil or margarine

Combine 1/2 cup whey with flour and stir until smooth. **Heat** remaining whey in sauce pan. **Stir** flour mixture into boiling whey. **Stir** until thickened. **Let cook** on low heat for 5 minutes.

Serve rice on large platter. **Top** with chicken-like sauce. **Arrange** tofu cubes on top. **Serve** extra sauce in pitcher or gravy boat. **Yield: 4 servings.**

Akara Balls
(Nigerian Dish)

2 cups black-eyed peas
1½ cups water
1 teaspoon chicken-like
  seasoning

1 teaspoon salt
½ cup savory crumbs
  (see recipe)

Soak the peas for 30 minutes or longer; skins should slip freely.

Remove from water and place on pastry board, a little at a time. **Roll** with rolling pin with enough pressure to separate peas into two pieces.

Return all peas into mixing bowl and fill with tap water. The hulls will float to the top of the bowl. **Pour** the top away. **Refill** the bowl with water, stir, and **pour** the top away. **Continue** until the hulls are removed. **Drain** all water away and leave in refrigerator overnight. This will make peas easier to grind.

Put ½ cup of water in blender. **Add** ⅓ of the skinned peas. Use a spatula to turn the top of the peas as they grind so that they will rotate easily and continuously. **Grind** until smooth. **Complete** grinding the others in the same way.

Put ground beans in a mixing bowl. **Add** salt and chicken seasoning. **Beat** with a wooden spoon 100 strokes.

Dip with dessert spoon and drop in bowl of Savory Crumbs. **Roll** over to coat with crumbs.

Place on cookie sheet. **Cover** with foil. **Bake** at 350°F, 20 minutes. **Remove** cover and bake another 15 minutes.

Serve plain or with mushroom or tomato sauce.

Gluten Entrées

Gluten itself does not offer a high quality protein and has other nutritional deficiencies characteristic of "fractioned foods," foods not in their whole, original state. Yet, because gluten is widely used as a vegetarian protein, these recipes and suggestions are offered for convenience sake. Nevertheless, they should be used with nutritional supplementation in mind. See pages 21; 236-238.

Gluten from Whole Wheat Flour
(Pilot Recipe)

6 cups high-protein whole   2 cups cold water
   wheat flour

To prepare dough: Measure flour into bowl. **Add** water slowly, while stirring with a fork to moisten as evenly as possible. **Use** just enough water to make a stiff dough. **Knead** well to develop the gluten. **Place** in bowl and flatten slightly. **Cover** with 2½ cups cold water and let stand at least one-half hour.

To wash out gluten: Use water in which the gluten was soaked. **Work** the dough with the fingers, beginning at the edge. **Break** off sections as starch is washed out and place in another bowl.

Continue until the whole mass has been worked. The water will become thick. **Drain** through wire strainer into a bowl. **Use** a rubber spatula to lift the bran from the sides and bottom of the strainer and allow the liquid to drain through.

Pour into wide-mouth glass jars. **Use** 2 cups cold water at a time. **Pour** over gluten. **Work** with fingers until water becomes thick with starch and bran.

Drain through strainer and repeat until most of the starch and bran have been washed out and the gluten is smooth and elastic. Total amount of water used, about 3 quarts. A small amount of bran improves texture.

Gluten is now ready to be made into a roast, or it may be cut into slices and boiled to be used as "steaks" or "burger." All by-products may be used.

Dip one cup of liquid from the tops of jars of rinse water. **Pour** over one cup of bran and let soak.

Set gluten and jars of rinse liquid to chill gluten and allow rinse water to separate. Three layers will form.

Layer	Content	Uses
1	Clear liquid	Boiling gluten, making sauces, soups, gravy, cooking cereals.
2	Mixture of gluten, small particles of bran and water	With clear liquid for making bread, rolls, waffles.
3	Starch	Thickening or laundry starch. Some may be used at once; the rest, dry quickly and store.

Gluten Supreme
(with nutritional reinforcement)

gluten produced by
  Pilot Recipe
3 cups clear rinse liquid
1 cup soaked bran
1 cup water
1 large onion
1 cup celery tops and stalks
1/4 cup brewers powdererd
  yeast with B$_{12}$

1/2 cup chopped parsley
2 tablespoons chicken-like
  seasoning
1 teaspoon salt or 2 tablespoons beef-like seasoning
2 tablespoons soy sauce
1/2 teaspoon salt
1 tablespoon oil

Blend soaked bran and one cup rinse liquid at high speed about one minute. **Pour** through strainer into large kettle. **Return** bran to blender. **Add** one cup rinse liquid. **Repeat** blending and straining process. **Rinse** bran with one cup clear water. **Press** out as much liquid as possible. **Discard** bran. **Add** remaining rinse liquid.

Peel onion. **Chop** fine. **Add** all seasonings to liquid. **Cover.** **Bring** to boiling point.

Shape gluten into long roll. **Cut** with kitchen shears or sharp knife into ten equal pieces. **Bring** liquid to rapid boil.

Flatten pieces of gluten with fingers into "steaks" and add one at a time to boiling broth. If boiling stops put cover on kettle until full boil is resumed. **Continue** adding gluten pieces one at a time.

Keep boiling. Gluten will sink to bottom and rise when partly cooked. **Move** with large fork if too crowded. **Cover.**

Boil gently for one hour. Most of liquid should be absorbed. Steaks should not stick. **Add** oil when liquid is nearly gone. **Reduce** heat.

◆

Savory Steaks with Mushroom Sauce

6 gluten steaks (see above)	1 4-ounce can chopped
1/2 cup savory crumbs	mushrooms
(see recipe)	2 tablespoons brewers flake
2 teaspoons moist starch	yeast with B_{12}
from above process	1 teaspoon chicken-like
2 tablespoons wheat germ	seasoning

Roll steaks in crumbs. **Bake** on ungreased cookie sheet 20 to 25 minutes at 350°F.

To make sauce, **drain** chopped mushrooms and put in kettle. **Simmer.** Combine mushroom liquid with starch. **Stir** until smooth. **Add** liquid if necessary to make two cups.

Boil. Add starch mixture. **Stir** until thickened and smooth. **Add** seasoning and salt if necessary. **Serve** on steaks.

Variations

1. One can undiluted cream of mushroom soup may be used in place of chopped mushrooms, liquid, and starch if liquid is mostly absorbed.

2. Steaks may be cut in strips before rolling in crumbs. Bake 15 to 20 minutes. Follow recipe for making sauce for Savory Pepper Steaklets.

3. Steaks may be ground and made into burgers; follow recipe.

Savory Steaks
(with restored vitamins and minerals)

2 cups bran	¹/₄ cup wheat germ
6 cups water	¹/₄ cup soy flour
2 tablespoons soy sauce	1 teaspoon beef-like
1 cup chopped celery tops	seasoning
1 cup chopped onions	¹/₂ teaspoon onion powder
1 teaspoon salt	¹/₈ teaspoon garlic powder
1 cup pure gluten flour	¹/₂ teaspoon salt
("do pep")	1 cup savory crumbs
¹/₄ cup brewers flake yeast	(see recipe)

Soak bran in 2 cups of water overnight. **Add** 1 cup water. **Blend** at high speed. **Strain. Return** bran to blender. **Add** 2 cups water. **Blend. Strain. Rinse** bran with 1 cup water. **Measure** 1 cup bran water into bowl. **Add** soy sauce.

Combine "do pep," brewer's yeast, wheat germ, soy flour, seasonings in another bowl. **Mix** well. **Add** gradually to bran water, stirring while adding.

Beat mixture and knead to develop gluten. **Shape** into a long roll, cut into 12 equal pieces. **Chill.**

Heat remaining bran water in large kettle. **Add** celery, onion, and seasoning, bring to boil.

Flatten pieces of gluten one at a time and drop into boiling water. **Repeat** until all gluten has been used. **Cover.** The pieces will sink to bottom until partly cooked and then will rise. **Boil** for an hour. Liquid should be mostly absorbed.

To prepare for serving: **Roll** in Savory Crumbs. **Place** on ungreased cookie sheet. **Bake** at 350°F for 25 minutes. **Serve** plain or with sauce of your choice. **Yield: 10 3-ounce steaks.**

Savory Pepper Steaklets

6 to 8 gluten steaks from above process	2 medium peppers, green or green and red
2 tablespoons oil	2½ cups water
½ cup sautéed onions	1 tablespoon soy sauce

Cut steaks into thin strips. **Roll** in savory crumbs. **Brown** lightly in oil, turning occasionally. **Stir** in sliced peppers, onion soup and 2 cups water and soy sauce. **Cover. Simmer** 10 minutes.

If not thickened sufficiently stir in flour or cornstarch moistened with water. **Serve** over rice with a green salad. **Yield: 6 servings.**

Gluten Roast

1 cup sautéed onions	½ cup chopped nuts:
1 cup chopped celery	walnuts, Brazil nuts,
½ cup bran	or others
2 cups soaked garbanzos	salt to taste
1 teaspoon chicken-like seasoning	basting liquid:
2 tablespoons wheat germ	¼ cup water
1 tablespoon oil	1 teaspoon chicken-like seasoning

Shape gluten into long roll. **Cut** into pieces. **Grind** through food chopper with other ingredients using medium-fine blade. **Grind** through a second time.

Shape into roast. **Place** in greased baking dish. **Cover. Bake** at 350°F for 30 minutes.

Surround with dressing. **Cover.** Bake 30 minutes. **Uncover. Baste** with basting mixture. **Bake** uncovered 15 minutes.

Beefless Burgers

5 gluten steaks from
   above process
1 cup soaked garbanzos
1 cup sautéed onions
2 tablespoons oil

$1/8$ teaspoon garlic salt
salt to taste
$1/2$ cup savory crumbs
   (see recipe)

Grind steaks using medium blade. **Grind** garbanzos using fine blade. **Combine** all ingredients except Savory Crumbs. **Mix** well. **Shape** into patties. **Roll** in crumbs.

Bake on ungreased cookie sheet at 350°F for 25 minutes. **Serve** plain or in burger buns with onion slices, lettuce, and burger relish.

Loma Linda Vegeburgers

1 cup vegetarian "burger"
1 cup soaked garbanzos
$1/2$ cup bran water
   (see recipe)
2 tablespoons wheat germ

$1/2$ cup sautéed onions
$1/2$ teaspoon salt
$1/2$ teaspoon sage
1 tablespoon oil

Measure vegeburger into a mixing bowl. **Blend** soaked garbanzos in bran water. **Add** to vegeburger. **Add** remaining ingredients. **Mix** well. **Shape** into patties. **Bake** in lightly oiled covered skillet at 350°F, 10 minutes. **Turn. Cover. Bake** an additional 10 minutes.

Note: Test the heat by baking a trial patty. It should be a nice, light brown. If too hot lower heat.

The bran gives a very desirable crunchiness as well as adding to the nutritive value. **Yield: 6 servings.**

Preparation of Bran Water

Crude bran produced in the milling of white flour is an excellent source of minerals and vitamins of the B complex. This bran may be secured at low cost at specialty food stores or the manager of your market may honor the request of a group to obtain it. Bran has extra leavening ability and will produce extra lightness when added to bread. To obtain a large portion of the nutritive value without the roughage, the bran may be soaked and the water used. When flours having low percentages of gluten are used in breadmaking, volume or lightness may be greatly improved by adding small amounts of gluten flour or refined white flour. Bran water and wheat germ may be used with these flours to improve nutritive quality.

Bran Water

2 cups bran, crude   3 cups water

Soak bran overnight in water. **Put** in blender. **Blend** one minute. **Drain** through the strainer. **Return** bran to blender. **Add** 2 cups hot water. **Blend** about one minute.

Strain into the same dish with first lot. **Squeeze** out as much of the liquid as possible. **Rinse** with 1 cup water. **Discard** the remains of the bran.

Note: This bran water may be used as liquid in making any bread, in cooking cereal, in making entrées, stuffings, and whenever white flour or gluten flour is used in a recipe.

Approximate proportions: Bran is 14% of wheat. Wheat germ is $1^1/_2$-$2^1/_2$% of wheat.

The mother's gift of love — with the loaf of bread she is giving herself, her strength to her family. Her hands are intimately in contact throughout the process of kneading, shaping, slicing, and serving. Her strength is required in developing the dough to impart the quality of lightness, tenderness, and texture which makes the bread more digestible and health-promoting.

Her intelligence and love promotes the selection of ingredients that will provide the best development for her family, physically and mentally, and will insure steady nerves and happy dispositions. Her gift is a symbol of the greater gift, given us by our loving Father, the gift of the Bread of Life.

Breadmaking
— With Artistry and Love

*Here are some of the steps described on Page 82
in the making of Pioneer Soy Bread — similar
to those that will produce any of the
delightful breads in this book.*

Ingredients assembled

Order of mixing is important

Beating incorporates air

. . . and develops gluten

Kneading on floured board

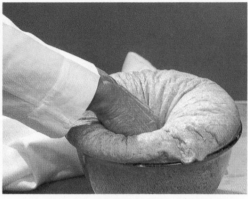

Punching down after rising

Dividing into loaves

Forming the loaves

. . . and into the pans

. . . and out of the oven!
(oiling optional)

Breads

Can you think of bread as a basic source of protein? Listen: "Grain products are still the staff of life, . . . the largest contributors of calories and protein to . . . the world as a whole."[1]

As to our future diet, "The bulk of . . . future needs will be met by conventional plant proteins; . . . even now cereals furnish a larger proportion of protein in human diets than all other sources combined in both developing countries and the world as a whole."[2]

How can your daily bread become a high-quality protein source? "About 5 percent soy flour is added to breads without adversely affecting baking characteristics and makes combined proteins in a bread more nutritious and comparable to quality of proteins in milk or meat. . . . Yet, it doesn't impair grain, loaf volume, texture, and crumb color. Because of its moisture-retaining property, it enhances eating quality through improved tenderness."[3]

The staff of life! "Bread is the real staff of life, and therefore every cook should excel in making it. . . . There is more religion in a good loaf of bread than many think."[4]

1. Henry C. Sherman, "The Nutritional Improvement of Life," *Journal of the American Dietetic Association* 22: 557. July, 1946.

2. Nevin S. Schrimshaw, "Nature of Protein Requirements; Ways They Can Be Met in Tomorrow's World," *Journal of the American Dietetic Association* 54:94. February, 1969.

3. John V. Ziemba, *Food Engineering* 38 (5) 82, 1966.

4. Ellen G. White, *Counsels on Diet and Foods.* (Washington, D.C.: Review and Herald Publishing Association, 1948), pp. 315-316.

Home-Baked Bread — Secrets for Success

Ingredients — Flour

Breadmaking: hard wheat, high protein (gluten)
Pastry: soft wheat, low protein (gluten)

Hard, red spring wheat	14.0% protein
Hard, red winter wheat	12.3% protein
Soft, red winter wheat	10.2% protein

Whole Wheat Flour

Protein: adequate for adult maintenance — biological value, 65; minerals and vitamins — excellent source.

A rating of 60 meets adult requirements; 70, childrens' requirements.

Fine grind better for breadmaking — can be used by more people.

White Flour

Protein: inadequate for adult maintenance — biological value, 52; loss in refining (in amount), 11 percent; loss in refining (quality), 20 percent.

Minerals and vitamins: losses ranging from 10 to 90 percent.

Number of minerals and vitamins with known losses, 20; number of minerals and vitamins replaced in "enrichment" process, 4 — 16 vitamins and minerals *not replaced*.

Gluten Flour

Often called "do pep" — 75 percent gluten, 25 percent patent flour.

Protein: biological value, 40; small quantities added to improve bread — increases volume — used by bakers for years. Add flours highest in gluten first and beat to develop the gluten texture.

Especially desirable when ingredients low in gluten are used: soy flour, wheat germ, rye, and other flours. Available at bakeries, food specialty stores, or request your market manager to stock.

Soy Flour

Excellent in supplementary value. "About 5 percent soy flour is added to breads without adversely affecting baking characteristics. Incorporation makes combined proteins in a bread more nutritious and comparable to quality of proteins in milk or meat. . . . Yet, it doesn't impair grain, loaf volume, texture and crumb color. Because of its moisture-retaining property it enhances eating quality through improved tenderness." — John V. Ziemba, *op. cit.*

Prevents staling; browns crust nicely.

Rye, Oat, other Flours

A combination of flours is more nutritious than one flour alone. Variety in breads is desirable.

Wheat Germ

Very good supplementary value; high vitamin values.

Other Ingredients

Dry Active Yeast

Available by pound, half pound, quarter pound, or $1/4$ oz. package.

Package = 1 tablespoon; 1 pound = 64 tablespoons.

Cost by package may be four to five times cost by pound.

Compressed Yeast

Available by pound at bakeries. Cut in pieces approximately $1^1/2''$ square and $1/2''$ thick, individually wrap in waxed paper, put in plastic bag, freeze. Will keep for a month; possibly much longer.

Sugars, Malt, etc.

Food for yeast and flavor. Only natural forms are free of harmful effects. Sugars, of course, in a variety of forms add flavor to the bread and give color to the crust. They furnish food for the yeast causing it to rise faster — if not used in excessive amounts.

Liquid
May be water, potato water, bran or vegetable water. Soft water gives extra lightness.

Bran
Bran is very high in minerals and vitamins. It is a very valuable supplement. Bran water should be used with refined flour.

Salt
Salt improves flavor, conditions gluten, slows yeast action.

Shortening
Shortening improves flavor, makes bread and crust more tender, aids in browning of crust, improves volume.

Temperature

In preparation of dough, keep it at even temperature at all times — 85° - 90°F unless you wish to delay the rising for a period of time. Keep room warm and free from drafts when mixing. Test water (with thermometer, 98°F). Check with fingers to get the "feel." Warm bowls and flour (in extremely cold weather).

Provide warm place for fermenting and proofing periods:

Gas oven warmed only by pilot light — 85°-90°F, check with thermometer.

Electric oven — turn on for seconds only and then turn off, check with thermometer.

A bowl of hot water placed in oven helps to keep an even temperature and provides humidity to prevent drying of dough. If placed in a dry place to rise, cover.

Caution! Guard against heat being turned on accidentally. A note on door, "DO NOT TURN ON!", is good protection.

Large kettle or canner, with very warm water in bottom, and with a cover is very satisfactory. Set bowl of bread in canner and cover. Be sure bowl is large enough so bread won't run over as it rises.

Enclosed cupboard or cabinet with large kettle of hot water placed in bottom.

Techniques

The Sponge Method
Advantages: improves flavor, prevents staling, and may save time and yeast by setting the night before. (A method popular in grandmother's day.)

Method: measure yeast into small bowl, add 1 teaspoon sugar and $1/2$ cup warm water, stir and let stand.

Pour rest of water (very warm — 100° - 110°F) into a large bowl. Add equal amount of flour. Use highest gluten flour first.

Beat vigorously to develop gluten and incorporate air (about 100 strokes). Add softened yeast. Beat lightly with about 30 strokes to mix well.

Cover and set in warm place to rise. Let rise until double — 20 to 30 minutes.

Add remaining ingredients and knead until smooth and elastic and springs back when pressed.

Place dough in oiled bowl. Turn over to oil surface.

Cover. Place in warm, moist place to rise. Best results are secured when bread rises quickly — temperature, 80° - 90°F.

Too long fermenting periods or too high temperature impairs the flavor.

Straight Dough Method

Follow the same steps as above but omit the period for sponge to rise.

Fermenting

The First Period requires from 30 to 45 minutes. When double in volume knead down with a few punches.

The Second Period may be omitted. It requires from 30 to 45 minutes. When double in volume it is ready to be molded into loaves.

Molding

Punch down well to expel air bubbles. Turn out on bread board. Avoid using flour on the board at this time as it will cause streaks in bread. Cut into loaf-sizes and let rest on board for 10 minutes. Flatten and fold sides, then ends, to center. (Or, dough may be flattened lightly with rolling pin and rolled as for jelly roll.)

Place in well-greased pans. Seal by pressing edges together. When there is more than can be baked at one time or if it is more convenient to bake later, the loaves may be set in the refrigerator. When raised just the right amount they may be put directly into hot oven.

Proofing

Loaves should not be put into oven before properly *proofed,* or raised — otherwise a heavy, compact loaf results.

Nor should it be allowed to rise too long — coarse grain, impaired flavor, lack of browning will result.

Bread will double and rolls will triple in volume in *proofing.* When pressed with the finger, dough will spring back into shape. If a dent remains it is overproofed and should be mixed down, reshaped, and allowed to rise again. Watch carefully to avoid overproofing.

Moisture while proofing will prevent crust from forming on loaf. When bread is placed in a dry place to rise, cover with paper or damp towel. Proofing in the pan requires 30 to 45 minutes.

Oven-spring: bread should rise an additional inch and a half while baking. This is called the "oven-spring." Bread that has been overproofed will lose its oven-spring, will lose its sweetness, will not brown properly, and will have a coarse texture.

Baking

Bread should be thoroughly baked — 350° - 375°F — for 50 to 60 minutes for one and one-half pound loaves; 40 to 45 minutes for one pound loaves; and 25 to 30 minutes for rolls — at 400°F.

Greasing the crust after baking gives a shiny appearance and softens the crust. It may be omitted if preferred.

Cooling

Lay loaves on side on rack. Store in covered bread box.

Short Cuts

For the working homemaker, bread may be kneaded when one has a few minutes, put into a well-greased, covered bowl or large covered kettle and put into the refrigerator. After work it may be shaped into loaves, allowed to rise and bake while preparing the evening meal and doing the dishes. Or loaves in pans may be placed in the refrigerator to be baked at a more convenient time.

Time for mixing, about 15 to 30 minutes; time for shaping into loaves, about 5 minutes.

Cold Storage

Bread may be kept in frozen storage for weeks and retain much of its original flavor and texture, if carefully wrapped and sealed.

Preparation for freezing: cool, wrap well in waxed paper, seal with hot iron, or place in plastic refrigerator bag, seal, or wrap with foil. Make sure it is completely sealed. Bread sliced before freezing is more likely to dry out.

Preparation for serving: allow to stand at room temperature until completely thawed. Sprinkle crust lightly with water, cover, and heat in oven -— 400°F, 10 minutes.

Something Special

Steamed Bread is a real delicacy and provides an excellent way to use stale bread.

Directions: slice bread and place in steamer with space to allow for circulation of steam. Bread may be placed on rack in deep-well cooker. Be sure that ample steam can reach the bread. Steam for about 10 minutes, until thoroughly softened. Serve directly from steamer as desired. Serve with honey, herb butter, your favorite spread, or sprinkled with onion or garlic salt.

Reheated Bread. Stale bread may be made fresh by reheating.

Directions: sprinkle crust lightly with water or place in paper bag, heat in oven at 400°F for 10 minutes.

Zwieback: cut slices thin, place in oven at about 250°F and allow to dry thoroughly. Then let it be browned slightly all the way through — a light straw color.

Healthful, twice-baked zwieback is a versatile accompaniment to many menus.

Barley Bread

2 tablespoons yeast
1 tablespoon brown sugar
2 cups warm water, 100°F
4½ cups barley flour

¼ cup soy flour
1 tablespoon oil
2 teaspoons salt

Measure yeast into a small bowl. **Add** sugar and warm water. **Put** in warm place to rise. **Put** remaining water in large mixing bowl. **Add** half of flour and beat vigorously to develop gluten and incorporate air. **Add** sugar, salt, and oil and mix well.

Add softened yeast and beat briskly. **Add** soy flour and enough barley flour to make dough that can be kneaded. **Place** on floured board. **Knead** until smooth and elastic. **Shape** into two round loaves on a cookie sheet. **Slash** diagonally. **Let rise** until double in bulk.

Bake at 350°F one hour. Oil top lightly, if desired. **Remove** from pans. **Cool** on rack.

Whole Wheat Bread

3 cups warm water (100°F)
7½ cups whole wheat flour
    (approximate)
3 tablespoons oil

2 tablespoons dry yeast
3 tablespoons brown sugar
1 tablespoon salt

Measure yeast into small bowl. **Add** ½ teaspoon sugar and ½ cup of the warm water. **Let rise.**

Put the remaining 2½ cups warm water into a large mixing bowl. **Add** sugar and 3 cups flour. **Beat** vigorously, about 100 strokes, to develop gluten and to incorporate air in batter. **Add** softened yeast. **Mix** well with about 25 light strokes. **Cover. Set** in a warm place to let rise, 20 to 30 minutes, until double in bulk.

Add oil and salt stirred into two cups of flour. **Mix** well.

Put remaining flour on board. **Empty** dough onto flour. **Scrape** the bowl well with rubber spatula so that no dough will be wasted.

Knead until smooth and elastic and springs back when pressed with fingers. **Place** in oiled bowl. **Turn** over to oil top. **Cover. Let rise** until double. **Punch** down.

Divide into three equal sections and let rest on board 10 minutes. **Grease** three pans, 4"x 7½" (top measure), with solid shortening. **Shape** loaves by flattening and rolling, or fold first sides and then ends over center. **Pinch** edges together.

Place loaf topside down in pan and roll over to oil top. **Make** sure it is in center of the pan. **Cover** unless in moist air. **Let rise** in warm place until double in bulk. Should spring back when pressed lightly with fingers.

Bake one hour at 350°F. **Place** loaves on side on rack to cool. Brush with oil, if desired to soften crust.

Variations
1. Rolls: (a) make dough a little softer, leave out approximately ½ cup flour; (b) add one extra tablespoon of oil; or, (c) use soy milk for liquid.

2. Add chopped nuts, raisins, dates, or combination, to loaf or rolls.

Breadmaking in Electric Mixer
(Whole Wheat Bread)

Ingredients are the same as for Whole Wheat Bread.

Measure yeast into largest bowl of electric mixer. **Add** sugar and water. **Let stand** while assembling other ingredients. **Add** 3 cups flour. **Beat** at low speed for 2 minutes. **Increase** speed to medium. **Add** gradually 2 more cups of flour with salt. **Add** oil. **Remove** and clean beaters.

Stir in enough flour to make a soft dough, using a large mixing spoon. **Scrape** sides of bowl clean. **Turn** out onto a generously floured board. Rest of process is the same as in recipe for whole wheat bread.

Note: If bowl is large enough the final mixing may be done in bowl.

Variation

Batter Bread: Follow instructions above. Stir in as much of the flour as possible with a large spoon. Fill greased tin cans a little less than half full. Let rise until double. Bake at 350°F, 45 minutes or longer as desired.

Oatmeal Bread

2 tablespoons dry active yeast or 2 cakes compressed
2¼ cups warm (100°F) bran water (see recipe)
2 tablespoons brown sugar
¼ cup "do pep" (gluten flour)

4½ cups flour (whole wheat, white, or mixture)
2 cups rolled oats
¼ cup wheat germ
¼ cup soy flour
2 tablespoons oil
2 teaspoons salt

Measure yeast into small bowl. **Add** ½ teaspoon sugar and ½ cup warm bran water. **Stir. Place** in warm place to rise. **Put** remaining bran water (very warm, 100°F) into bowl. **Add** sugar and "do pep" and half of flour. **Beat** vigorously 100 strokes to develop gluten and to beat air into batter. **Add** softened yeast. **Beat** about 30 strokes. **Add** 2 cups rolled oats to make soft sponge. **Mix. Let** stand in warm place until very light, 20 to 30 minutes.

Add oil. **Combine** wheat germ, soy flour, salt, and remaining rolled oats, and stir into sponge. **Turn out** on floured board and knead until smooth and elastic. **Place** in oiled bowl and turn over to oil top. **Set** in warm place to rise until double in bulk. **Punch** down.

Turn out on board. **Divide** into two equal portions. **Let rise** for 10 minutes. **Shape** into loaves. **Place** in greased pans. **Cover. Let rise** until double in size. **Put** into oven at 350°F, let bake 60 minutes. **Brush** top lightly with oil, if desired. **Remove** from pans. **Cool** on side on rack.

Pioneer Bread

1⅛ cups unground high
   protein wheat, water
   to cover
1 cup whole wheat flour,
   high protein, fine grind
½ cup water
1 tablespoon oil

1 tablespoon yeast, dry
   active, or 1 cake
   compressed
1 tablespoon molasses or
   brown sugar
1 teaspoon salt

Look over wheat and wash. **Soak** in water to cover, 24 hours. **Drain** off water, use ½ cup for bread. **Heat** to 100°F.

Grind wheat through household food chopper, using the finest blade. When about half of the wheat is ground, **put** yeast to soak in small bowl with ½ cup warm water and ½ teaspoon sugar or molasses.

As soon as it is light, **mix** yeast with ground wheat in bowl to let rise, while finishing the grinding of the rest of the wheat.

Combine all ingredients. **Knead** until smooth and elastic. **Let rise** on board 10 minutes. **Shape** in loaf. **Let rise** until double in size.

Bake at 350°F for 1 hour. **Remove** from pan. Oil if desired. **Cool** on side on rack.

Hardy, tasty Pioneer Bread
is made from the most
simple, natural ingredients.

Modified Pioneer Bread

1¹/₈ cups unground high
    protein wheat, water
    to cover
2¹/₂ cups water
6 cups whole wheat flour
2 tablespoons dry active
    yeast or 2 cakes compressed

¹/₂ cup soy flour
3 tablespoons "do pep"
    (gluten flour)
3 tablespoons molasses or
    brown sugar
3 tablespoons oil
1 tablespoon salt

Look over wheat and wash. **Soak** in water to cover for 24 hours. **Drain** and use water in breadmaking, warm to 100°F.

Measure yeast and ¹/₂ teaspoon sugar and place in a small bowl. **Add** ¹/₂ cup warm water. **Set** in warm place to rise.

Put 1 cup of the soaked wheat in blender with sugar and half of the remaining water (about 100°F). **Blend** until fine. **Add** soaked yeast and blend for a few minutes. **Put** into bowl.

Blend the remaining wheat with "do pep" and water until wheat is very fine. **Add** to the first portion and mix. **Let rise** in a warm place 10 minutes.

Mix salt with soy flour and add to sponge. **Stir. Add** oil, and enough flour to make a soft dough. **Mix.**

Turn out on floured board and knead until smooth and elastic, and springs back when pressed with fingers. **Place** in oiled bowl, turn over to oil top, set in warm place, let rise until double in bulk. **Punch** down. **Turn** out on board. **Divide** in two or three equal portions, and let rest on board in a warm place for 10 minutes.

Shape into loaves, and put into greased pans. **Let rise** in a warm place until double in size. **Bake** at 350°F, 50 to 60 minutes. **Remove** from pans. **Brush** top lightly with oil, if desired. **Cool** on side of rack.

Variation
1¹/₂ cups quality white flour may be used to replace 1¹/₂ cups whole wheat flour instead of using "do pep."

Pioneer Soy Bread

2¼ cups soaked, unground wheat, high gluten (start with 1⅛ cup dry wheat)	2 tablespoons dry active yeast or 2 packages compressed
2 cups soaked soy beans (1 cup dry)	¼ cup molasses or brown sugar
8 cups whole wheat flour (high protein, fine)	¼ cup oil
¼ cup pure gluten flour ("do pep") (optional)	1⅓ tablespoons salt
	2½ cups warm water (100°F)

Follow method in preceding recipe, using the same method for soaking soy beans as for wheat. **Continue** with the instructions given until wheat is all blend and mixed.

Chop soaked soybeans medium-fine in blender with extra cup of water and add to sponge. **Mix. Knead.** Finish according to directions in preceding recipe.

Pita
Middle East Bread

To be used with Falafels (see recipe). Follow instructions for recipe for Whole Wheat Bread, except omit most or all of the oil, to the point of punching down.

Turn dough out on board. **Divide** in half. Form each half into a long roll. **Divide** into six equal sections. **Make** ball of each section. **Flatten** into circle ¼ inch thick. **Use** rolling pin. **Roll** from center out in each direction. Or **pat** into shape with fingers held flat.

Cut with 5½-inch plastic bowl for more perfect circle. **Use** any leftover scraps in next ball. **Place** on greased cookie sheet. **Let rise** until double in bulk. **Bake** 8 minutes at 475°F. (The Pitas will puff up and be hollow inside. They should brown lightly.)

Note: Pitas may be cut in two crosswise or a slit may be made on the top. They are then filled with Falafels, chopped lettuce, ripe tomatoes, green onions, and Tahini Sauce (see recipe). This is sometimes called the "Middle East or Israeli Taco."

Swedish Limpa Bread

2 tablespoons dry active
   yeast, or 2 cakes
   compressed
3½ cups warm water
   (about 100°F)
⅓ cup brown sugar
5 cups whole wheat flour

¼ cup gluten flour
   ("do pep")
¼ cup oil
1½ tablespoons fennel
   seeds
1 tablespoon salt
3 cups rye flour

Dissolve yeast and ½ tablespoon sugar in warm water in a small bowl. **Let stand** in warm place. **Add** 4 cups whole wheat flour and "do pep" to 4 cups warm water in bowl. **Beat** vigorously 100 strokes with large spoon or wire whip to develop gluten and to incorporate air. **Add** yeast and beat again 30 strokes. **Add** sugar and enough flour to make thick batter.

Let rise in warm place, 20 to 30 minutes. **Add** oil, salt, soy and rye flour, fennel seeds, salt, and enough whole wheat flour to make a soft dough. **Put** on floured board and knead until smooth and elastic and dough springs back when pressed with fingers. **Place** in lightly oiled bowl and put in warm place to rise until double in bulk. **Punch** down.

Place on bread board and divide into three equal portions. **Let rest** on board for 10 minutes while greasing pans. **Shape** into loaves. **Let rise** until double in size. **Put** in oven that has been heated to 350°F. **Bake** 60 minutes. **Remove** from pans. **Brush** crust with oil if desired and let cool on side on rack.

Note: fennel seed may be crushed in mortar or small grinder or may be soaked in part of the liquid and oil and blended briefly to intensify flavor.

Really Enriched White Bread
Good for the Bland Diet

2 tablespoons dry active
   yeast, or 2 cakes
   compressed
$2^1/_4$ cups warm bran water
   (100°F) (see recipe)
5 cups enriched flour

2 tablespoons brown sugar
2 tablespoons wheat germ
3 tablespoons soy flour
2 tablespoons oil
2 teaspoons salt

Measure yeast into small bowl. **Add** $^1/_2$ teaspoon sugar and $^1/_2$ cup warm bran water. **Stir. Place** in warm place to rise.

Put remaining bran water into large bowl. **Add** $2^1/_2$ cups flour and sugar. **Beat** vigorously 100 strokes to develop gluten and incorporate air into the sponge.
Add softened yeast. **Beat** about 30 strokes. **Cover** and let stand in warm place to rise, 20 to 30 minutes.

Add oil. **Combine** $1^1/_2$ cups flour, wheat germ, soy flour, and salt, and stir into sponge. **Turn out** on board and knead until smooth and elastic.

Note: this recipe is especially for those who cannot tolerate roughage. Even so, eaten in large quantities it can be somewhat constipating.

Extra Special Bread

3 cups first rinse waters from
   gluten (not starch layer)
   (see recipe for gluten)
2 tablespoons yeast

$^1/_4$ cup sugar
6 cups whole wheat flour
1 tablespoon salt
$^1/_4$ cup oil

Combine and mix as for Holiday Bran Rolls. **Knead** until smooth and elastic and dough springs back when pressed with fingers. **Place** in oiled bowl and let rise until double in bulk. **Punch** down. **Let rise** a second time.

Shape into three loaves. **Let rise** until double in size.

Place in 400°F oven for 10 minutes. **Reduce** heat to 350°F. **Bake** 50 minutes. **Yield: 3 1-lb. loaves.**

Variation
Make into burger buns for Beefless Burgers.

Orange Date Bread

1 tablespoon dry active
yeast, or 1 cake
compressed
1¹/₂ cups water, 100°F
2 tablespoons brown sugar
3 cups whole wheat flour
3 tablespoons "do pep"
(gluten flour)
1¹/₂ cups chopped dates

¹/₄ cup grated orange rind
(including white part)
2 tablespoons honey, com-
bine with orange rind
¹/₂ cup chopped nuts
2 tablespoons soy flour
2 tablespoons oil
1¹/₂ teaspoons salt

Measure yeast into small bowl. **Add** ¹/₂ teaspoon sugar. **Add** ¹/₂ cup water. **Stir. Let stand** until light.

Add "do pep" and 1 cup flour to remaining water in bowl and beat vigorously 100 strokes until very light. **Add** sugar and softened yeast, beat about 30 strokes. **Let rise** 20 to 30 minutes.

Add other ingredients except flour. **Mix. Add** flour to make dough firm enough to handle. **Put** on floured board. **Knead** until smooth, elastic, yet soft. (Springs back when pressed.) **Let rise** until double in bulk. **Punch** down; put out on board. **Let rest** on board 10 minutes.

Shape into loaf. **Place** in greased pan. **Cover. Let rise. Put** bread in oven, at 350°F. **Bake** 1 hour. **Remove** from pans. **Brush** lightly with oil if desired. **Cool** on side of rack.

Variations
1. Rolls
2. Fruit Bread
3. Orange Bread
4. Orange Rolls

Holiday Bran Rolls

1 cup water (water from
   gluten)
1 cup bran washed
   from gluten
   (see recipe above)
1 tablespoon yeast
2 tablespoons brown sugar

2 teaspoons salt
2¹/₂ cups (approximately)
   flour, half fine whole
   wheat and half white
   may be used or all fine
   whole wheat

Warm the water. **Soak** yeast in part of the warm water
to which 1 teaspoon sugar has been added. **Combine** all ingredients except flour and beat until blended.

Add flour to make soft dough and knead until smooth and
elastic, but not sticky. **Place** in oiled bowl and let rise until
double in bulk. **Punch** down. **Let rise** a second time.

Shape into round balls about the size of a large walnut.
Some may be rolled in evaporated or soy milk and sesame
seeds before placing on the cookie sheet. **Let rise** until
double in bulk.

Place in 400°F oven for 10 minutes. **Reduce** heat to 350°F
for an additional 10 minutes. If browned enough they are
ready to be taken from the oven. Otherwise allow a little
more time. **Yield: 36 rolls.**

Variations

1. Use ¹/₂ cup orange honey (honey with grated orange
rind added) instead of brown sugar.

2. Substitute ¹/₂ cup sieved cooked squash or pumpkin for
¹/₂ cup water and add 1 cup raisins.

3. Add ¹/₂ cup chopped nuts and ¹/₂ cup chopped dates.

4. Add ¹/₂ cup cranberry relish and 1 teaspoon honey
instead of the brown sugar.

Date-Pecan Rolls

½ cup dry soy milk powder	2½ cups chopped dates
1½ cups boiling water	1½ cups pecans

Follow recipe for Whole Wheat Bread except substitute ½ cup dry soy milk powder for ½ cup flour and use ¼ cup oil. Mix and add 1 cup chopped dates. Set dough to rise.

Put boiling water into a small saucepan or skillet. **Add** 1½ cups chopped dates. **Reduce** heat. **Simmer** and mash with fork until dates are softened, well-blended, and slightly thickened.

Grease muffin pans or, if preferred, a large baking pan. **Determine** how many pecans to allow for each roll. **Arrange** nuts topside down in center of spot allotted for roll.

Punch down dough. **Turn out** on very lightly floured board. **Divide** into three equal parts. **Shape** each portion into long roll. **Cut** each roll into 12 portions. **Let rest** on board.

Spoon 1 tablespoon of date mixture on top of each cluster of nuts, add more if any is left over. **Shape** rolls and place each on top of nut cluster. **Let rise** until triple in bulk.

Bake at 400°F, 10 minutes. **Reduce** heat to 350°F for 15 minutes. Should be nicely browned.

Variations

1. Walnuts, or other nuts may be used in place of pecans.

2. Slices of raw apples and chopped dates may be rolled inside of a cinnamon type bun. Shredded raw apple may be added to the date mixture for the topping.

3. Coarsely shredded apples, and raisins, may be stirred into softened date mixture. Spread part on flattened dough before rolling and put the rest in the bottom of the pan. Cut rolls in 1-inch sections and place close together in pan. Cut in 1½-inch sections if placed farther apart. One or two teaspoons of grated orange rind may be stirred into the mixture before using.

Potato Rolls

2 cups warm bran water
  (see recipe)
2 cups mashed potatoes
1 cup whole wheat flour
4 cups (approx.)
  "enriched" flour
3 tablespoons "do pep"
  (gluten flour)

¹/₄ cup wheat germ
2 tablespoons dry active
  yeast, or 2 cakes
  compressed
3 tablespoons brown sugar
¹/₄ cup soy flour
2 tablespoons oil
2 teaspoons salt

Measure yeast into small bowl. **Add** 1 teaspoon sugar and ¹/₄ cup warm water. **Stir. Put** in warm place to rise.

Mix bran water (100°F), mashed potatoes, whole wheat flour, 3 cups white flour, and "do pep." **Beat** vigorously to develop gluten and incorporate air, 100 strokes. **Add** softened yeast. **Beat** briskly, 30 strokes. **Add** 2 cups white flour and remaining ingredients. **Mix.** Put out on well-floured board. **Knead** until smooth and elastic and dough springs back when pressed. Dough should be soft. **Oil** lightly, **place** in bowl. **Cover.**

Let rise in warm place until double in bulk. **Punch** down. **Place** on board. **Form** in long roll, and **cut** 24 equal portions. **Let rest** on board while greasing pans. **Mold** by rolling balls and flattening slightly. **Place** two inches apart in pan. **Let rise** until triple in size. **Bake** at 400°F for 25 to 30 minutes.

Refrigerator Rolls

1¹/₃ cups water
1 cup potato water
2 cups enriched flour
2 cups whole wheat flour
¹/₄ cup "do pep"
  (gluten flour)

¹/₃ cup cornmeal
1 tablespoon yeast
2 tablespoons brown sugar
¹/₄ cup oil
2 teaspoons salt

Measure yeast into small bowl. **Add** ¹/₂ teaspoon sugar and ¹/₄ cup warm water. **Stir. Put** in warm place to rise. **Bring** 1 cup water to boiling point in kettle. **Add** salt. **Add** cornmeal which has been mixed with ¹/₃ cup cold water. **Stir** until thickened and smooth. **Let cool.**

Combine potato water, gluten, 1 cup whole wheat flour, and sugar. **Beat** vigorously 100 strokes to develop gluten and incorporate air.

Add softened yeast. **Beat** briskly. **Add** warm cornmeal mixture and 2 cups flour and other remaining ingredients. **Mix. Turn out** on floured board. **Knead** until smooth and elastic. Should be a soft dough. **Oil** lightly, place in bowl and let rise until double in bulk. **Punch** down. **Cover** and place in refrigerator until ready to use.

Form into long roll. **Cut** in 24 equal pieces. **Shape** into rolls by rolling into balls and flattening. **Let rise** in warm place until triple in size. **Bake** at 400°F, 25 to 30 minutes.

Sandwich Buns

2¹/₂ cups warm water	1 tablespoon yeast
²/₃ cup soy milk powder	¹/₄ cup water (warm)
¹/₃ cup brown sugar	¹/₂ cup wheat germ
1¹/₂ cups whole wheat flour	2 eggs (large)
3 cups white flour	¹/₃ cup oil
1 cup oatmeal (dry)	2 teaspoons salt

Measure yeast, ¹/₂ teaspoon of the sugar, and water into a small bowl. **Mix** and let rise.

Put warm water and soy milk powder into a large bowl. **Add** sugar, 1¹/₂ cup whole wheat flour, and 1 cup white flour. **Beat** vigorously with wire whip, slotted spoon or foley fork to develop the gluten and incorporate air — about 100 strokes.

Add softened yeast. **Stir** briskly to mix well, about 30 strokes. **Set** in warm place to rise, about 20 minutes.

Add 1/4 teaspoon salt to eggs and beat to mix well. **Add** to sponge. **Mix. Add** wheat germ, oil, oatmeal, remaining salt and one cup white flour. **Stir** to mix well.

Put remaining flour on board. **Knead** until dough is smooth and elastic and springs back when pressed with fingers. The dough should be soft but not sticky. **Place** in oiled bowl, turn over to oil top. **Cover. Let rise** until double in bulk. **Punch** down.

Place on board. Form into long roll, cut into 16 equal portions. **Let rest** 10 minutes. **Shape** into sandwich buns by forming a ball and flattening. **Place** on greased cookie sheets about 2 inches apart on all sides. **Let rise** until triple in size.

Bake at 400°F about 25 minutes. Should be nicely browned.

Variation

Substitute 1/2 cup soy flour and 2 tablespoons "do pep" for eggs; and bran water in place of water. (May need to reduce flour a little.)

Squash-Raisin Rolls

2 tablespoons dry active yeast, or 2 cakes compressed	1/4 cup "do pep" (gluten flour)
3 tablespoons brown sugar	5 cups enriched flour
2 cups warm bran water (see recipe)	1/4 cup soy flour
4 cups squash (yellow winter)	1/4 cup wheat germ
2 cups whole wheat flour	3 tablespoons oil
	1 tablespoon salt
	1 1/2 cups raisins

Measure yeast into small bowl. **Add** 1/2 teaspoon sugar and 1/2 cup warm bran water. **Stir,** place in warm place to rise.

Mix squash and bran water (100°F). **Add** "do pep," whole wheat flour, and 1 cup white flour. **Beat** vigorously to develop gluten and beat air into batter — 100 strokes. **Add** softened yeast. **Beat** briskly — 30 strokes. **Add** 2 cups flour and other remaining ingredients. **Mix.**

Turn out on well-floured board. **Knead** until smooth and elastic. Dough should be soft. **Let rise** in warm place until double in bulk.

Punch down. **Turn out** on board. **Form** into long roll. **Cut** into 36 equal portions. **Let rest** on board while greasing pans. **Mold** by rolling in balls. **Place** two inches apart in pan. **Let rise** until triple in size. **Bake** at 400°F, 25 to 30 minutes.

Quick Breads

Apple-Oatmeal Muffins
(Pilot Recipe)

1 cup medium shredded
  raw apple
1¹/₂ cups rolled oats
¹/₄ cup oil

¹/₂ teaspoon salt
¹/₂ cup raisins or chopped
  dates
¹/₄ cup nuts, chopped

Wash apples, quarter, cut out core. **Shred** cut side down on medium shredder. **Pack** into cup.

Combine ingredients. **Let stand** for a few minutes to absorb moisture. **Mix** together firmly with fingers or fork. **Spoon** into oiled muffin pans, filling pans well and rounding nicely.

Bake at 375°F, 25 minutes. **Yield: 8 muffins.**

Barley-Oat Muffins

1 cup barley flour
1 cup rolled oats
  (quick cooking)
¹/₂ cup raisins
³/₄ cup water

¹/₂ cup dried apple, ground;
  or 1 cup fresh shredded
  apple
¹/₄ cup oil
¹/₂ teaspoon salt

Follow method in **Pilot Recipe** for Apple-Oatmeal Muffins for shredding apple. **Combine** dry ingredients and mix well.

93

Measure water into cup, add oil. **Beat** with fork to emulsify. **Pour** slowly into dry mixture, stirring with fork to moisten as evenly as possible.

Let stand for a few minutes to absorb moisture. **Spoon** into greased muffin pans. Make as large as desired for finished muffins.

Bake at 350°F, 25 minutes or until nicely browned. **Yield: 8 muffins.**

Note: If fresh grated apples are used, combine apple with water and oil mixture and add to dry ingredients.

Cornbread

1 cup hot milk	1/4 cup oil
1 cup cornmeal	1 teaspoon salt
1/2 cup flour	2 eggs

Add cornmeal all at once to hot milk. **Stir** until it is all moistened and holds together in one mass. **Remove** from fire. **Add** flour and beat. **Add** oil and salt. **Stir** well and set aside.

Separate 2 eggs. To the egg whites add 1 tablespoon water and a pinch of salt. **Beat** until stiff. To the 2 yolks, add 1/4 cup boiling water and beat until light and thick. **Fold** the beaten yolks and then the beaten whites into cornmeal mixture.

Pour into greased pan (8″x 8″) and bake at 400°F for about 25 minutes. **Yield: 8 slices, 2″ x 4″.**

Cornmeal-Rice Muffins

1 cup cooked brown rice	1/2 teaspoon salt
1 cup boiling water	1/4 cup oil
1 1/4 cups cornmeal	2 tablespoons soy flour
(not degerminated)	

Mash rice with fork. **Bring** water to boil in pan that is large enough for mixing muffins. **Mix** dry ingredients and add all at once to boiling water. **Remove** at once from fire and stir until moisture is absorbed. **Add** mashed rice and mix well with fork. **Add** oil. **Beat.**

Fill greased muffin pans. (Make the finished muffins as large as you want and round nicely; they will not rise any higher. Or place in mounds on greased cookie sheet.)

Bake at 400°F, 30 minutes or until nicely browned. **Yield: 8 muffins.**

Corn Muffins

1 cup soybean concentrate (see recipe) blended with ¼ cup oil	1 teaspoon salt
1 cup water	1¼ cups cornmeal, not degerminated

Follow method for Whipped Soybean Concentrate. **Bring** water to boil in sauce pan, large enough for mixing muffins. **Add** salt. **Add** cornmeal all at once and stir until it gathers in a mass and leaves the side of the pan.

Add whipped soybean concentrate. **Mix** with fork until well-blended. **Drop** from tablespoon into greased muffin pans or on greased cookie sheet. **Make** as large as desired for finished product. (They rise only slightly.)

Bake at 350°F, 30 minutes or until nicely browned and well-done. **Serve** directly from oven. **Yield: 6 muffins.**

Hoecake

1½ cups cornmeal	1¼ cups boiling water
1 tablespoon sugar	2 eggs
¼ cup oil	½ teaspoon salt

Bring water to rapid boil in a kettle large enough to use in mixing hoecake. **Mix** salt and sugar with cornmeal. **Add**

all at once to boiling water. **Stir** until it gathers into one mass and leaves the sides of the pan. **Remove** from fire.

Add oil and beat vigorously. Add unbeaten eggs one at a time and beat hard after each addition. The secret of success lies in thorough beating.

Drop from tablespoon on greased cookie sheet. **Bake** at 400°F about 30 minutes. Should be nicely browned. **Serve** directly from oven. **Yield: 6 2-cake servings.**

Oatcake

1 cup oatmeal
¼ cup chopped walnuts
½ teaspoon salt

1 cup whipped soybean
    concentrate (see recipe)
2 tablespoons oil, optional

Combine dry ingredients and mix. **Add** oil to Whipped Soybean Concentrate if desired, and beat lightly with fork to blend. **Stir** dry ingredients into whipped concentrate and stir with fork until well-mixed.

Spread into greased 9″ x 12″ pan. **Bake** at 350°F, 25 minutes. **Serve** hot. **Yield: 6 servings.**

Variations

1. Spread quite thin on greased cookie sheet. Bake at 350°F, 15 minutes. Reduce heat to 250° F. Bake until crisp and completely dry. Watch carefully to avoid scorching.

2. Grind ¼ cup unrefined sesame seeds and add to recipe or replace chopped nuts. Spread thin. Sprinkle ¼ cup unground sesame seeds over top and sprinkle lightly with salt. Bake as above.

Note: Remove from oven after 15 minutes and work in 2″ squares with pastry wheel or sharp knife. Return to oven and bake until dry.

Crackers and Flat Breads

Barley Sticks

1½ cups barley flour
1½ cups macaroon coconut
¼ cup soy flour
½ teaspoon salt

½ cup water
¼ cup oil
1 tablespoon sugar

Combine and mix dry ingredients in a bowl. **Measure** water and oil **together** into glass measuring cup. **Beat** with fork to emulsify. **Pour** over dry ingredients, stirring with a fork to moisten as evenly as possible.

Gather into a ball and knead lightly. **Place** on board and roll to about one-half inch thickness. **Cut** in sticks one-half inch wide and about 3 inches long.

Place on ungreased cookie sheet. **Place** in oven preheated to 400°F. **Reduce** heat to 350°F and bake 25 minutes or until lightly browned. **Reduce** heat and allow to dry thoroughly.

Variation
Use 2½ cups barley flour and ½ cup chopped walnuts, other nuts or sesame seeds.

Crackers

3 cups rolled oats
2 cups fine whole wheat
  flour
1 cup wheat germ

1 tablespoon sugar
1 teaspoon salt
1 cup water
⅔ cup oil

Combine dry ingredients in large bowl. **Mix** well. **Measure** water and oil in a two-cup measuring cup. **Beat** with a fork to emulsify. **Pour** slowly into dry mixture, stirring with fork all the while to distribute the moisture evenly. **Mix** well and knead lightly.

Divide into two equal portions. **Place** each portion on a 10"x 15" well-greased cookie sheet.

Flatten with fingers and roll with small rolling pin or cylindrical glass until the crackers are thin and even and entirely fill the space. **Sprinkle** lightly with salt and roll to embed in dough.

Cut with pastry wheel into 2"x 3" rectangles. A clean yardstick is useful in obtaining uniform size.

Heat oven to 400°F. **Place** trays in oven. **Reduce** heat at once to 325°F and bake 25 minutes or until lightly browned. **Reduce** heat and let dry thoroughly. **Watch** very carefully when nearly done as they brown very quickly at this stage. (It may be necessary to remove some of the crackers along the edges if they start browning before the ones in the center.) **Loosen** with wide spatula or pancake turner and let cool on cookie sheet.

These crackers are crisp, tender, and delicious as well as of good nutritive value. They should be browned very slightly.

Flat Bread

1 cup rye flour
1¹/₂ cups whole wheat flour
1 cup soy flour

1 cup oat flour or quick
    cooking oats

Combine dry ingredients in bowl. **Boil** water, add oil, salt, and sugar. **Stir** into flour. Use enough water to make a soft pliable dough, not sticky. **Knead** 10 minutes.

Divide into 12 equal portions. **Roll** small pieces paper-thin. **Roll** lightly from center out to control shape.

Bake on top of clean stove or ungreased griddle, or on baking sheet in oven at 300°F, until thoroughly dried and slightly browned. (If baked on top of the stove, it may be turned and browned slightly, and put into the oven to crisp.)

Note. This is crisp, tender, and very delicious.

Sesame Seed-Oatmeal Crackers

5 cups rolled oats
1 cup soy flour
1 teaspoon salt
1 cup water
1/2 cup oil

1/2 teaspoon salt to sprinkle over top
1/2 cup sesame seeds (not refined)

Follow method in recipe for Crackers, except sesame seeds should not be combined with other dry ingredients. When crackers have been rolled thin **moisten surface** with a pastry brush dipped in water and **sprinkle** liberally with sesame seeds and lightly with salt. **Roll** and bake according to instructions.

Wheat Lefse

3 cups whole wheat pastry flour
1/4 cup oil

1 cup water
1/2 teaspoon salt

Add salt to flour. **Combine** oil and water and beat with fork until oil is emulsified. **Pour** over flour, stirring all the while to wet the flour as evenly as possible. **Gather** into a ball. **Knead** lightly.

Dough should be moist and pliable but not sticky. If not wet enough, a small amount of water may be added; if too moist, dust lightly with flour.

Roll dough thin and cut to desired size. A few drops of oil on the surface of the dough, instead of flour, prevents sticking while the dough is being rolled out. (Or, instead of rolling, divide the dough into balls a little larger than a walnut, and pat out with fingers until thin and even and nicely rounded.)

Bake on grill, heavy skillet, or on iron stove top. (The surface does not require greasing and should be medium-hot to bake quickly and still be pliable enough to roll.)

Serve with mashed beans, green onion, tomatoes, etc. — as tacos. They are good with a variety of other spreads of your choice.

Variation

Crisp Lefse: Roll lefse very thin. Cut in circles about 5" in diameter. Place on ungreased cookie sheet. Bake in hot oven until slightly browned and crisp. Watch carefully. Dry thoroughly. Serve with Soy-Oat Tomato Topping.

Whole Wheat Bread, Page 77

Pioneer Bread, Page 80

Crackers, Potato Rolls, Swedish Limpa Bread, Pages 83, 86, 89

Crackers with Garbanzo-Pimiento Cheese, Page 32

Granola, Page 119

Soy-Oat Waffles, Buckwheat Waffles, Pages 109, 112

Date-Pecan Rolls and Variations, Page 87

Miniature Fruit Cakes, Page 156

Breakfast Breads
and Cereals

Protein, iron, and the B vitamins, notably thiamine and niacin, are among the chief contributions of cereals to the diet. The minerals and vitamins are more highly concentrated in the germ and outer layers than in the inner portions of the grain.

Cereal grains undergo fairly sizable physical losses when they are processed into the forms we use most. The nutritive losses are directly related to the physical losses. The kind and extent of processing determine the proportions of nutrients remaining in the finished product.

Milling wheat for white flour for breadmaking and for general home use involves removing some 28 to 37 percent of the weight of the kernel. Even more is removed for very highly refined cake flours. About 72 pounds of straight-grade white flour are obtained from 100 pounds of cleaned, hard wheat. This amount of flour has about a third of the amount of iron in the unmilled kernel, about a fourth of the thiamine and niacin, and about a third of the pantothenic acid, another important B vitamin in cereals.

Refining losses. Losses in milling are even higher for some less familiar nutrients. For example, vitamin E is present in high concentrations in the oil of wheat germ. Nearly all of this vitamin is removed with the germ and outer layers of the wheat kernel in the milling of white flour. The importance of the loss cannot be estimated until more is known about the role of vitamin E in human metabolism.

Rice and other cereal grains also lose much of their nutrients in milling.

The highly milled, polished rice commonly referred to as white rice contains smaller amounts of iron and the B vitamins than either parboiled or brown rice. Brown rice has the value of the whole grain.

Parboiled rice, also called converted rice, is prepared by a special adaptation of the milling process wherby it retains much more iron and vitamins than ordinary white rice, although it looks like white rice. The nutritive value of parboiled rice is intermediate between regular white rice and brown rice.

Whole-grain or nearly whole-grain forms of cereals are available generally. Among them are whole wheat flour, sometimes called graham flour, brown rice, dark rye flour, and wholeground cornmeal. They retain the germ and outer layers and thus the high nutritive values of these portions. They are preferred by many for their flavor and roughage.

Cooking losses. Cereals cooked in only enough water to be absorbed lose only small amounts of thiamine — probably 5 to 10 percent.

Such products as macaroni, other Italian pastas, and rice lose some of their thiamine by heat destruction in cooking. When they are cooked in an excessive amount of water, they also lose fairly large portions of the remaining thiamine and other water-soluble nutrients when the cooking water is thrown away.

The handling of rice has changed considerably in recent years. It was once sold from bins in the stores and it had to be washed. Some people still wash rice, although for the cleaned, packaged rice of today washing is unnecessary and nutritionally expensive.

Washing once before cooking can cause a thiamine loss of 10 percent in brown and converted white rice and 25 percent in regular white rice. After changing water three times, the loss of thiamine may increase to 55 percent in white rice, 20 percent in brown rice, and 10 percent in parboiled rice. The loss of riboflavin and niacin is not so great — 10 to 15 percent.

Cooking rice by boiling in an excessive amount of water and discarding the cooking water leads to high losses of nutrients in all types of rice. The loss of B vitamins is roughly proportional to the volume of water used and the amount of water drained off.

If a poor cooking method is used, such as cooking 1 cup in 8 to 10 cups of water and draining the cooking water and rinsing afterward, the loss is about one-third of the original thiamine in the white and enriched rice. Rice cooked in the top of a double boiler with a minimum amount of water, until all the water is absorbed, with no rinsing afterward, loses 10 to 20 percent of the thiamine and less than 10 percent of the riboflavin and niacin. The use of a double boiler is desirable to avoid the high temperatures at the bottom surface of the cooking utensil, which tend to accelerate losses of vitamins.

Another good method is to bake the rice after just enough water is added to it in a casserole to produce a palatable but not too soft rice by the time the cooking water is absorbed. The loss of thiamine then is 10 to 30 percent, depending on whether the rice is washed once or not at all.

The label on some packages of rice says, "To retain vitamins, do not rinse before or drain after cooking." If that principle is followed in the preparation of rice for eating and if the amount of water used is just enough for absorption, the values will be retained.

— *Bernice Kunerth Watt and Woot-Tsuen Wu Leung,*
Yearbook Separate No. 2986,
U.S. Department of Agriculture.

Ingredients for light, flavorful waffles? The very best, in fact, and as nourishing as a breakfast meat dish.

Waffles

The waffles in this section are wholesome, of high nutritive value and easy to prepare. They contain a substantial amount of protein of high quality and no cholesterol.

The Soy-Oat Waffles were used in a study to supply the sole source of protein for experimental animals. The growth was very good, the same as from casein (a protein of milk). The biological value based on content of essential amino acids was 77 — excellent.

One nine-inch waffle contains approximately the same amount of protein as a three-ounce serving of T-bone steak, or six slices of bacon and two medium eggs. But the cost for ingredients for the waffle is only about one-eighth that of the steak or bacon and eggs.

One six-inch waffle (one-fourth of recipe) provides as much protein as three strips of bacon together with one medium egg.

Waffles for breakfast satisfy. There will be no desire for mid-morning snacks and no let-down in energy.

Secrets for Success in Baking Waffles

Conditioning the waffle iron. For best results the waffle iron needs to be conditioned occasionally.

When: 1. After scouring or washing grids.
2. After overheating (if it just gets smoking hot, greasing before the first waffle is usually sufficient).
3. After long usage.
4. Even teflon-coated irons require greasing the first time used after washing or overheating.

With what: 1. Use solid shortening of good quality.
2. Do *not* use safflower oil on grids.
3. Do *not* use margarine or low-grade shortening.

How: 1. Heat iron hot — *not smoking.*
2. Brush on a liberal coating of solid shortening.
3. *Let cool.*
4. Heat the second time.
5. Brush on more shortening.
6. Cool. Absorb as much of the grease as possible with paper towels.
7. Heat medium-hot — not smoking. Add waffle batter. Bake 7 or 8 minutes. Discard the first waffle if grease-soaked.
8. The waffle iron should work well for a long while, if it is not overheated, or if it is not scoured or washed. Should there be a tendency to stick, brush lightly with solid shortening. Lecithin added to waffle batter will help to prevent sticking. "Pam" is a lecithin product.

Short cuts.
1. Presoak soybeans or other ingredients.
   a. Store in refrigerator.
   b. Freeze.

2. Baking requires 8 minutes.
   a. Stack and reheat for group.
   b. Freeze for stockpile.

3. To reheat:
   a. Place single layer on cookie sheet in very hot oven.
      1. For moist waffles cover with foil.
      2. For crisp waffles leave uncovered.
      3. Heat quickly — do not dry out.
   b. Heat in toaster.
   c. Heat in waffle iron.

4. To freeze:
   a. Freeze quickly, uncovered in single layer on cookie sheets or cooling rack. (Prevents crushing or bending out of shape.)

b. Stack three or four with pieces of wax paper between.
c. Put in plastic bag. Seal.

Yield of following recipes. All of these waffle recipes will yield 2 9-inch waffles on deep grids; 4 6-inch waffles on deep grids; or 6 6-inch waffles on shallow grids.

Soy-Oat Waffles
(Pilot Recipe)

2¼ cups water
1½ cups rolled oats
1 tablespoon oil

1cup soaked soybeans
(½ cup dry)
½ teaspoon salt

Soak soybeans several hours or overnight in sufficient water to keep covered. **Drain,** discard water. (Soaked, drained soybeans may be kept in the refrigerator for a week or stored for longer periods in the freezer. Keep on hand for use at a moment's notice.)

Combine all ingredients and blend until light and foamy, about half a minute. **Let stand** while waffle iron is heating. The batter thickens on standing. **Blend** briefly. **Pour** into a pitcher for convenience.

Grease iron with solid shortening for first waffle. (Do not use margarine.) **Bake** in hot waffle iron 8 minutes, or until nicely browned. **Set timer** for 8 minutes and do not open before time is up. If waffle iron is hard to open, leave a few seconds longer.

Note: When serving a large number, bake waffles ahead of time. Stack and cover with waxed paper. Just before serving, reheat in hot waffle iron just long enough to heat through for soft waffles or longer to make crisp. Sections may be heated in the toaster or in very hot oven, briefly. **Do not** allow to dry.

Barley-Soy Waffles

2¼ cups water
1¼ cups barley flour
1 tablespoon oil

1 cup soaked soybeans
   (½ cup dry)
½ teaspoon salt

Follow method in **Pilot Recipe** for Soy-Oat Waffles except use barley flour in place of rolled oats.

Variation
Use 1¼ cups whole barley, soaked, in place of barley flour.

Cornmeal-Soy Waffles

1 cup boiling water
1¼ cups cornmeal
1 cup soaked soybeans
   (½ cup dry)

1¼ cups cold water
1 tablespoon oil
½ teaspoon salt

Follow method in **Pilot Recipe** for Soy-Oat Waffles, except use cornmeal in place of rolled oats. Bring water to boil in medium-size kettle. **Add** cornmeal all at once. **Remove** from heat. **Stir** until cornmeal is moistened. **Add** cold water. **Proceed** with pilot recipe.

Pinto Bean-Wheat Waffle

2¼ cups water
1 cup soaked wheat
   (½ cup dry)
1 tablespoon oil

1 cup soaked pinto beans
   (½ cup dry)
1 tablespoon sugar
½ teaspoon salt

Follow method in **Pilot Recipe** for Soy-Oat Waffles, substituting soaked pinto beans for soaked soybeans, and soaked wheat (entire grain) for rolled oats.

Garbanzo-Oat Waffles

2$^1/_4$ cups water
1$^1/_2$ cups rolled oats
1 cup soaked garbanzos
  ($^1/_2$ cup dry)

1 tablespoon oil
1 tablespoon sugar
$^1/_2$ teaspoon salt

Follow method in **Pilot Recipe** for Soy-Oat Waffles, substituting garbanzos for soybeans.

Lentil-Oat Waffles

2$^1/_4$ cups water
1$^1/_2$ cups rolled oats
1 cup soaked, raw lentils
  ($^1/_2$ cup dry)

2 tablespoons oil
1 tablespoon sugar
$^1/_2$ teaspoon salt

Follow method in **Pilot Recipe** for Soy-Oat Waffles substituting lentils for soybeans.

Millet-Soy Waffles

2$^1/_4$ cups water
1$^1/_4$ cups millet flour
  or 1 cup millet seeds

1 cup soaked soybeans
1 tablespoon oil
$^1/_2$ teaspoon salt

Follow method in **Pilot Recipe** for Soy-Oat Waffles, except for 1$^1/_4$ cups millet flour (or 1 cup millet seeds) in place of rolled oats.

Pinto Bean-Oat Waffles

2$^1/_4$ cups water
1$^1/_2$ cups rolled oats, regular
1 cup soaked pinto beans
  ($^1/_2$ cup dry)

1 tablespoon oil
1 tablespoon sugar
$^1/_2$ teaspoon salt

Use method in **Pilot Recipe** for Soy-Oat Waffles, substituting pinto beans for soybeans.

Rice-Soy Waffles

1¹/₂ cups soaked
   brown rice
1¹/₂ cups water (from
   soaked rice)

1 cup soaked soybeans
1 tablespoon oil
¹/₄ teaspoon salt

Follow method in **Pilot Recipe** for Soy-Oat Waffles except for rice instead of rolled oats. **Soak** 1¹/₂ cups brown rice 24 hours. **Drain.** Use water in making waffles.

Variation
Use ¹/₃ cup raw cashew nuts instead of the soybeans.

Buckwheat-Oat Waffles
(Pilot Recipe)

2¹/₄ cups water
¹/₂ cup buckwheat flour
1¹/₂ cups rolled oats

¹/₄ cup soy flour
¹/₂ teaspoon salt
1 tablespoon oil

Combine ingredients and blend until light and foamy. **Let stand** while waffle iron is heating. The batter thickens on standing. **Blend briefly. Bake** on hot waffle iron 8-10 minutes. **Do not** raise lid until timer sounds. **Allow** more time, if necessary, to brown.

Note: Ingredients may be combined and allowed to soak for 30 minutes or overnight in refrigerator, then beaten in the electric mixer or by hand, using rotary egg beater or wire whip. Vigorous beating is required. Chilling will aid in forming steam for rising.

Pecan-Oat Waffles

¹/₂ cup pecan meal   1 tablespoon oil
1¹/₂ cups rolled oats   ¹/₂ teaspoon salt
2¹/₄ cups water

Follow method in **Pilot Recipe** for Buckwheat-Oat Waffles substituting pecan meal for buckwheat.

Multi-Grain Waffles

¹/₂ cup rolled oats   ¹/₂ cup soy flour
¹/₂ cup rye flour   2¹/₄ cups water
¹/₂ cup whole wheat flour   ¹/₂ teaspoon salt

Follow method in **Pilot Recipe** for Buckwheat-Oat Waffles, except use rolled oats, rye, whole wheat, and soy flour in place of buckwheat, rolled oats, and soy.

Filbert-Oat Waffles

¹/₂ cup filbert meal, packed   ¹/₄ cup wheat germs
  or ¹/₃ cup filbert nuts   1¹/₂ cups rolled oats
2¹/₄ cups water   1 tablespoon oil
¹/₂ teaspoon salt

Follow method in **Pilot Recipe** for Buckwheat-Oat Waffles, substituting filbert meal for buckwheat or filbert nuts for cashew nuts, in Cashew-Oat recipe.

One Soy-Oat Waffle has protein equal in quantity and quality to that in a serving of steak.

Cashew-Oat Waffles
(Pilot Recipe)

2¹/₄ cups water
1¹/₂ cups rolled oats
¹/₃ cup raw cashew nuts

1 tablespoon oil
¹/₂ teaspoon salt

Combine all ingredients and blend until light and foamy, about half a minute. **Let stand** while waffle iron is heating. The batter thickens on standing. **Blend** briefly.

Grease iron with solid shortening for first waffle. (Do not use margarine.) **Bake** in hot waffle iron 8 to 10 minutes, or until nicely browned. **Set timer** (or check time carefully by the clock) for 8 minutes and do not open before time is up. If waffle iron is hard to open, leave a few seconds longer.

Almond-Oat Waffles

2¹/₄ cups water
1¹/₂ cups rolled oats
¹/₃ cup almonds
¹/₄ cup wheat germ

1 tablespoon oil
1 tablespoon sugar
¹/₂ teaspoon salt

Follow method in **Pilot Recipe** for Cashew-Oat Waffles, substituting almonds for cashew nuts.

Sunflower Seed-Oat Waffles

¹/₂ cup sunflower seeds
2¹/₄ cups water
2 cups rolled oats

¹/₄ cup wheat germ
2 tablespoons oil
¹/₂ teaspoon salt

Follow method in **Pilot Recipe** for Cashew-Oat Waffles, substituting ¹/₂ cup sunflower seeds for cashew nuts.

Cornmeal-Cashew Nut Waffles

1 1/4 cups cornmeal
1 cup boiling water
1/3 cup raw cashew nuts
1 1/2 cups cold water

1 tablespoon oil
1/2 teaspoon salt
1 tablespoon sugar

Follow method in **Pilot Recipe** above (or for Cashew-Oat Waffles) except — **bring** water to boil in medium-size kettle. **Add** cornmeal all at once. **Remove** from heat. **Stir** until cornmeal is moistened. **Add** cold water.

Peanut-Oat Waffles

2 1/4 cups water
1 1/2 cups rolled oats
1/3 cup raw peanuts

1/4 cup wheat germ
1 tablespoon oil
1/2 teaspoon salt

Follow method in **Pilot Recipe** for Cashew-Oat Waffles, substituting peanuts for cashew nuts.

Variation
Peanut Butter-Oat Waffles: substitute peanut butter for raw peanuts.

Eggless French Toast

1 cup soybean concentrate
  (see recipe)
1 cup cold water

1/2 teaspoon salt
2 tablespoons oil
8 slices whole wheat bread

Put Soybean Concentrate into flat bowl. **Add** water, salt, and oil and beat with fork until blended.

Dip one slice of bread at a time into the mixture. **Turn over** to moisten all the way through. **Stir** well before adding another slice.

Put into hot skillet — 350°F, or on a lightly oiled cookie sheet and put in oven at 400°F. **Turn** when nicely browned — about 10 minutes. **Cover. Let cook** 10 minutes longer.

Soya French Toast

1 cup soybean concentrate	2 tablespoons oil
(see recipe)	1 tablespoon lemon juice
1 teaspoon sugar	$\frac{1}{2}$ cup soy milk
$\frac{1}{2}$ teaspoon salt	6 slices bread

Blend concentrate, sugar, and salt together until light and foamy. **Add** oil gradually. **Add** lemon juice. **Empty** into a flat bowl. **Rinse** blender top with soy milk and add to whipped concentrate. **Mix** lightly. **Soak** slices of bread one by one in soy concentrate.

Bake in medium-hot covered skillet, 350°F. **Turn** when nicely browned, about 5 minutes. **Bake** on other side an additional 5 minutes, or until well-browned.

Garbanzo French Toast
(Another Eggless Version)

1 cup soaked garbanzos	2 tablespoons oil
$\frac{2}{3}$ cup water	$\frac{1}{2}$ teaspoon salt
1 cup soy milk (see recipe)	6 slices stale bread

Blend garbanzos with water until very fine. **Add** salt, oil, and Soy Milk. **Blend** to mix. **Pour** into a flat dish.

Soak slices of bread until they absorb as much garbanzos as possible. **Spread** a little of the thick part of mixture on slice with spatula.

Cook on a very lightly oiled skillet until browned nicely on both sides and well-done all the way through — about 10 minutes to a side.

(May be baked on a greased cookie sheet in a hot oven 20 to 25 minutes. Should be turned to brown on both sides and have a crusty texture.) **Yield: 6 servings.**

Variation
Soy French Toast: Follow recipe above except use 1¹/₂ cups soaked soybeans and 1¹/₂ cups water and no soy milk.

Fruit Toast

1 pint cooked fruit, apricots	4 tablespoons peanut butter
2 tablespoons cornstarch or	or other nut butter, or
minute tapioca	4 tablespoons finely
4 slices whole wheat toast	chopped nuts

Heat fruit and thicken with cornstarch or tapioca. **Cover** and let simmer 10 minutes or longer. **Stir** occasionally. **Spread** toast with peanut butter and top with hot fruit. **Yield: 4 servings.**

Variations
1. With cold apple sauce.
2. Put fruit over buttered toast and sprinkle nut meal over top.

Cornmeal with Soy Grits

²/₃ cup cornmeal (whole not degerminated)	3 cups water
¹/₃ cup soy grits	1¹/₂ teaspoon salt

Put 2 cups water and salt into a heavy kettle or top of a double boiler. **Bring** to rapid boil. **Combine** cornmeal and soy grits and moisten with 1 cup cold water.

Stir into boiling water. **Let boil** rapidly for a few minutes.

Stir occasionally to prevent sticking. **Cover.** Reduce heat to simmer or put over boiling water and let cook 30 minutes or longer.

Corn Granola

1 cup cornmeal	1 cup water
1 cup rice flour	$1/4$ cup oil
$1/2$ cup soy flour	1 teaspoon salt
$1/2$ cup wheat germ	

Heat water to boiling point in a kettle large enough to use to mix granola. **Add** cornmeal all at once. **Remove** from heat. **Stir** until all is moistened. **Add** oil. Beat until well mixed. **Add** rice flour. **Stir** to mix. **Add** soy flour and wheat germ. **Mix** with fork. **Knead** lightly.

Dough should crumble but still be moist enough to hold together in small, flat pieces. **Crumble** onto a greased cookie sheet. **Bake** at 350°F, until slightly browned. **Reduce** heat to 200°F and leave until thoroughly dry. **Stir** occasionally. **Yield: 8 $1/2$-cup, 2 ounce servings.**

Variations

Autumn Leaves: Follow recipe above until kneaded. Break off little balls the size of a small marble. Roll on floured board. As they flatten out, points and various shapes will develop. Encourage them to assume the shapes of leaves. Sprinkle lightly with salt.

Pick them up with wide spatula or pancake turner and place on greased cookie sheet. Bake at 350°F approximately 25 minutes. As edges begin to brown, reduce heat. The leaves should be only lightly browned around the edges.

— An idea from Marion Vollmer

Corn Crumbles: Follow method in Corn Granola recipe above until kneaded. Crumble rather sparingly on greased cookie sheet. Sprinkle lightly with salt. Roll quite thin with small rolling pin. The pan should be filled with flakes of various shapes and sizes, from small fingernail to large postage stamp. Bake until lightly browned and thoroughly dry and crisp.

Corn Crumbles may be served with salad or soup, as a breakfast cereal or in a variety of other ways.

Other suggestions: may be used to make Corn Crackers or Corn Sticks.

Good Earth Granola

2 cups rolled oats
2 cups rolled wheat
3/4 cup soy flour
1/2 cup chopped almonds or other nuts (optional)

1/2 cup dates, chopped
1 cup water
1/4 cup oil
1 teaspoon salt

Combine oats, wheat, rye, salt, and nuts in a large bowl and mix. Add dates to water to soften. **Mash** and mix with water. **Add** oil. **Beat** with fork until oil is emulsified. **Pour** over dry mixture, stirring to moisten as evenly as possible. **Mix** with fingers until all is thoroughly dampened.

Crumble in thin layer on greased cookie sheets. **Bake** at 350°F for 10 minutes. **Reduce** heat to 250°F. **Bake** an additional 30 minutes or until thoroughly dry. Should brown very slighty. **Reduce** heat even more if there is a tendency to brown too much. **Yield: 1 quart, or 8 1/2-cup servings.**

Thermos-Cooked Wheat

For 1-quart bottle:
1 1/3 cups unground wheat
2 2/3 cups water
1 teaspoon salt

For 1-pint bottle:
2/3 cup wheat
1 1/3 cups water
1/2 teaspoon salt

Soak wheat 8 to 10 hours. **Drain** soaking water into kettle. **Bring** to boiling point. **Add** salt. **Add** wheat and bring to vigorous boil. **Heat** thermos bottle by filling with hot water. **Empty.**

Fill bottle with boiling wheat. If there is not enough liquid to come up to neck, add a little boiling water. **Make** sure that there is air space in neck of bottle. **Place** stopper and screw cap on securely. **Lay** bottle on side; leave for at least 8 hours.

For breakfast cereal, put to soak the morning before. **Place** in thermos bottle in evening. Wheat will be cooked and piping hot for breakfast. **Yield: 4 ¹/₂-cup servings per pint.**

Variation

Follow method above for soaking wheat and bringing to boiling point. Cover and allow to boil gently, until tender and kernels break open. Time about 45 to 60 minutes.

Whole-grain wheat cooked overnight with hot water in a thermos bottle makes a pleasant and nourishing breakfast.

Soybean Magic!

What delights and what good health come from the once-lowly soybean! Using the methods and basic products presented in this section a tempting variety of good things can be made.

Soy milk, as nutritious as whole milk — for pennies a quart; tofu and soy cheese; soybean concentrate which can take the place of milk and eggs in many recipes in this book; "cream" and cream sauces, "mayonnaise" and whipped topping to grace many dishes . . .

Yes, the soybean lives up to its reputation as the "magic" ingredient of healthful and pleasant dining — the vegetarian way.

Forget any old ideas you may have about "bean taste" in the new soybean products. Cornell University has developed a method for eliminating the strong bean flavor in making soy milk directly from the soybeans — any variety may be used. Formerly only the mildest flavored beans were selected for making milk and even so there was a characteristic soybean flavor. Careful study disclosed that as soon as the bean was broken the enzyme action began to produce the strong flavor. By blending in very hot water the enzymes were inactivated as fast as the beans were broken and so no strong flavor developed. This method is well-adapted to home use.

One pound of beans may produce three and one-half to four quarts of soy milk with approximately the same amount of protein as dairy milk — at a cost only slightly higher than the price of the beans.

This method is a gift of Cornell University to the people.

Soy milk and soy milk products. The same method has been used in nutrition research at Loma Linda University in California to develop a wide variety of interesting and nutritious foods:

1. Soy milk
2. Concentrated soy milk or soy bean concentrate
   a. Cream sauces
   b. Whipped topping
   c. Soy sour cream
      Variation: Garlic sour cream dressing
   d. Mayonnaise
      Variation: Mayonnaise without added oil

Soybean Concentrate
Replaces Milk and Eggs in Many Recipes

Concentrate made from the entire soybean is used in place of milk and eggs in making many interesting dishes. It may be in the form of milk or whipped topping to be used in making foods with a texture that would mask its slight graininess.

Suggestions for use are in making: muffins, cookies, pies, sauces, soy cheese and other foods in an interesting assortment.

Equipment and procedure. Some of the equipment needed and the methods are the same for the first part of both the concentrate and the whipped topping:

Blender	Measuring spoons
Large kettles	Rubber spatula
Large double-boiler	Large strainer
Shallow bowl	About 24″ square of fine mesh
Colander	nylon curtain material

The following ingredients:

1 pound soybeans	7 cups water (for soaking)
2 kettles of boiling water for preheating	4½ to 5 quarts of boiling water for blending

Sort and measure 2¹/₄ cups (1 pound) unbroken soybeans. **Wash** and soak in 7 cups water from 4-16 hours. Have ready large kettles of boiling water.

Drain beans. **Sort** out beans which have been broken while soaking. **Fill** top of blender with hottest water from tap and let stand. **Measure** 1¹/₂ cups sorted, soaked beans into flat bowl or pan. **Set** bowl of beans in sink. **Let** hottest water from tap fill bowl and continue to run slowly over beans.

Empty top of blender and fill with boiling water. **Drain** beans in colander or strainer. **Pour** water from blender over beans in strainer. **Put** hot beans into hot blender. **Cover** with 2 cups boiling water. **Put** lid on securely, place thick hot pads or folded towel on top. **Cover** with folded pastic. **Press** down firmly on cover while starting blender or steam may cause water to spurt out. **Blend** 2 to 3 minutes at high speed.

Caution: Do not allow children around while working with boiling water.

To this point the process for making Soy Milk, Concentrated Soy Milk and Soybean Concentrate is the same — only **proportions of water** are different.

For Soybean Concentrate, empty the slurry (blended soybeans) into a pan. If raw concentrate is desired, cool. Refrigerate. If cooked concentrate is to be used, cook in top of double boiler over hot water, then cool and chill.

To fortify with calcium, add ¹/₂ teaspoon calcium lactate per cup of milk, concentrate, or cream.

Soy Milk and Concentrated Soy Milk

Soy Milk

Use concentrate as prepared above.

Place large strainer over deep kettle or bowl. **Put** square of nylon curtain material over strainer. **Pour** slurry (blended soybean concentrate) into cloth-lined strainer. **Gather** up edges of strainer-cloth in fingers and twist. **Press** lightly with rubber spatula.

Empty contents of strainer-cloth back into blender. **Add** 2 cups cold water. **Blend** briefly. **Pour** again into cloth-lined strainer. **Twist** strainer-cloth and squeeze with hands until most of liquid is extracted. (Some sediment will come through mesh. This will settle to bottom and milk can be drained off.)

Pour into top of a large double boiler. (If a large double boiler is not available, improvise by setting a large pan in a large kettle.)

Repeat process until all of the beans are used. **Heat** pan of soy milk over large kettle of boiling water, 20 to 30 minutes.

Cool quickly by emptying boiling water and filling bottom of double boiler with cold water and setting container of soy milk over the cold water. **Set** in refrigerator to chill.

To flavor/fortify Soy Milk. This step is of extreme importance and may need to be worked out to suit individual or family tastes. Flavorings commonly used and amounts per quart are :

Oil	1 tablespoon
Salt	$1/8$ teaspoon
Sugar, brown	1 to $1\frac{1}{2}$ tablespoons
Vanilla	1 to $1\frac{1}{2}$ teaspoons
Butter flavoring	1 or 2 drops
Coconut flavoring	$1/4$ teaspoon
Vitamin B_{12}	Dissolve one 50 mg. tablet of vitamin B_{12} in 1 tablespoon of hot water. Stir. Use 1 tablespoon of liquid per quart.

Blend one quart of milk at a time, add oil gradually. Add flavorings. The milk is now ready to serve. It is essential that people on a total vegetarian diet have a dependable source of Vitamin B_{12}. It should be used to fortify all soy milk products.

To fortify with calcium, add $1/2$ teaspoon calcium lactate —mixed with a teaspoon of lemon juice—per cup of milk, concentrate, or cream.

Concentrated Soy Milk

Follow method for making Soy Milk except use one-half the amount of water or less.

Cream Sauces

1 cup uncooked concentrated   ¹/₄ cup vegetable juice
   soy milk (see above)

Stir uncooked, Concentrated Soy Milk into hot vegetable juice in sauce pan. **Boil** gently. **Stir** until thickened. **Serve** over cooked vegetables.

Soy Whipped Topping

1 cup chilled, cooked,   ¹/₂ teaspoon vanilla
   concentrated soy milk   1 tablespoon brown sugar,
   (see above)   molasses, honey, sorghum
speck of salt   or 2 tablespoons chopped
2 tablespoons to ¹/₄ cup   dates
   chilled oil   few drops lactic acid

Measure Soy Milk and put in blender. **Add** seasonings. **Blend** until light and foamy. **Add** oil gradually while blending.

Add lactic acid, a few drops — only enough to thicken. (Lemon juice may be used if desired. Use sparingly — only enough to thicken.)

Soy Cream

1 cup chilled, cooked   speck salt
   concentrated soy milk   ¹/₄ teaspoon vanilla
   (see above)   1 tablespoon oil
1 teaspoon brown sugar

Blend all ingredients except oil until well-mixed. **Add** oil gradually. **Chill. Serve** on cereal or pudding.

Note: For creaming vegetables or for use in cooking, use uncooked, Concentrated Soy Milk.

Soy Sour Cream

1 cup chilled, cooked
   concentrated soy milk
1 tablespoon to ½ cup oil
¼ teaspoon salt

1 to 2 teaspoons lemon juice
   or few drops to ⅛ tea-
   spoon lactic acid

All ingredients should be **chilled. Blend** until light and foamy. **Add** salt. **Add** oil gradually. **Add** lemon juice or lactic acid to thicken.

Sweet Cream Custard Sauce

2 cups uncooked soy cream
⅛ teaspoon salt

1 tablespoon brown sugar
½ teaspoon vanilla

Heat Soy Cream in top of double boiler over boiling water, 20 minutes. **Add** flavorings. **Chill.**

Note: If not thickened enough add 1 tablespoon of starch mixed with cold milk or cream before removing from heat. Cook until thickened.

Desserts for Health

The objective of this dessert section is simplicity, attractiveness, natural goodness, and low or no sugar. This is accomplished through the use of fruits, fresh and dried in their natural state; or as ingredients, with little or no sugar, in making a variety of simple cookies, pies, fruit bars, compotes, fruit soup and a nice assortment of other dishes.

Fresh fruits provide the dessert prepared especially for our use by an all-wise and loving Creator; their excellence of beauty, delicacy, deliciousness, and their health-promoting qualities cannot be surpassed. Apples, fresh-picked and crunchy, strawberries with their little green caps and the bloom that is reminiscent of the morning dew, speak of a hospitality that is warm, genuine, and based on true values. A slice of melon in season is appetizing, appealing, low in calories, and refreshing; a sprig of fresh mint adds interest. Or the melon-half may be the center of a fruit plate with a note of elegance to grace any table.

The fruit plate with cornmeal muffins, a scoop of cottage cheese (dairy or soy), and a warm beverage would suggest an interesting menu for a light luncheon or supper.

An arrangement of dried fruits and nuts may be very attractive and appealing. Home-dried fruits may provide a quality that is unsurpassed. Remember their high concentration when planning and serving the meal.

The use of fruit for dessert is time-saving and provides excellence of taste and quality which cannot be improved by any amount of mixing, baking, whizzing or blending, and enables the mother to spend less time in the kitchen and more time with her children, and to honor her guests as a relaxed, unhurried hostess.

The meal should be planned with the dessert in mind. Even an apple or a slice of melon should not be served after a large meal when a sufficient quantity of food has already been eaten. At breakfast or as a part of a light luncheon or evening meal, fruit or simple fruit dessert "fits" perfectly. Meals should be satisfying, attractive, and delicious, with a keynote of simplicity. Desserts should be occasional and fit into the meal pattern supplying their due portion of calories, minerals, and vitamins.

Fruits, grains, and nuts may be combined to make simple desserts of excellent quality and taste appeal which may be used occasionally to add variety and interest. In most of our dessert recipes, unsweetened fruit or fruit juice supplies sufficient sweetening. A moderate amount of sugar may be added occasionally when absolutely necessary and even that should be unrefined sugar if at all possible. As a guideline, two teaspoons of such sugar per serving may be safely used for the normal person. Many of the desserts sweetened by fruits only may be used by those on a diet in which sugar is restricted.

The use of wholesome, low-sugar desserts will be enjoyed by the children and other members of the family if their initial appearance is not prefaced by, "These desserts are good for you." Overenthusiasm sometimes engenders suspicion and predisposes to an attitude of dislike. There are times when "silence is golden."

Sugar vs. Fruit Sugar

Some may question the use of large amounts of fruit in the diet on account of their natural sugar content. The results of a study by Selma Chaij Lukens at Loma Linda University in which 34 subjects on such a diet were tested for serum lipids (fats & cholesterol) are given herewith:

"In this study we attempted to observe the effect of 275

grams (.61 lb.) of fruit carbohydrate in the serum lipids of 34 subjects. The fruit sugar was added in the form of fresh fruits to an otherwise regular diet which was devoid of other sources of sucrose.

"No significant differences were observed in the serum triglycerides (fat), cholesterol, or electrophoretic impressions of the subjects after two weeks on this diet; except in three cases of initial carbohydrate-induced hyperglyceridemia, in which the high fruit diet markedly elevated their serum triglycerides.

"It appears possible then that a generous amount of fruit included in a regular low-sucrose diet which contained enough roughage, bulk and polyunsaturated fats, may not elevate the serum triglycerides of normal subjects. This may be due to some compensatory physiological or nutritional response from fresh fruits. Further studies should be encouraged to fully elucidate the proper management of lipid disorders and the control of lipid metabolism."

Sugar as Food

Sugar is not a *poison* as some pople say. *As it occurs in nature,* in dilute form and accompanied by the minerals and vitamins necessary for its use by the body, it is a wholesome energy food.

Moderate amounts of concentrated sugars for flavoring when used with a well-balanced diet containing ample minerals and vitamins will not be harmful to the normal person. But the rich cakes and pastries high in sugar are not wholesome for any person at any time.

Sugar when eaten alone has the quickest gastric emptying time. Sugar ferments readily when held in the stomach by foods such as fats and coarse vegetables. This causes a sour stomach and indigestion.

In addition it is extreme concentration and lack of the essential vitamins and minerals that make sugar a health hazard. This applies also to the less highly refined sugars. Even in the process of concentrating honey, the bees do not pack in enough of the elements really necessary for use by the body.

Honey is a wholesome food when used in moderation with a diet of unrefined foods high in the necessary minerals and vitamins. Thus is has been used throughout countless ages. Its excessive use with refined foods is not so wholesome.

Little sugar of any kind should be used in cooking and baking. Heat in the presence of sugar is destructive of protein value. This is true in a larger degree when honey or glucose, such as corn syrup, is used in baking or cooking of any kind.

Two important statements, the first made nearly a century ago by an inspired writer on nutrition, Ellen G. White; the second from a recent study reported in the journal of the Southern California Dental Association dramatize the importance of avoiding the super-sweet desserts:

". . . No one can have good digestive powers and a clear brain who will eat largely of sweet cookies and cream cake and all kinds of pies and partake of a great variety of food at one meal. When we do this we take cold, the whole system is so clogged and enfeebled that it has no power of resistance, no strength to combat disease."

"Experimental study has shown the relation between sugar intake and the ability of the body to resist disease. The human body is protected from microorganisms by the white blood cells, which increase in numbers in the blood stream when there is a bacterial infection. They are the body's soldiers of defense. Under normal conditions these white cells are very active and engulf the bacteria and destroy them. However when the level of the blood sugar goes up the cells become sluggish and inactive and the body's defense against disease decreased."

So . . . with every good reason to avoid what is harmful, let us use knowledge and ingenuity to create desserts that are naturally delicious — and healthful.

Apple Pie

2 cups sliced apples
1/2 cup apple juice
  concentrate
1 tablespoon margarine

1/2 tablespoon cornstarch or
  minute tapioca
1 teaspoon fennel seeds
  or 1/2 teaspoon cinnamon

Wash apples. **Peel,** quarter, and remove core. **Slice. Heat** apple juice concentrate in a saucepan. **Add** apple slices, cover, and simmer. **Stir** in cornstarch which has been blended with a little water, or tapioca.

Fill pastry shell (see recipe) with apples. **Dot** margarine over top. **Moisten** edge of crust and put on top crust. **Flute** edge by pinching firmly. The edges should be well-sealed together to prevent juice from leaking out. **Bake** 30 minutes at 350°F. **Yield: 1 9-inch pie.**

For fuller pie, use 4 cups shredded apples and 1 6-oz. can apple juice concentrate.

Orchard Apple Pie

2 cups apple, grated raw
4 cups unsweetened
  pineapple juice

2 tablespoons cornstarch to
  thicken

Select sweet, ripe apples. **Wash,** quarter and cut out the core. **Shred** on medium shredder into bowl containing pineapple juice. **Keep** cut side down to remove skins. **Press** pulp down so that juice completely covers.

Cover bowl and set in refrigerator until ready to serve. (It may stand overnight or longer.)

Pour pulp into a large strainer and let drain for a few minutes.

Heat two cups of the drained juice and **thicken** with cornstarch blended with a little cold juice. **Cool.**

Spoon fruit filling into baked pie shell (see recipe). **Pour** thickened juice over it. **Serve** with your favorite topping. **Yield: 1 9-inch pie.** (See Variations, next page.)

Variations

1. Apple Date Pie: Follow method in recipe above, except add chopped dates and nuts.

2. Cranberry Delight: Follow recipe above, except use 2 cups apple juice concentrate instead of pineapple juice, and

a. add 1 cup ground raw cranberries, 2 tablespoon grated orange rind, and ¼ cup chopped walnuts; or,

b. add 1 cup cooked raisins, 2 tablespoons grated orange rind, and ¼ cup chopped walnuts.

Date-Pumpkin Pie

1 cup water	¼ teaspoon salt
⅔ cups (scant) chopped dates	1 cup uncooked soybean concentrate (see recipe) whipped with 2 table-
2 cups cooked pumpkin	spoons oil
1 teaspoon butterscotch flavoring	1 uncooked pie shell

Heat water in a saucepan. **Add** chopped dates. Mash and stir until smooth and well-blended. **Add** pumpkin and salt. **Simmer,** stirring occasionally until about two-thirds of the original volume. **Fold in** Whipped Soybean Concentrate. **Add** butterscotch flavoring. **Mix** well.

Fill unbaked pie shell. **Bake** at 350°F, 30 to 40 minutes. It should be well set and slightly browned. May be served with Whipped Soy Topping (see below).

Variations

1. In sweetening: ½ cup brown sugar and 2 tablespoons mild molasses or sorghum may be used in place of dates for sweetening. Topping sweetened with molasses or sorghum is a pleasing variation.

2. Chiffon Pumpkin Pie: Use ingredients and method above except use cooked Soybean Concentrate whipped with ¼ cup oil and chilled. Simmer pumpkin until reduced about

$^1/_2$ in volume. Chill. Fold topping into chilled pumpkin, until evenly blended. Fill baked pie shell. Garnish with Whipped Soy Topping (see below) and mint leaves.

Lemon Pie Deluxe

1$^1/_2$ cups unsweetened
  pineapple juice
$^1/_3$ cup cornstarch
$^1/_4$ cup sugar (may be brown)
$^1/_4$ cup lemon juice
2 tablespoons lemon rind

1 tablespoon margarine
Few drops natural yellow
  food coloring
1 cup whipped soy topping,
  chilled (see recipe)

Mix sugar and cornstarch and moisten with $^1/_4$ cup of pineapple juice. **Put** rest of the pineapple juice into saucepan and bring to boil. **Stir** in the cornstarch and sugar mixture and stir until thickened and clear. **Reduce** heat.

Add lemon juice, grated rind, and margarine. **Stir** until blended. **Let cook** slowly an additional 10 minutes.

Chill. Spoon half of filling into baked pie shell (see recipe). **Chill** other half of filling. **Add** chilled, whipped topping and mix just enough to give a marbleized effect. **Spoon** lightly on top of pie. **Yield: 1 9-inch pie.**

Variations

1. Lemon Cream Pie: Follow method in recipe above. except combine all of chilled lemon filling with Whipped Soy Cream Topping. Mix lightly until evenly blended.

2. Lemon Pie with Coconut: Follow method in recipe above, except put all of chilled filling into baked pie shell. Sprinkle $^1/_4$ cup macaroon coconut over top.

Prune Pie

$^3/_4$ cup pitted prunes
$^1/_3$ cup pitted dates
1$^1/_3$ cups apple juice

$^1/_2$ teaspoon natural vanilla
$^1/_4$ teaspoon salt
2 tablespoons lemon juice

Blend all ingredients in a blender until smooth. **Pour** into a baked pie shell (see recipe). **Cover** with Whipped Soy Topping.

Raisin Pie

2 cups raisins	$1/4$ cup water
2 tablespoons lemon juice	$1/8$ teaspoon margarine
1 cup water	1 tablespoon grated orange
$1/2$ to 1 tablespoon creamed flour	rind

Combine raisins, lemon juice, and water in a saucepan. **Bring** to boiling. **Simmer** until raisins are puffed, add flour which has been moistened with water and stirred smooth. **Add** grated orange rind and margarine.

Place in unbaked pastry shell (see recipe) and follow method in recipe for Apple Pie for top crust and baking.

Note: The amount of water needed will depend upon the moisture content of the raisins. If dry, more water may be added. The pie should be moist with a rich, slightly-thickened juice. **Yield: 1 9-inch pie.**

Strawberry Pie

1 quart very ripe strawberries	Few drops of natural red coloring
$1/2$ cup apple juice concentrate	$1/8$ teaspoon salt

Select very ripe, sweet berries. **Stem** and wash berries very carefully. **Drain.** Some may be cut in half if desired. **Save** out $1/2$ cup berries and add to apple juice concentrate. **Blend** until smooth (or berries may be pressed through a fine strainer and added to apple juice).

A Fruit Plate Dessert, Page 127

Ambrosia and Other Fruit Desserts, Page 146

Fruit Nectar, Page 201

Lemon Pie Deluxe, Page 133

Fruit Empanadas, Page 154

Mixed Home-dried Fruits, Page 207

Banana-Date Cookies, Page 148

Strawberry Waffles – Whipped Soy Topping, Page 141

Boil briefly. (It should give a good jelly test: dip up a spoonful of the liquid, hold above the pan and pour out slowly: two or three drops cling to edge of spoon and break off.)

Add a few drops of food coloring. **Cool** and spoon over berries which have been arranged nicely in baked pie shell (see recipe). **Chill. Top** with Whipped Soy Topping (see recipe). **Yield: 1 10-inch pie.**

Variations

Other fresh berries in season may be used: blueberries, raspberries, blackberries; unsweetened crushed pineapple. Drain, thicken juice, and pour over.

Pie Pastry

1 cup whole wheat pastry flour	¹/₄ cup oil
¹/₄ teaspoon salt	3 tablespoons water

Place flour and salt in pie pan to be used. **Measure** oil in measuring cup, add 2 tablespoons water. **Beat** with fork until

Healthful pie crust can be made directly in the pan – fewer dishes to clean and a cradle of good nutrition for your pie filling!

oil is emulsified. **Pour** over flour, stirring with the fork to distribute moisture as evenly as possible. **Mix** until well-blended. **Press** into shape with fingers and **prick** with fork. **Bake** at 375°F for 20 minutes. **Yield: 1 9-inch pie shell.**

Variation

Follow first step in above recipe. Then blend oil in blender. Add 3 tablespoons boiling water gradually. Add ¹/₂ teaspoon lecithin. Remove from blender. Mix with fork into flour in pie pan until well-blended. Then follow last two steps. **Note:** This method produces a very flaky crust.

Other Variations

1. Whole Wheat Pie Pastry (from bread flour):

²/₃ cup whole wheat flour	¹/₄ teaspoon salt
¹/₂ cup (half wheat germ & half soy flour)	¹/₃ cup oil
	3 tablespoons cold water

2. Pie Pastry from White Bread Flour:

²/₃ cup bread flour	¹/₄ teaspoon salt
¹/₃ cup (half wheat germ & half soy flour)	¹/₃ cup oil
	3 tablespoons cold water

Barley Pie Pastry

²/₃ cup barley flower	¹/₄ cup water
¹/₆ cup soy flour	3 tablespoons oil
¹/₆ cup wheat germ	¹/₃ teaspoon salt

Stir barley flour and fill measuring cup to ²/₃ mark with tablespoon. **Fill** cup with approximately half soy flour and half wheat germ. **Add** salt. **Put** into a 9-inch pie pan. **Mix.**

Measure 3 tablespoons oil into cup. **Add** 3 tablespoons water. **Beat** with fork to emulsify. **Add** slowly to dry mixture while stirring with fork. **Mix** until evenly moistened. **Gather** into a ball. **Knead** lightly. **Flatten.**

Place in pan and press into shape with fingers. **Prick** with fork on bottom and sides.

Bake at 400° for 10 minutes or until slightly browned and well done. **Yield: 1 9-inch pie shell.**

Whipped Soy Topping

²/₃ cup fortified soy milk powder
1 cup water
2 tablespoons oil

1 tablespoon lemon juice
1 tablespoon grated lemon rind
Speck of salt

Combine soy milk powder and water in blender until well-mixed. **Add** just enough lemon juice to thicken. **Put** in covered container. **Chill.**

Baked Apples

8 large apples
¹/₂ cup raisins
¹/₄ cup brown sugar

¹/₂ cup water
¹/₄ teaspoon salt

Wash apples carefully. **Cut** in quarters. **Cut** out cores. **Slice** each quarter in two. **Arrange** with raisins in large baking dish. **Combine** sugar, water, and salt. **Pour** over apples. **Bake** at 350°F, 30 minutes or until well done. **Yield: 8 servings.**

Variations

1. Half-cup apple juice concentrate may be used in place of sugar.

2. Apples may be left whole. Core. Fill center with raisins and pour sugar water into centers.

Note: Length of cooking time, amount of water and sweetening depends upon kind of apples.

Golden Apple Dessert

$^1/_2$ cup unsweetened
  pineapple juice
2 large unpeeled, cored
  golden apples

5 medium-size pitted dates
3 tablespoons finely cut
  walnuts
$^1/_8$ teaspoon salt

Place juice and salt in blender. Gradually **add** sliced apples and dates. **Start** on low speed. When mixture is well blended, **stir** in walnuts. **Spoon** into sherbet dishes and garnish, using a stem-on cherry, sliced apple dipped in pineapple juice, or walnut pieces. **Yield: about 4 $^1/_2$-cup servings.**

Dutch Barley Fruit Pudding

1 cup whole barley
3 cups water
1 cup chopped dried apples

$^1/_2$ cup raisins
$^1/_2$ teaspoon salt

Soak barley 24 hours or longer. **Add** dried apples, raisins, and salt. **Bake** in covered baking dish at 350°F for one hour or until juice is thickened. The barley will be chewy.

Note: for softer texture of barley, drain water from soaked barley into a saucepan and bring to boil. Add cold, soaked barley. Let boil two or three minutes. Add fruit and put in baking dish and bake as directed.

Variation

Other fruits may be added as desired.

Grandmother's Old Fashioned Bread Pudding

2 cups cubed stale whole
  wheat bread (6 slices)
1 cup soybean concentrate
  (see recipe)
$^1/_4$ cup brown sugar

$^1/_4$ teaspoon salt
1 teaspoon vanilla
2 tablespoons oil
1 tablespoon lemon juice
$^1/_2$ cup raisins

Cube bread or break into about 1-inch square bits. **Pack lightly** into measuring cup. **Blend** Soybean Concentrate, sugar, salt, and vanilla until very light. **Add** oil gradually. **Add** lemon juice to thicken. **Combine** with cubed bread. **Mix. Add** raisins.

Bake in uncovered casserole or baking dish at 350°F, 30 to 35 minutes. **Brown** lightly. **Serve** with Grandmother's Sweet Cream Dressing (see below) or Whipped Topping. **Yield: 6 servings.**

Grandmother's Sweet Cream Dressing

1 1/2 cups soy cream (see recipe) or other healthful non-dairy creamer

1 tablespoon brown sugar
1/8 teaspoon salt
1/2 teaspoon vanilla

Combine. Mix well. Serve in small pitcher to be poured over pudding as desired.

Variations
1. One-fourth cup chopped dates may be used instead of brown sugar; 1/2 cup chopped dates may be used instead of raisins; 1/4 cup chopped walnuts may be added.
2. One-half cup chopped, dried apples may be used with dates or raisins.
3. Other fruit combinations may be used as desired.

Creamy Rice Pudding

1/4 cup chopped dates
1/2 cup hot water
1 teaspoon ground fennel seeds
2 cups cooked brown rice

1/2 cup raisins
1/2 teaspoon salt
1 1/2 cups whipped, uncooked soybean concentrate (see recipe)

Soften chopped dates in hot water, add ground fennel seeds. **Add** to rice. **Add** raisins and salt. **Mix** well. **Fold** in whipped concentrate.

Bake in covered baking dish at 350°F, 30 minutes. **Uncover** and **bake** an additional 15 minutes. **Yield: 6 servings.**

Variation

Vanilla or other flavoring may be used instead of fennel seed.

Peach Crisp

4 cups sliced peaches	½ cup rolled oats
¼ cup sugar	¼ cup sugar
1 tablespoon tapioca	¼ cup margarine

Combine peaches, sugar, and tapioca in glass baking dish or casserole. **Set** in hot oven while making topping.

Combine rolled oats, sugar, and margarine. **Mix** well with fingers. **Crumble** over top of peaches. **Bake** at 375°F until peaches are well-done and topping is lightly browned. **Yield: 6 servings.**

Variations

Other fruits may be used — apricots, apples, prunes, or berries.

One-fourth cup apple juice concentrate may be used to sweeten the fruit.

Peach Sherbet

1 cup soy cream (see recipe)	1 to 2 tablespoons lemon
1 tablespoon brown sugar	juice
1 tablespoon oil	1 pint frozen peaches

Unmold peaches by dipping in hot water. **Place** on chopping board. **Cube** with French knife.

Blend Soy Cream until foamy. **Add** oil gradually and

blend for a few seconds longer. **Add** lemon juice to thicken. **Drop** peach cubes in one or two at a time until all are blended. **Yield: 1 quart sherbet.**

Note: This sherbet may be placed in cartons and frozen in deep-freeze.

Variations

Use other frozen fruits of your choice.

Fruit Plate Deluxe

Cantaloupe half	Grapes
Cherries	Peach or apricot sherbet
Strawberries	Fresh mint leaves

Wash all fruit carefully and dry. **Place** cantaloupe half in center of plate. **Fill** with fruit sherbet. **Surround** with fresh strawberries with caps and stems left on, cherries, green grapes, and mint leaves. **Yield: 1 serving.**

Variation

Cottage cheese or Soy Cottage Cheese (see recipe) may be placed in cantaloupe center instead of sherbet. Garnish with mint leaves.

Fruit Soup

2 cups fruit juice	1 banana
1/2 cup dried fruits	mint leaves
2 tablespoons minute tapioca	

Heat fruit juice in sauce pan. **Chop** fruits medium-fine and add to juice. **Add** minute tapioca. **Stir** until thickened. **Serve** hot or cold. **Slice** banana on top. **Garnish** with mint leaves and section of dried fruit. Serve hot or cold.

Ambrosia

2 oranges
2 bananas
1/2 cup coconut

1 cup pineapple wedges,
   with juice (fresh or
   canned unsweetened)

Wash and dry fruit before peeling. **Peel** oranges. **Slice** on board. **Cut** into wedges. **Peel** bananas, put into bowl, add orange and pineapple wedges and coconut. **Mix** lightly with fork.

Serve in individual fruit dishes or sherbet glasses.

Garnish with fresh mint leaves and wedge of orange. **Yield: 4 servings.**

Variation

Just plain orange and banana slices with a little extra orange juice served as sauce are delightful. Pineapple wedges may be added for variety. Garnish with mint leaves.

Carrot Cake

4 large eggs
1/2 teaspoon salt
1/4 cup hot water
2 tablespoons lemon juice
1/3 cup corn oil
3/4 cup brown sugar
1 cup grated raw carrot

1 tablespoon grated orange
   rind
1 2/3 cups whole wheat pastry
   flour, sifted 4 times
1/2 cup coconut
1/2 cup pecans, chopped

Drop egg whites into a small mixing bowl and the yolks into a large bowl, adding 1/2 the salt to each. **Beat** the egg yolks until thick; **adding** the hot water while continuing to beat until like meringue. **Add** 1 tablespoon lemon juice, add oil slowly while continuing to beat; **add** sugar slowly while continuing to beat; remove egg beater.

Mix grated carrot and orange rind. **Using** a wire whip, very gently fold in small portions of the sifted flour, alternately with portions of carrot (use as few strokes as possible). **Fold** in coconut.

Beat egg white until stiff; continuing to beat, **add** lemon juice and sugar. **Fold** meringue carefully into batter with the wire whip.

Sprinkle half the nuts on bottom of cake pan. **Pour** batter into a tube pan (or other type pan); sprinkle remaining nuts over top. **Bake** at 325°F for 1 hour. **Test** with toothpick.

Make glaze while baking. **Let stand** for 5 minutes if tube pan is used, then invert to cool (see below). **Pour** glaze over cake when it comes from oven, if desired. **Yield: 16 servings.**

Carrot Cake Glaze

$^1/_2$ cup buttermilk
$^1/_4$ cup sugar (may be brown)

1 tablespoon corn syrup
1 tablespoon margarine

Mix in saucepan. **Bring** to a boil. **Pour** over warm cake.
— Marion Vollmer
from *It's Your World Cookbook.*

Carob-Apple Brownies

1 cup brown sugar
1 cup shredded raw apple
$^3/_4$ cup oil
$^1/_2$ teaspoon salt

1 teaspoon vanilla
$^1/_2$ cup chopped walnuts
2 cups rolled oats
$^3/_4$ cup carob powder

Combine sugar, apple, and oil and **beat** until well-blended. **Add** remaining ingredients. **Mix. Let stand** for 10 minutes for oats to absorb moisture.

Turn into oiled pan (should be about 1$^1/_2$" thick). **Bake** at 375°F, 25 minutes. **Cut** in squares when cool. **Yield: 24 squares.**

Banana-Date Cookies

3 bananas
1 cup chopped dates
$^1/_2$ cup chopped walnuts
$^1/_3$ cup oil

$^1/_2$ teaspoon salt
1 teaspoon vanilla
2 cups rolled oats

Mash bananas, leaving some pieces. **Add c**hopped dates and oil. **Beat** with a fork. **Add** remaining ingredients **Mix** lightly. **Let stand** a few minutes for oatmeal to absorb moisture.

Drop from spoon on ungreased cookie sheet. **Heat** oven to 400°F. **Bake** 25 minutes or until nicely browned. **Loosen** with spatula and let cool on cookie sheet. **Yield: 24 cookies.**

Banana-Date Cookies – simple steps for a tempting delight: add oil to mashed bananas, then brown sugar, wheat germ, dates and nuts.

Carrot-Oatmeal Cookies

1 cup finely grated carrots
  (packed lightly) and water
$^1/_2$ cup brown sugar
$^1/_2$ cup oil
2 cups rolled oats

1 cup macaroon coconut
$^1/_4$ cup soy flour
1 teaspoon vanilla
$^1/_2$ teaspoon salt

Pack carrots lightly in cup; add water to fill to cup mark. **Combine** carrots, sugar, and oil. **Beat** until oil is emulsified.

Add remaining ingredients. **Mix** well and let stand 10 minutes or longer to absorb moisture.

Drop from teaspoon on greased cookie sheet.

Heat oven to 400°F. **Put** cookies in oven and reduce heat to 350°F. **Bake** 20-25 minutes until nicely browned. **Loosen** cookies with spatula and let cool on cookie sheet. **Yield: 24 cookies.**

Date-Apple Cookies

1 cup dates
$^1/_2$ cup water
1 cup shredded raw apple
$^3/_4$ cup oil
$^1/_2$ cup chopped walnuts

$^1/_2$ teaspoon salt
1 teaspoon vanilla
$^1/_4$ cup chopped dates
3 cups rolled oats

Combine dates and water in saucepan. **Heat, mash,** and **stir** until smooth.

Add shredded apple and oil and **beat** until smooth and oil is emulsified. **Add** other ingredients. **Mix** well. **Let stand** 10 minutes to absorb moisture. **Beat** briskly.

Drop from teaspoon on ungreased cookie sheet. **Bake** at 375°F, 25 minutes or until nicely browned. **Yield: 36 cookies.**

Golden Macaroons

1 cup grated raw carrots,
  packed (two medium,
  large carrots)
$1/4$ cup water, or just as
  much as can be poured
  into cup of carrots
$1/2$ cup brown sugar
$1/2$ cup oil

2 cups unsweetened
  macaroon coconut
$1/4$ cup soy flour
$1/4$ cup whole wheat pastry
  flour
$1/2$ teaspoon salt
1 teaspoon almond flavoring

Wash. Peel and **grate** carrots. **Pack** into measuring cup.
Pour water into cup of carrots to fill to one cup mark. **Put**
carrot and water mixture into bowl. **Add** sugar and stir to
blend. **Add** oil. **Beat** with fork to emulsify. **Add** remaining
ingredients. **Mix** until blended.

Drop from spoon on lightly greased cookie sheet. **Bake**
at 325°F, 30 minutes or until nicely browned and well done.
Loosen with spatula and let cool on cookie sheet. (If they
soften on standing reheat to restore crispness before serving.) **Yield: 24 macaroons.**

Macaroons

1 cup soybean concentrate
  (see recipe)
$1/4$ cup sugar
$1/2$ teaspoon salt
$1/2$ teaspoon almond extract

$1/2$ cup oil
$1/8$ teaspoon lactic acid or
  1-2 tablespoons lemon
  juice
2 cups macaroon coconut

Measure chilled Soybean Concentrate and put into blender. **Add** sugar, salt, and almond extract.

Blend about half a minute before adding the oil gradually. **Add** only enough lactic acid or lemon juice to thicken
well.

Put whipped concentrate into a large bowl. **Add** coconut and fold in to mix well.

Drop from tablespoon on oiled cookie sheet. **Press** dough together when dipping with spoon.

Bake at 350°F, 25 to 30 minutes. Should be nicely browned and well-baked.

Loosen with spatula and let cool on cookie sheet. The cookies are very tender and will break easily when warm or if not baked long enough. **Yield: 30 macaroons.**

Yummie Oatmeal Cookies

1 cup soybean concentrate (see recipe)	1/2 cup oil
1/2 cup chopped dates	1/2 cup chopped walnuts
1 teaspoon vanilla	1/4 cup chopped dates
1/2 teaspoon salt	1/4 cup whole wheat pastry flour or very fine whole
1-2 tablespoons lemon juice	wheat flour
	2 cups rolled oats

Measure Soybean Concentrate and put into blender. **Add** chopped dates, vanilla, and salt. **Blend** until well-mixed and light. **Add** oil gradually. **Add** lemon juice to make very thick. **Empty** into a large bowl. **Add** remaining ingredients and mix well.

Drop from tablespoon onto oiled pastry sheet. **Bake** at 350°F, 25 minutes or until nicely browned. **Loosen** with spatula and let cool on cookie sheet. **Yield: 36 cookies.**

Variations
Replace:

1. Dates with other fruits: prunes, raisins, etc.

2. 1 cup rolled oats with 1 cup macaroon coconut.

3. Dates with 1/4 cup brown sugar and 1 cup shredded carrots. Walnuts and 1 cup rolled oats with 1 1/2 cups macaroon coconut.

Brittle Peanut Cookies

1 1/4 cups raw peanuts
1/2 cup water (scant)
1/2 cup brown sugar
2 cups rolled oats

1/2 cup oil
1 teaspoon vanilla
1/2 teaspoon salt

Blend 1 cup peanuts in water until fine (or grind with fine blade) reserving 1/2 cup to chop in medium pieces. **Combine** all ingredients.

Drop on oiled sheet, **press** dough together and **flatten** with side of spoon. **Bake** at 325°F, very lightly browned.

Reduce heat — let dry. **Loosen** with spatula and let cool on cookie sheet.

Peanut Butter Cookies

1 cup soybean concentrate
  (see recipe)
3/4 cup peanut butter
1/4 cup brown sugar
1 1/2 cups rolled oats

1/2 cup whole wheat pastry
  flour
1/2 teaspoon salt
1 teaspoon vanilla

Combine Soybean Concentrate with peanut butter. **Add** sugar. **Mix** well. **Add** rolled oats, salt, and vitamins. **Mix. Let stand** while oiling pan.

Drop from soupspoon. **Flatten** with fork by pressing lengthwise and then crosswise of the pan. **Bake** at 350°F for 25 minutes or until lightly browned. **Yield: 24 cookies.**

Fruit Bars

2½ cups rolled oats
½ cup whole wheat pastry
   flour
1 tablespoon brown sugar

2 tablespoons soy flour
½ teaspoon salt
⅓ cup oil
⅓ cup water

Measure into bowl. **Measure** water and oil in cup. **Beat** with fork until oil is moistened evenly. **Let stand** while preparing filling (see below).

Filling for Fruit Bars

1½ cups dates, raisins,
   or combination
½ cup water

¼ teaspoon salt
½ cup chopped nuts
1 tablespoon lemon juice

Grind raisins or chop in blender with water. **Combine** with chopped dates and nuts. **Add** salt and lemon juice. **Mix** well. **Mix** oat mixture well with fork or fingers.

Flatten a little less than half into bottom of greased 8″x 8″ pan. **Press** down firmly with fingers. **Spread** filling evenly over crust. **Put** remaining mixture over filling. **Press** firmly with fingers or fork.

Bake at 375°F for 25-30 minutes or until a delicate brown. **Cool** before removing from pan. **Loosen** edges, invert pan on cloth-covered tray by putting tray on top of pan and turning over. **Pat** sharply on bottom of pan. **Cut** in 2″ squares **Yield: 16 squares.**

Fruit Squares

2 cups shredded apple
½ cup dates, chopped fine
2 tablespoons orange juice
1 tablespoon grated
   orange rind

¼ cup chopped nuts
1 tablespoon minute tapioca
   or starch
speck of salt

Shred apples and pack in cup. (Add water if juice doesn't come to cup line.) **Combine** apples, dates, nuts, orange, and salt in heavy saucepan. **Mix** well and set over low heat. When hot, stir in tapioca or thickening if needed. **Let thicken** slightly.

Pastry for Fruit Squares

1 cup grated raw apple	1/2 teaspoon salt
2 1/2 cups rolled oats	1/4 cup chopped nuts
1/4 cup oil	1 tablespoon brown sugar

Combine ingredients and mix well. **Let stand** to absorb moisture. **Crumble** half of pastry mixture into 8" x 8" well-greased pan. **Press** down firmly with fork or fingers until pastry is even in thickness and covers the bottom of the pan.

Spoon in apple filling and spread evenly. **Crumble** the remaining pastry over top of apples. **Spread** evenly and press down firmly.

Bake at 375°F, 25-30 minutes until delicate brown. **Cut** in 2" squares.

Fruit Empañadas

6 lefse or tortillas	1 cup fruit spread

Sprinkle lefse or tortillas with water, place in pan. **Cover** with foil. **Heat** in oven at 350°F, 10-15 minutes.

Spread with fruit spread (see below). **Roll** and serve.

Fruit Spreads

1.
1/2 cup ground raisins	1/4 cup chopped nuts
1/2 cup chopped dates	speck salt
1 tablespoon juice	1/2 cup water

2. 1 cup shredded raw apples
   $\frac{1}{4}$ cup raisins
   $\frac{1}{4}$ cup chopped dates
   $\frac{1}{4}$ cup water

   speck salt
   $\frac{1}{4}$ cup orange juice
   1 tablespoon grated
      orange rind

3. 2 cups shredded raw apple
   $\frac{1}{2}$ cup apple juice
      concentrate

   $\frac{1}{4}$ cup chopped nuts
   speck salt

For all Spreads: Combine, simmer until softened and thick enough to spread. For Spread No. 2, add orange juice and rind when cooked.

Reason enough for avoiding ordinary desserts: just count the cubes representing the sugar content of one piece of pie with ice cream!

Mini-Fruitcakes

1½ cups grated apple
½ cup orange juice
½ cup chopped dates
¼ cup oil
1½ cups rolled oats

½ teaspoon salt
2 tablespoons grated orange
rind
¼ cup whole wheat pastry
flour

Make your own **selection** from the following:

1 cup each cut in medium
pieces:
    dried pineapple
    pitted dates
    dried apricots
    dried prunes or figs
    raisins

¼ cup each cut in medium
pieces:
    walnuts
    pecans
    almonds
    Brazil nuts

Shred apples fine and combine with orange juice in bowl. **Add** oil, softened date pieces, and **mix** well. **Add** remaining ingredients. **Mix.**

Let stand while cutting fruit. **Combine** fruits and nuts and mix. **Add** to first mixture and stir well. **Drop** from spoon into small greased muffin pans. **Put** half a cherry on top of each for garnish.

Bake at 350°F, 20 to 25 minutes. **Store** in tightly covered container to prevent drying. **Yield: 48 pieces.**

Yule Log

1 cup pitted dates
1 cup raisins
2 slices dried pineapple
½ cup dried apricots
¼ cup red candied cherries

¼ cup green candied cherries
½ cup walnut halves
½ cup Brazil nuts, whole
½ cup pecans or almonds,
whole

Follow method in recipe above for preparing dates and raisins. **Mix** well. **Set** aside. **Cut** pineapple into medium-size wedges. **Cut** apricots into pieces approximately the same size as pineapple. **Slice** cherries crosswise.

Reserve six rings of each kind and 6 of each of nuts for garnish.

Mix cut fruit and whole nuts together. **Add** date and raisin mixture bit by bit and mix through well. **Press** together and shape into two logs. **Arrange** slices of cherries and **brazil** nuts and halves of walnuts and pecans on top.

Wrap in waxed paper. **Chill.** To serve, slice one log and arrange slices attractively around uncut log on a long dish or platter.

Note: Steam the cut fruit slightly if too dry to hold together well. **Yield: about 60 pieces.**

Peanut Butter Fudge

$1/4$ cup honey
$1/4$ cup molasses (very mild
    or sorghum)
$1/2$ cup peanut butter

$1/2$ teaspoon vanilla
1 cup + 2 tablespoons
    soy milk powder

Combine honey, molasses, and peanut butter and beat until smooth. **Add vanilla. Stir** in dried soy milk powder. **Knead** a little after last addition. Should be firm, but not too dry.

Grease 8"x 8" pan lightly with margarine. **Flatten** fudge into pan by pressing with a rubber spatula until it is of even thickness and fills the corners. **Cut** in 1" squares. **Store** in covered dish. It dries quickly if exposed to air. **Yield: 64 squares.**

Variation
Add $1/2$ cup unrefined sesame seeds.

Coconut Candy

1 tablespoon margarine
$\frac{1}{2}$ cup honey
$\frac{1}{2}$ cup grandma's molasses
   or sorghum

$\frac{1}{8}$ teaspoon salt
$3\frac{1}{2}$ cups macaroon coconut
1 teaspoon vanilla

Grease 8"x 12" pan with margarine.

Combine honey, molasses, and salt in a heavy saucepan. **Boil. Stir** occasionally at first, then constantly as it thickens. **(Test:** a small amount forms a firm ball when dropped in cold water. Temperature 250°F.) **Remove** from heat.

Stir in 3 cups coconut or enough to make very stiff. **Sprinkle** $\frac{1}{4}$ cup coconut into bottom of pan.

Put candy into pan. **Flatten. Cover** with remaining coconut. **Cut** into inch squares before the candy hardens. **Yield: 128 pieces.**

Fruit Candy

1 cup pitted dates
1 cup raisins
1 cup chopped nuts

1 cup macaroon coconut
$\frac{1}{4}$ teaspoon salt

Chop dates. **Grind** raisins through food chopper using medium blade. **Combine** dates and raisins and **mix** well. **Add** chopped nuts and $\frac{3}{4}$ cup of coconut. **Mix** well.

Form into rolls about $1\frac{1}{2}$ inches in diameter. **Roll** in remaining coconut. **Wrap** in wax paper. **Chill. Slice. Store** in cool place in covered container. **Yield: 36 pieces.**

Variations

Dried apples, dates, pineapple, apricots, or other fruits of your choice.

Vegetables

A garden was one of God's first gifts to man. From it comes health-laden food. In the garden the family may find the joy of working together and the satisfaction of mutually contributing to provide the finest food for the family fare.

Vegetables fresh from the garden contain their maximum nutritive value. The shortest time possible should elapse between gathering and serving the vegetables. The methods used in their care and preparation should be those that have been found to retain the highest amount of nutrients.

Those who do not have a garden and must depend on buying from the market should find at what time the vegetables are brought in and should make it a point to buy the vegetables as soon as possible after they arrive.

Vegetables should be washed quickly under running water and dried on an absorbent towel. Excessive moisture should not be left on them, neither should they be left soaking in water, for there may be loss of water-soluble nutrients.

Store in a refrigerator tray. Take care not to crush or bruise leafy vegetables. Damage to cells causes loss of vitamins.

Store in plastic bag or in covered container in a cold place — and use as soon as possible. When vegetables are kept under these conditions the nutritive loss may be comparatively small over a period of two or three days.

The following information on conserving the nutritive value of vegetables is adapted from material provided by Bernice K. Watt and *Woot-Tsuen Wu Leung.*

Fresh vegetables such as kale, spinach, turnip greens, chard, broccoli, and salad greens need to be refrigerated as soon as possible. They keep their nutrients best near freezing and at high humidity.

Leafy, dark-green vegetables and broccoli keep practically all of their ascorbic acid for several days if they are packed in crushed ice. They retain about half of it after five days in

159

the refrigerator at 40° to 50°F. Although this represents a large proportional loss, deep-green leaves have such high initial values that they remain excellent sources of ascorbic acid and vitamin A even after this substantial loss. They could be expected to provide more vitamins C and A than freshly-harvested snap beans and head lettuce — perhaps more even than tomatoes.

Cabbage is a more stable source of ascorbic acid than most leafy vegetables. Kept in cold storage under 40°F, it retains three-fourths or more of its vitamin C as long as two months.

Cabbage should not be allowed to dry out. If it is to be held at home for a few days, it should be wrapped or put in a special compartment where the humidity is high. Cabbage holds its vitamin C well for a few days even at room temperature (usually considered to be 65° to 80°F.).

Among other vegetables that also retain their ascorbic acid well at room temperature and do not require high humidity are a number that stem from tropical plants, like peppers (a rich source of vitamin C), snap beans, lima beans, and tomatoes.

The ascorbic acid in tomatoes vine-ripened out-of-doors in summer sunlight is double that in those grown in greenhouses in winter. Green tomatoes just beginning to turn color also are a good source if they have been exposed to full sun; they may have more vitamin C than red tomatoes from the same plant that ripened under foliage.

Tomatoes picked before they turn red do not reach their best in appearance and nutritive value either on a hot window sill or in the refrigerator. The bright-red color does not develop when the temperature goes above 85°F for very long. A temperature between 60° and 75°F is desirable. Tomatoes become soft, watery, and easily subject to decay when they are ripened in the refrigerator.

Firm, ripe tomatoes can be held at room temperature several days, probably a week, without loss of ascorbic acid. They lose their value rapidly when they become overripe.

Why vegetables lose nutrients. The conditions causing nutritive loss are few and the methods for avoiding such loss are simple and easy to master.

Major loss is sustained through *discarding* peelings, outer leaves, and other parts of high nutritive value. (NOTE: If using vegetables that have been sprayed, it may be necessary to discard outer leaves.) The outer leaves of cabbage have been found to have many times more calcium than the inner bleached leaves. Use the parts high in nutritive value — usually discarded.

Both *light* and *room temperatures* are destructive of nutritive value. Do not allow vegetables to remain on the kitchen table or drainboard. Put at once into a cool, dark place. String beans have been found to lose half of their vitamin C content when allowed to remain out overnight after being picked.

Perhaps even greater nutritive losses are sustained in the cooking of vegetables.

Observe these two rules: a. do not allow vegetables to soak in water; b. use little water in cooking vegetables.

Fifty per cent and more of the soluble nutrients in vegetables may be found in the cooking water. If this water is discarded, considerable loss occurs. The water should all be absorbed by vegetables without scorching. If there is any water left over, use it at once. It is delicious.

Cooking to retain nutrients. Various methods of cooking have been found to retain approximately the same amounts of nutritive value. The principles are the same:

    1. Quick initial heating.

    2. Exclusion of air while hot.

    3. Short time of cooking.

Baking. Baked in their jackets, potatoes are of excellent quality. The initial temperature should be high and the baking time as short as possible. The time may be shortened by preheating the potato in a steam-filled kettle on the top of the stove. (Prick the skin to prevent possible "explosion.")

Broiling is a method that may be used effectively in the

preparation of vegetables. The quick heating tends to reduce vitamin loss.

Pressure cooking. In the pressure saucepan the air is forced out and the space filled with steam; also the length of the time of cooking is reduced. High values for the retention of nutritive value have been found for vegetables cooked on the rack in the pressure saucepan.

Steaming. Steaming has been found effective, especially for vegetables cooked whole in their jackets. With large cut surfaces or flat leaves, as in greens, there may be larger nutritive losses.

Steam-boil. "Steam-boil" is a term used for a method of cookery in which only enough water is used to produce steam — two to four tablespoons. It is sometimes called the "waterless" method. Consistently high values have been found for vegetables cooked by this method.

Add two to four tablespoons of water to kettle. Cover with tight-fitting cover.

Heat over high burner until the kettle is hot and filled with steam. Small head space and hot kettle and water are important.

Add vegetables quickly and cover. Leave on highest heat until kettle is filled with steam. Turn to simmer. Do not leave for any reason with burner turned on high.

Cook only until crisp-tender. Vegetable should be tender but still retain a pleasing firmness; not a soft, mushy texture. The green vegetables should retain their clear-green color.

This steam-boil method is well adapted to the cooking of potatoes in their jackets. Potatoes cooked by this method retain their maximum nutritive value. The skins may be slipped off and the potatoes mashed. Potatoes cooked in their jackets by this method may also be served like baked potatoes. Chopped parsley and/or chopped chives make a pleasing addition. May be served with Soy Sour Cream (see recipe).

Contrasted with these nutrient-saving cooking methods, boiling and draining cause great losses as the following tables show:

Asparagus Tips on Toast

24 asparagus tips
1 cup boiling water
1/2 teaspoon salt
2 tablespoons margarine
   or oil
1 to 2 tablespoons flour

1/2 cup evaporated milk,
   and liquid from asparagus
1/2 cup minced parsley
   (optional)
1 teaspoon salt
4 slices toast

Wash asparagus. **Break** off fibrous end of stem and save for Asparagus Soup (see recipe). **Drop** into rapidly boiling water. **Cook** until crisp-tender. **Remove** tips — keep warm.

Add milk. **Heat. Blend** flour with cold milk. **Add** salt. **Stir** until smooth. **Add** margarine — part may be reserved for toast.

Arrange tips on toast and cover with sauce. Toast may be buttered or not as desired. **Yield: 4 servings.**

Variations

1. Use 1/2 cup water in cooking asparagus and add 1 cup Soy Cream (uncooked) (see recipe). Omit flour.

2. Add 1/2 cup minced parsley.

Dilled Green Beans

2 cups green beans (cooked)
1 tablespoon margarine
1/2 teaspoon dill seed, or
   1 head fresh dill

dash garlic powder
1/8 teaspoon onion powder
1/2 teaspoon salt

Cook beans according to method suggested in recipe for Green Beans, or use canned or frozen beans. **Mash** or grind dill seed.

Add margarine to hot beans. **Add** dill seed to combine with melted margarine. **Add** other seasonings and stir. **Simmer** 2 or 3 minutes. **Yield: 4 1/2-cup servings.**

Beets with Greens

4 beets, 2″ in diameter, $1/2$ teaspoon salt
  with tops   2 tablespoons margarine
Water to cover

Wash carefully. **Cut** tops from beets leaving about $1^1/2$ inches of stems. **Put** beets in boiling water. **Boil** gently until tender. **Wash** greens well and cut in about 2″ lengths with kitchen shears or with sharp knife on chopping board.

Remove beets from kettle when tender and slip off skins while greens are cooking in small amount of beet liquid.

Cook greens 5 to 7 minutes. **Add** peeled beets to greens in kettle to keep hot. When greens are tender, juice should all be absorbed. **Add** salt and margarine, stir in lightly.

Arrange greens in mound in vegetable dish. **Cut** beets in slices or wedges and place around the outside of the greens. **Garnish** with slices of lemon if the beets are cut in wedges and with wedges of lemon if beets are cut in slices. **Yield: 4 servings.**

Harvard Beets

3 cups beets, cooked and   1 tablespoon flour or starch
  sliced $1/4$ cup water
$1/3$ cup beet liquor   3 tablespoons lemon juice
2 tablespoons honey, raw $1/4$ teaspoon onion powder
  or brown sugar   and dash garlic, if desired
$3/4$ teaspoon salt

Follow method in above recipe for preparing and cooking beets. **Remove** skins and slice. **Mix** beet liquor, honey, and salt. **Heat** in saucepan.

Combine flour and water and stir until smooth. **Stir** into boiling liquid and continue stirring until thickened and clear. **Add** lemon juice and sliced beets. **Heat** briefly and serve. **Yield: 6 servings.**

Just Plain Cabbage

8 thin wedges cabbage
1/4 cup water

1 teaspoon salt
1 tablespoon margarine

Put water into a flat, heavy, saucepan. **Cover.** Bring to rapid boil. **Place** cabbage wedges so that the steam can circulate readily. **Cover.** Let kettle fill with steam.

Reduce heat and boil gently 7-10 minutes or until cabbage is crisp-tender. Salt may be sprinkled over wedges as they are placed in the kettle, or after they are cooked according to preference. Margarine may be added just before serving. **Yield: 4 servings.**

Cabbage Baked in "Soy Sour Cream"

4 cups coarsely chopped
   cabbage or 8 thin wedges
1/4 cup water

1 cup soy sour cream
  (see recipe)
1 teaspoon salt

Follow method in recipe above. **Place** cooked cabbage in baking dish with cover. **Pour** cream over. **Cover. Bake** at 350°F, 15-20 minutes. **Yield: 4 servings.**

Panned Cabbage and Celery

1 cup celery, thinly sliced
4 cups shredded cabbage
1 tablespoon oil
1/2 teaspoon salt, or to taste

1/4 cup water
1/4 teaspoon beef-like
  seasoning

Sauté celery lightly. **Stir** in shredded cabbage. **Pour** in water, beef-like seasoning, and salt. **Cover. Steam** 5-7 minutes. **Serve.** May serve with sour cream if desired. **Yield: 4 1-cup servings.**

Carrots with Savory Crumbs

8 small carrots
1/2 cup boiling water
1/2 teaspoon salt
1/4 cup bread crumbs,
    whole wheat, fine

3 tablespoons brewers
    yeast, flake with B_{12}
1 1/2 teaspoons oil
few drops butter flavoring
    (optional)

Wash carrots, scrape lightly. **Place** in flat, steam-filled, heavy saucepan. **Sprinkle** with salt. **Cover. Heat** until steam begins to escape. **Reduce** heat.

Cook 10-20 minutes, until crisp-tender. (Carrots boil dry very readily. **Watch** carefully until you become accustomed to adjusting to heat and amount of water needed for your type of kettle.)

Mix crumbs, yeast, oil, and seasonings. **Roll** carrots in crumbs and serve at once.

Note: For slices or wedges, cooking time will be shorter depending on the size of the pieces and the age of the carrots. Small new carrots fresh from the garden will cook in half the time required for older carrots. **Yield: 4 servings.**

Creamed Carrots with Evaporated Milk

4 medium carrots or 8 small
1 cup water
1 tablespoon margarine

1/2 cup evaporated milk
1 teaspoon salt
1 tablespoon flour

Wash carrots, scrape lightly. **Leave** whole or slice or dice as desired. **Bring** water to boil in flat saucepan. **Add** carrots to rapidly boiling water. **Cover.** Reduce heat. **Boil** gently 15 minutes or until tender but not soft. **Salt.** Liquid should be reduced by half.

Add a part of the milk to the flour in a small bowl and stir until smooth. **Add** remaining milk. **Stir. Add** to carrots and stir until thickened. **Serve** at once. **Yield: 4 servings.**

Variation

Creamed Carrots with Soy Cream: Follow method in recipe above using the same ingredients and method, except use ½ cup Soy Cream (see recipe) instead of evaporated milk; no flour is required for thickening.

Parsleyed Carrots

4 medium carrots, whole,
slices, or wedges
¼ cup boiling water

½ teaspoon salt
½ cup parsley, minced
1 tablespoon margarine

Follow method in recipe above, for preparing and cooking carrots. **Add** salt, margarine, and parsley. **Mix. Serve** at once. **Yield: 4 servings.**

Cauliflower with Savory Buttered Crumbs

4 cups cauliflower florets
(medium)
¼ cup water
1 teaspoon salt

1 teaspoon lemon juice
½ cup savory buttered
crumbs (see recipe)

Follow recipe above for preparing and cooking cauliflower. **Let cook** gently 20 minutes or until crisp-tender. Dip each floret in buttered crumbs and **arrange** attractively in serving dish. **Garnish** with parsley. **Yield: 4 1-cup servings.**

Cauliflower Baked in Soy Cream

4 cups cauliflower florets
½ cup water
1 teaspoon salt
1 teaspoon lemon juice

1 cup soy cream (may be
sour or sweet cream —
see recipe)

Wash cauliflower and separate into medium-size florets. **Put** water and lemon juice into heavy, flat saucepan. **Cover. Bring** to rapid boil.

Put cauliflower into pan. **Salt. Cover. Bring** to rapid boil. **Reduce** heat and cook gently 5-7 minutes. **Place** in baking dish. **Add** liquid, if any. **Add** Soy Cream. **Cover. Bake** 15-20 minutes. **Yield: 4 1-cup servings.**

Celery and Green Beans

2 cups green beans (cut in 1″ pieces)	1 teaspoon salt
	½ cup water
2 cups celery, cut diagonally	1 tablespoon margarine

Bring water to boil in flat saucepan. **Add** vegetables. **Cover. Fill** kettle with steam. **Lower** heat, keep boiling gently, 15-20 minutes, or until crisp-tender. Salt may be added before or after cooking according to preference. **Add** margarine just before serving. **Yield: 4 servings.**

Variation

Creamed Celery and Green Beans: Follow method in recipe above for amounts and ingredients, except add ½ cup Soy Cream (see recipe) just before serving and let simmer briefly to thicken. Or add ½ cup evaporated milk. Thicken if desired with ½ tablespoon flour blended with 2 table-spoons water.

Corn on the Cob

6 ears corn	½ cup water

Remove husks and silks. (To remove silks easily hold ear under cold running water and brush with soft vegetable brush.) **Bring** water to boil in heavy covered kettle. **Place** corn in kettle, uncrowded.

Cover. Bring to rapid boil. **Reduce** heat. **Boil** gently 7 or 8 minutes. **Serve** at once. (A rack in the bottom of the kettle so corn may be cooked in steam is very good.)

Note: Corn cooked in this manner retains its maximum sweetness. It is at its best when the time from the garden to the table is only 15 minutes.

Escalloped Corn and Tomatoes

2 cups tomatoes	2 cups soft bread crumbs,
2 cups corn	or 1 cup dry
1 cup soaked garbanzos	1 tablespoon raw or brown
¹/₂ cup water	sugar
1 teaspoon salt	2 tablespoons margarine

Drain juice from tomatoes and corn. **Save. Blend** garbanzos until fine with water. **Add** tomato and corn juice. **Mix.**

Fill baking dish with alternate layers of tomatoes, corn, bread crumbs and part of the juice mixture. **Sprinkle** each layer lightly with sugar and salt, and dot with margarine. **Bake** uncovered at 350°F, 30 minutes. **Yield: 8 servings.**

Variation
Chopped green bell peppers and sweet basil may be added.

Corn Fritters

1 cup corn with liquid	1 cup uncooked whipped
¹/₂ teaspoon brown sugar	soybean concentrate
¹/₂ teaspoon salt	(see recipe)
2 tablespoons flour	

Mix sugar and salt with flour. **Stir** into corn. **Fold** Whipped Soybean Concentrate into corn.

Drop from tablespoon onto medium-hot (350°F) skillet. **Cover. Cook** 10 minutes. **Turn. Cook** 10 minutes longer. Should be nicely browned on both sides. **Serve** at once. **Yield: 4 2-fritter servings.**

Eggplant

4 slices eggplant, ³/₄″ thick   ¹/₄ cup water
¹/₂ teaspoon salt

Bring water to boiling point in covered saucepan. **Arrange** slices so that steam can penetrate each. **Cover,** until kettle is filled with steam. **Reduce** heat. **Cook** until tender, 15-20 minutes.

Broiled Eggplant

4 slices eggplant, ³/₄″ thick   1 tablespoon margarine
¹/₂ teaspoon salt

Peel and slice eggplant ³/₄″ thick. **Broil** on both sides until nicely browned and tender. **Sprinkle** with salt and **dot** with margarine.

Eggplant with Garbanzo Batter

8 slices eggplant   ¹/₂ cup water
1 teaspoon salt   1 tablespoon oil
1 cup soaked garbanzos   ¹/₄ teaspoon salt

Wash, peel, and slice eggplant into ¹/₂″ slices. **Sprinkle** slice lightly on both sides with salt.
Blend 1 cup soaked garbanzos with ¹/₂ cup water and

Retaining Vegetable Nutrients, Page 161

Green, Leafy Vegetables Rival Milk in Protein

Root Vegetables, Pages 164-167

Split Pea Chowder, Page 183

¼ teaspoon salt until very fine. **Spread** garbanzo mixture on both sides of slices. **Place** in lightly oiled skillet at 350°F. **Cover.**

Cook 10 minutes **Turn. Cover** and cook 10 minutes longer.

Variations

1. Eggplant with Garbanzo Batter and Savory Crumbs: Follow method in recipe above, except sprinkle ¼ tablespoon of savory crumbs on each side after spreading on the garbanzo mixture.

2. Eggplant with Egg and Savory Crumbs: Follow method in recipe above, except roll in beaten egg and crumbs before cooking.

Eggplant with Tomato Sauce

2 cups diced eggplant	¼ cup chopped green
¼ cup water	peppers
½ teaspoon salt	2 teaspoons raw or brown
1 cup cooked tomatoes	sugar
¼ cup onions	¼ teaspoon salt
½ tablespoon oil	¼ teaspoon sweet basil

Cook diced eggplant 10 minutes, or until tender and water is mostly absorbed. **Put** sautéed onions and chopped green peppers in skillet.

Add juice of the tomatoes and **let boil** gently until reduced about half in amount. **Cut** tomatoes in small pieces and add with seasonings.

Add cubed eggplant. **Mix** well and **let simmer** a few minutes to absorb flavor. Sauce should be quite thick.

Parsleyed Parsnips

1 large parsnip	1 tablespoon oil
1/4 to 1/2 cup water	1/2 cup chopped parsley
1/2 teaspoon salt	

Wash and peel parsnip. **Cut** in slices, dice, shred, or grind according to personal preference. **Bring** water to boiling in flat, heavy saucepan. **Add** salt and parsnip. **Heat** on high steam.

Reduce heat. (Caution: do not turn attention to anything else until heat is turned down.) **Allow** to simmer gently until parsnips are tender. Water should be absorbed. **Add** oil and chopped parsley. **Serve** at once. **Yield: 4 servings.**

Parsnip Patties

1 large parsnip	1/4 cup water
(2 cups shredded)	1/2 teaspoon salt
1/2 cup soaked garbanzos	1 tablespoon oil

Shred raw parsnips on medium-coarse shredder. **Blend** raw soaked garbanzos in water until fine or grind using fine blade in grinder. **Combine** all ingredients.

Drop from tablespoon on lightly oiled skillet (about 325°F). **Cover. Let cook** 5 minutes, or until nicely browned. **Turn. Cover. Reduce** heat to 300°F and let cook 15 minutes. **Yield: 6 servings.**

Note: May be spread thin for crisp texture or made into a regular patty.

Variation

Parsnip Patties with Egg: Follow method in above recipe except use egg instead of garbanzos and water.

Green Peas

2 cups green peas
1/4 cup water

1/2 teaspoon salt
1 tablespoon margarine

Bring water to boil in covered, flat, quart-size kettle. **Add** peas quickly. **Cover. Bring** to boiling. **Reduce** heat. **Boil** gently 3 to 5 minutes depending upon the size of the peas. **Add** salt and margarine and serve at once. **Yield: 4 1/2-cup servings.**

Creamed Peas

2 cups green peas
1/4 cup water
1/2 cup soy cream (see recipe)

1/2 teaspoon salt
1 tablespoon margarine
1/2 tablespoon flour

Follow method in recipe above for cooking peas. **Combine** Soy Cream and flour and **stir** until smooth. **Add** to peas when they have cooked 3 minutes. **Stir** and cook until thickened about 2 minutes.

Note: a. Flour that has been previously heated is best for creaming.

b. When uncooked Soy Cream is used flour may be omitted.

c. Evaporated milk may be substituted for Soy Cream.

Creamed Peas in Toasted Shells

2 cups green peas
1/4 cup water
4 slices whole wheat bread
1/2 cup soy cream

1/2 teaspoon salt
2 tablespoons margarine
1/2 tablespoon flour

Follow generally recipe for Green Peas. **Cut** crusts from slices of whole wheat bread, making squares. **Put** squares into muffin pans with points up. **Put** crusts into pan and toast for dried crumbs.

Toast shells and crumbs in oven at 400°F while peas are cooking. **Spread** lightly with margarine. **Fill** with creamed peas. **Serve** at once.

Creamed Peas and New Potatoes

2 cups green peas
4 small new potatoes
   (approximately one pound,
   2 inches in diameter)
1 cup soy cream

1 tablespoon margarine
$^1/_2$ cup water
$^1/_2$ teaspoon salt
1 tablespoon flour

Wash potatoes and **scrape** off skin with a paring knife or plastic scouring pad. **Cut** out any spots. **Divide** into quarters. **Boil** water in covered kettle. **Add** potatoes and salt. **Cover.** **Let** kettle fill with steam. **Reduce** heat. **Simmer** until tender, 15 to 20 minutes. **Follow** generally recipe for Green Peas. **Add** creamed peas. **Stir** lightly to mix. **Serve** at once. **Yield: 4 servings.**

Note: Peas should be cooked in the shortest possible time. Do not put on to cook until everything is in readiness.

Mashed Potatoes

2 large potatoes
   (1 lb.)
1 cup boiling water
1 teaspoon salt

$^1/_2$ cup evaporated milk
   (or soy cream – see recipe)
1 tablespoon margarine

Scrub potatoes. **Cut** out any spots. **Avoid** breaking skin as much as possible. **Put** whole potatoes into boiling water.

Cover. Bring to full boil. **Reduce** heat to keep boiling gently. **Cook until tender.** Water should be mostly absorbed.

Peel the skins off, holding with fork. **Do not** peel away any of the potato, unless spots make it necessary. **Place** potatoes in heated kettle and mash. **Add** Soy Cream or evaporated milk, salt, and margarine and whip until light and fluffy. **Serve** at once. **Yield: 4 servings.**

Russian Mashed Potatoes

2 large potatoes	1/2 cup soy sour cream
1 cup chopped onions	(see recipe)
1/2 to 1 cup boiling water	1 tablespoon margarine
1 teaspoon salt	

Wash potatoes. **Cut** out any spots. **Scrub** off skin with plastic scouring pad and knife. **Quarter** potatoes and add with onions to boiling water. **Salt. Cover. Bring** to full boil. **Reduce** heat to keep boiling gently.

Cook 25 minutes or until tender. Water should be absorbed. **Mash. Add** sour cream and margarine. **Beat** until light and fluffy. **Serve** at once. **Yield: 4 servings.**

Steam-Boiled Potatoes

4 medium potatoes	1/2 cup water

Select uniform potatoes. **Scrub** with a vegetable brush. **Cut** out any spots. **Bring** water to boil in covered, heavy kettle. **Add** potatoes. **Cover. Let** steam fill kettle. **Reduce** heat to gentle boiling. Steam should continually fill kettle.

Cook 30 minutes, or until tender. (The length of time depends upon the size and variety of potatoes. The potato skin is nonpermeable and potatoes steam-boiled with unbroken jackets should contain their maximum of original nutrients.)

Rutabagas

4 cups rutabagas, diced	1 tablespoon margarine
1 teaspoon salt	¹/₂ cup water

Wash and peel rutabagas. **Dice. Bring** water to boil in heavy saucepan. **Add** diced rutabagas. **Cover. Let** kettle fill with steam. **Reduce** heat and let boil gently until rutabagas are tender, 20 minutes or longer. **Season.**

Variation

Cook 30 minutes and mash rutabagas with salt and margarine. Serve piping hot.

Zucchini — Plain

4 small zucchini, about 4″ long (1 lb.)	1 teaspoon salt
2 tablespoons water	1 tablespoon margarine

Wash zucchini. **Trim** off stem and blossom ends. **Slice** into ¹/₂″ sections or shred on coarse shredder. **Put** water in heavy sauce pan. **Cover. Bring** to boiling. **Put** zucchini in kettle. **Cover. Heat** until kettle is full of steam. **Reduce** heat to keep a good live steam.

Cook 5-7 minutes, or until crisp-tender. Water should be absorbed. **Salt** after cooking. (Salting before cooking draws out juices and makes the zucchini soupy.) **Serve** plain or with Savory Crumbs, or Soy Sour Cream, or Sour Cream Dressing (see recipes). **Yield: 4 servings.**

Zucchini Slices with Garbanzos

8 slices zucchini	1 cup soaked garbanzos
¹/₂ teaspoon salt	¹/₂ cup water
1 tablespoon oil	¹/₄ teaspoon salt

Wash zucchini slices. **Place** on cookie sheet. **Sprinkle** both sides lightly with salt. **Heat** skillet medium-hot, 350°F. **Blend** garbanzos with water and salt until very fine. **Spread** garbanzo mixture on top of slices. **Pick** up slices one at a time. **Spread** mix on other side.

Put into lightly oiled skillet. When all are in the skillet, **cover. Let cook** 10 minutes. **Turn. Let cook** 10 minutes longer. **Yield: 4 servings.**

Zucchini in Tomato Sauce

½ cup sautéed onions	2 cups zucchini, small,
½ cup minced green	unpeeled, cut in slices or
bell peppers	small chunks (1 lb.)
2 cups cooked tomatoes	2 tablespoons water

Put sautéed onions and minced green bell pepper into saucepan. **Add** juice of cooked tomatoes. **Let simmer** until about half in quantity. **Cut** tomatoes in small pieces or mash. **Add** to juice, **add** sugar and salt to taste, and **let simmer.**

Select small, tender zucchini. **Wash.** Do not peel. **Cut** as desired. **Put** 2 tablespoons water in small sauce pan. **Cover,** bring to rapid boil. **Add** cut zucchini. **Cover. Let** pan fill with steam. **Reduce** heat.

Simmer gently for 8-10 minutes, or until tender. Water should be absorbed. **Salt. Add** to tomatoes. **Add** 1 teaspoon basil, crushed fine. **Mix** well. **Simmer** for a few minutes. **Serve** at once. **Yield: 4 servings.**

Soups and Salads

Asparagus Soup

2 cups fibrous ends of
asparagus
$1/2$ cup soy cream or
uncooked soybean con-
centrate (see recipe) or
evaporated milk

2 cups boiling water
$1/2$ teaspoon salt
$1/4$ teaspoon onion powder
1 tablespoon margarine
or oil

Wash and cut asparagus ends into one-inch pieces. **Drop** into rapidly boiling water. **Let boil** gently for 3 minutes. **Cool.**

Blend until chopped fine. **Strain. Reheat.**

Add onion powder. **Stir** in Soy Cream or Concentrate or evaporated milk. **Add** oil or margarine, more salt if necessary. **Serve** piping hot with zwieback, breadsticks, or croutons. **Yield: 2 1-cup servings.**

Creamy Bean Soup — With Evaporated Milk

2 cups cooked beans
(brown, white, or a
mixture of string beans
and shell beans)

$1/2$ teaspoon onion powder
2 cups water
$1/2$ teaspoon salt
1 cup evaporated milk

Follow method in **Pilot Recipe** for cooking beans. **Measure. Blend** beans with water, onion powder, and salt. **Bring** to boiling point. **Add** evaporated milk. If too thick, thin with water. **Serve** piping hot, garnished with parsley. **Yield: 5 1-cup servings.**

Variation

May use Soybean Concentrate (thinned with water) or Soy Cream (see recipe).

180

Old Homestead Bean Soup

1 cup navy beans
4 cups boiling water

1 teaspoon salt
2 tablespoons margarine

Follow method in **Pilot Recipe** for cooking beans. Cook very well-done. **Thin** as desired with water or milk. **Add** margarine. **Mash** lightly, or serve as is. Other seasonings may be used as desired.

Ye Olde Time Soup

$^1\!/_2$ cup barley, whole,
   unrefined
5 cups water
1 cup split peas
1 cup sautéed onions

1 teaspoon salt
1 tablespoon margarine
$^1\!/_2$ teaspoon thyme or
   sweet basil

Soak barley in one cup water several hours or overnight. **Boil** 4 cups water. **Add** split peas, soaked barley, and onions. **Cover.** Boil gently until barley is cooked and peas are tender.

Add salt, margarine, and herbs. **Simmer** 10 minutes. **Serve** with zwieback, breadsticks, or croutons.

Creamy Bean Soup, rich in nutrition and taste appeal. Soups are not "extras" in good meal planning but rather are part of the basic nutritional pattern.

Cream of Corn Soup

1 cup cooked soybean concentrate (see recipe)	1 tablespoon lemon juice
	2 cups cooked corn with juice
³/₄ cup cold water	¹/₂ cup sautéed onions
1 tablespoon oil	1 teaspoon salt

Blend concentrate and water together. **Add** oil gradually. **Add** lemon juice. **Add** corn and salt. **Blend** until smooth. **Heat,** do not boil. **Serve** with crackers, zwieback, croutons, or bread sticks.

Kale Soup

¹/₂ cup sautéed onions	4 cups boiling water
1 cup diced potatoes	1 tablespoon oil
2 cups minced kale	1 teaspoon salt

Combine onion, diced potatoes, minced kale, salt, and water and cook 20 to 25 minutes. Evaporated or Soy Milk may be added if desired. **Serve** with zwieback or bread sticks. **Yield: 6 servings.**

Variations

Soup may be blended if desired.
One-half cup evaporated milk may be added.

Cream of Pea Pod Soup

1 quart fresh pea pods	¹/₂ to 1 teaspoon salt
3 cups cold water	1 tablespoon margarine, or
¹/₂ cup soy cream (see recipe) or evaporated milk	1 tablespoon oil with 2 drops butter flavoring

Blend half of the pea pods with 1¹/₂ cup water until pulp is separated from fiber. **Pour** into strainer placed over sauce pan. **Press** out all the liquid possible. **Rinse** with ¹/₂ cup water and press to get all the liquid. **Repeat** with second half of pea pods using part of liquid in blending. **Discard** fibers.

Heat liquid in heavy saucepan. **Add** Soy Cream (see recipe). (If you use evaporated milk instead, blend with 1 tablespoon flour before adding.) **Let simmer,** stirring until slightly thickened. **Reduce** heat to lowest. Boiling may curdle. Short cooking is essential.

Dish into soup bowls. **Garnish** with 1 tablespoon Soy Sour Cream (see recipe), 1 tablespoon cooked peas, and 1 tablespoon grated carrots. **Yield: 4 servings.**

Split Pea Soup

1 cup (slightly rounded) split peas	4 cups water
¹/₂ cup sautéed onions	2 teaspoons salt
1 tablespoon oil	¹/₂ teaspoon sweet basil

Wash peas. **Add** to rapidly boiling water. **Add** onions. **Cover. Boil** gently until tender or if desired until a smooth texture. **Add** seasonings. **Yield: 4 servings.**

Variation
Add ¹/₂ cup Soy Cream or evaporated milk.

Split Pea Chowder I

6 cups water	1 tablespoon oil
¹/₂ cup brown rice	¹/₂ cup finely diced carrots
2 cups split peas	¹/₂ cup finely diced celery
2 teaspoons salt	¹/₂ teaspoon sweet basil
1 cup sautéed onions	

Add rice to rapidly boiling water in large kettle. **Cover. Bring** to full boil and let cook 30 minutes. **Add** peas and cook

30 minutes. **Add** salt and sautéed onions. **Add** carrots and celery to soup and let cook 10 or 15 minutes. Vegetables should be "crisp and tender." **Add** sweet basil, test and season to taste.

Serve over slices of whole wheat bread.

Split Pea Chowder II

1 cup split peas
½ cup sautéed onions
4 cups boiling water
2 cups diced potatoes
¼ cup minced celery tops

1 teaspoon salt
1 cup evaporated milk, or
    soy milk
1 tablespoon margarine

Combine peas and sautéed onions and add boiling water. **Bring** to boil. **Cook** 15 minutes. **Add** diced potatoes, celery tops and salt. **Cook** until potatoes are tender, 15-20 minutes. **Add** milk and margarine. **Serve** at once. Additional water may be added if necessary. **Yield: 6 servings.**

Variation
Beans may be used instead of peas.

Potato Soup

1 cup sautéed onions
2 cups diced potatoes
1 cup chopped celery
2 teaspoons salt
4 cups boiling water

1 cup soy cream or
    evaporated milk
1 tablespoon margarine,
    optional

Combine vegetables and salt. **Add** to boiling water. **Cover. Boil** gently 30 minutes or until vegetables are tender. **Add** Soy Cream (see recipe). **Let simmer** 10 minutes. **Add** margarine. **Mash** if desired. **Yield: 8 servings.**

Variations

1. Corn Chowder: Add one cup of corn.

2. Add ½ cup lentils to combined vegetables before adding to boiling water, or add 1 cup tomatoes.

3. Creamy Potato Soup: Blend cooked potato soup until creamy and serve at once.

Russian Mashed Potato Soup

2 cups diced potato	1 cup soy sour cream
½ cup sautéed onions	(see recipe)
1 teaspoon salt	1 tablespoon margarine
3 cups boiling water	

Add diced potatoes, onions, and salt to rapidly boiling water in a heavy sauce pan. **Cook** 20 minutes, or until potatoes are tender.

Blend briefly until potatoes are fine. **Add** Soy Sour Cream and margarine. **Serve** hot or cold.

Note: Leftover Russian Mashed Potatoes may be used. Add one cup of milk or soymilk and ⅓ cup of soy sour cream for each cup of mashed potatoes. **Yield: 6 1-cup servings.**

Variation

Buttermilk may be used in place of milk and sour cream if desired.

Instant Russian Mashed Potato Soup

3 cups boiling water	1 teaspoon salt
½ cup sautéed onions	1 cup soy sour cream
1 cup instant mashed potato	concentrate (see recipe)
potato flakes	¼ cup chopped parsley

Add onions and salt to boiling water, remove from heat. **Add** ³/₄ cup Soy Sour Cream Concentrate. **Pour** flakes into liquid, pressing flakes under liquid.

Let set for 30 seconds. **Stir** gently, do not beat. **Garnish** with chopped parsley and a tablespoon of whipped sour cream. **Yield: 4 1-cup servings.**

Note: ¹/₂ teaspoon of onion powder or ¹/₄ cup of dried onion flakes may be used instead of sautéed onions.

Cream of Tomato Soup

1 cup cooked soy cream concentrate (see recipe)	1 tablespoon sugar
	1 teaspoon salt
³/₄ cup cold water	1¹/₂ cups tomatoes
2 tablespoons oil	

Blend concentrate and water together. **Add** oil gradually. **Add** seasonings. **Add** tomatoes. **Blend. Heat** in sauce pan. **Serve. Yield: 4 servings.**

Vegetable Soup with Lentils

1 cup sautéed onions	2 small carrots or 1 large – sliced or diced
2 cups diced potatoes	
1 cup chopped celery	1 tablespoon salt
¹/₂ cup lentils	8 cups boiling water

Put sautéed onions in large kettle. **Add** lentils, vegetables and salt. **Add** boiling water. Boil gently 30 minutes. May be served as a thick chowder or vegetables mashed and more water added if desired. **Yield: 8 servings.**

Variation
Add 1 cup cooked tomatoes cut in medium size pieces.

Hearty Vegetable Soup

1 quart water
1/2 cup commercial textured
   vegetable protein (TVP),
   beef-like chunks (small)
1/4 cup barley
1/4 cup split peas

1 cup onions, chopped
1 cup diced carrots
1 cup diced turnips
1 cup chopped cabbage
1/2 tablespoon salt
1/4 cup parsley, chopped fine

Soak TVP chunks and barley in water 30 minutes or longer. **Bring** to boiling point, add split peas. **Let cook** 20 minutes. **Add** remaining ingredients, except parsley. **Cook** an additional 20 minutes. **Add** parsley a few minutes before serving. **Serve** with whole wheat zwieback, bread sticks, or croutons: **Yield: 4 servings.**

Vitamin Cocktail Soup

discarded outer leaves,
   stems, peelings. tops of
   various vegetables
1 cup boiling water, and
1/4 teaspoon salt for each
   cup chopped vegetables

1 medium onion
1 cup diced potatoes
1 cup soy cream (see recipe)
   or evaporated milk
1 tablespoon margarine

Store carefully washed and dried vegetable parts in plastic bag or refrigerator tray until preparation of vegetable for meal is complete or until there is sufficient quantity for use.

Cut chilled vegetable pieces into medium pieces with a sharp knife or kitchen shears.

Add to rapidly boiling water using equal amounts of vegetables and water. **Add** salt. **Boil** gently for 15 minutes. **Blend. Strain** as much pulp through strainer as possible. **Add** soy or evaporated milk and margarine. **Serve** hot. **Yield: 2 servings for each cup vegetables.**

Variation

Vitamin Broth: Use 2 cups boiling water, omit milk, add 1 teaspoon chicken-like seasoning.

Washington Chowder

½ cup sautéed onions	1 teaspoon salt, or to taste
2 cups sliced potatoes.	¼ teaspoon savory
1 cup corn	4 cups water
2 cups stewed tomatoes	1½ cups evaporated milk, or
½ cup chopped celery	soymilk (see recipe)
2 tablespoons oil	

Put oil, onion, celery, and savory into a sauce pan and let simmer for a few minutes. Do not brown.

Add the potato, water, and salt and let boil 15 minutes. **Add** corn and tomato. **Let boil** gently for 20 minutes. Just before serving add evaporated or Soy Milk. **Yield: 6 servings.**

Chilled Zucchini Buttermilk Soup

½ cup sliced onion	1 teaspoon chicken-like
1 tablespoon polyun-	• seasoning
saturated vegetable oil	½ teaspoon salt
2 cups sliced zucchini	2 cups buttermilk

Sauté onion in oil (do not brown). **Add** sliced zucchini, **steam** until zucchini is tender. **Sprinkle** on seasonings; **turn** a time or two to distribute seasonings. **Chill** slightly.

When ready to serve soup, **place** 1 cup chilled buttermilk in blender; **add** ½ cup chilled zucchini-onion mixture. **Whiz** until well-blended. **Taste** for seasoning. **Add** more salt and chicken-like seasoning if desired. **Yield: 4 servings.**

Beet Salad

2 cups coarsely-shredded
   beet pickles
1/2 cup chopped bread and
   butter pickles

1 cup cooked garbanzos
3/4 cup soy sour cream
   (see recipe)

Combine beet pickles, cooked garbanzos, and bread-and-butter pickles. **Add** Soy Sour Cream. Mix lightly. **Serve** on nest of dark-green lettuce leaves, whole or shredded.

Carrot Salad

2 cups ground carrots
1 cup macaroon coconut
1/2 teaspoon salt

1/2 cup soy mayonnaise
   (see recipe)

Grind carrots or shred on coarse shredder to give chunky texture. **Combine** all ingredients. Serve on dark-green lettuce leaves — or nest. **Yield: 4 servings.**

Variation
Substitute 1/2 cup coarsely chopped peanuts for macaroon coconut.

Cole Slaw

4 cups cabbage
1 teaspoon salt
1/2 teaspoon onion powder
2 tablespoons lemon juice

1/2 cup soy sour cream
   (see recipe)
2 tablespoons sugar

Select very crisp, firm cabbage. **Wash. Place** in plastic bag. **Store** in refrigerator. **Shred** very fine with sharp knife on cutting board. (There is evidence that cabbage cut with a sharp knife retains more nutrients than when put through a grinder.)

Combine with sour cream and seasonings and **keep** in refrigerator until ready to serve. **Chopped** cabbage may be placed in a covered bowl and stored in the refrigerator briefly to avoid last minute rush. **Yield: 4 1-cup servings.**

Variation

Hot Slaw: Use same amounts and ingredients only steam boil cabbage 7 minutes in heavy kettle with about 2 tablespoons water. Add other ingredients. Heat thoroughly. Serve at once.

Eggplant Caviar (Lebanese)

1 eggplant	1 clove garlic
1 green pepper	1/2 cup lemon
1 red pepper (or 2 green)	1/4 cup oil
1/2 cup chopped parsley	1 teaspoon salt

Wash eggplant. **Bake** whole eggplant in oven at 375-400° F, 30 minutes, until skin starts peeling. **Peel. Cool. Chop** peppers medium or fine according to preference. **Chop** cooled eggplant. **Combine. Marinate** for several hours or overnight. **Yield: 8 servings.**

Delightful Fruit Dressing

1 cup pineapple juice or mixture of fruit juices	2 tablespoons cornstarch cold juice or water to moisten
1 tablespoon lemon juice	1 cup whipped soy topping
sprinkle of salt	(see recipe)

Combine juices in a sauce pan. **Add** salt. **Bring** to boil.

Stir in moistened cornstarch. **Stir** until thickened. **Chill.** Fold **into** Whipped Soy Topping.

Fruit Salad Suggestions

1. Unsweetened pineapple sections, fresh pear cubes, sliced bananas, Thompson seedless grapes, fruit dressing.

2. Apple, chopped walnuts, unsweetened pineapple tidbits, delightful fruit dressing.

Hot Potato Salad

1 1/2 cups soybean concentrate, sour cream style (see recipe)
1 tablespoon dill seed

4 cups sliced hot potatoes
1 teaspoon salt
1/2 cup chopped green onions or chives

Combine concentrate and dill seed. **Heat** in top of double boiler. **Slice** potatoes and **sprinkle** with salt while slicing, or cook with salt.

Add with chopped green onions to hot concentrate. **Mix** lightly. **Serve** hot.

Variation

Chopped celery may be used in place of dill seed.

Sour Cream Potato Salad

4 cups diced potatoes
1 teaspoon salt
1/2 cup diced cucumbers
1/2 cup chopped celery
1 cup garbanzos (chicken-style seasoning)

1/2 cup chopped green onions
1 1/2 cups soybean concentrate, sour cream style (see recipe)
parsley and tomato slices

Cook potatoes with salt, or sprinkle with salt when dicing.

Chill in refrigerator while preparing other ingredients. **Combine. Mix** lightly. **Garnish** with parsley and tomato slices. **Yield 8 cups.**

Variations

1. Bread-and-butter pickles may be used instead of diced cucumbers.
2. Chives or dry onions may be used instead of green onions.

Salad Suggestions with
Garlic Sour Cream Dressing

1. Sliced cucumbers.
2. Combination of crisp vegetables.
3. Lettuce wedges.
4. Green beans.
5. Bean salad.
6. Broccoli — hot or cold.
7. Any hot greens.

Tomato Rosette Salad

4 medium tomatoes
lettuce or watercress
   for nest
parsley

2 cups soya curd cheese
   (see recipe) or cottage
   cheese

Wash tomatoes carefully and **cut** out stem end. **Peel** if desired. **Arrange** nest of lettuce or watercress on salad plates. **Place** tomato, stem side down, in center of nest.

Cut three-fourths of the way through tomato to divide it into 6 equal wedges. **Spread** apart and place mound of Creamy Soy Curd Cheese, or cottage cheese in center.

Garnish with a mound of Soy Mayonnaise and a sprig of parsley or watercress. **Yield: 4 servings.**

Piquant Tomato Dressing

1 cup tomato sauce   1 cup sour cream

Combine.
See recipe for Soy-Oat Patties with tomato sauce.

Salad Suggestions
with
Piquant Tomato Dressing

1. **Salad wedges.** Generous serving of dressing over center of wedge. Garnish with parsley.
2. **Torn, dark-green lettuce.** Mound on salad plate or in bowl. Generous serving of dressing in center and dribbled from center to edge to form artistic pattern.
3. **Combination of crisp vegetables.** Dressing added and tossed lightly.
4. **Chilled, cooked green beans.** In mounds on lettuce leaf. Generous serving of dressing.
5. **Combination bean salad.** String beans, red beans, pinto beans, and garbanzos. Combine. Mix with dressing. Serve on lettuce.

Sour-Sweet Memory Salad

torn chilled lettuce in
   individual bowls
2 tablespoons lemon juice
   per bowl

1 teaspoon brown sugar
   (may use apple juice
   concentrate or honey
   instead)

Dribble lemon juice over lettuce. **Sprinkle** sugar over lettuce as evenly as possible. **Serve** at once.

Note: The Sour-Sweet Memory Salad dates back to a day when salads were practically unknown.

Winter Garden Salad

2 cups kale or other greens
1 cup green or dry onions
   or chives

1 cup parsley
lemon-honey French
   dressing (see recipe)

Wash kale quickly with cold water. **Dry. Chill. Cut** very fine with kitchen shears or with sharp knife on chopping board. (A number of leaves may be fitted together and cut at the same time.) **Mince** onions (using tops if green onions are used) **cut** chives with kitchen shears. **Mix** with dressing and serve at once.

Lemon-Honey French Dressing

$1/2$ cup salad oil
3 tablespoons lemon juice
1 tablespoon honey
$1/2$ teaspoon celery salt

$1/2$ teaspoon paprika
$1/2$ teaspoon onion salt
2 tablespoons purée

Combine chilled ingredients. **Place** in bottle or jar and shake until thick, or mix in blender.

Spreads and Relishes

Orange-Honey Whipped Margarine

½ lb. whipped margarine ¼ cup grated orange rind
½ cup honey

Combine, whip, and serve. **Yield: 32 servings.**

Soy Mayonnaise

1 cup chilled, cooked
 concentrated soy milk
¼ teaspoon paprika, Spanish
½ teaspoon salt
2 teaspoons sugar

¼ teaspoon onion powder
⅛ teaspoon garlic powder
2 to 4 tablespoons lemon
 juice
¼ cup oil, chilled

Measure Soy Milk and put in blender. **Add** seasonings. **Blend** until light and foamy. **Add** oil gradually while blending. **Add** enough lemon juice to give the desired thickness and flavor.

Variation

Soy Mayonnaise without Oil: Use the same ingredients as above except the oil. Add lemon juice to thicken as soon as light and foamy.

Peanut Butter-Yeast Spread

$1/2$ cup peanut butter   2 tablespoons oil
$1/2$ cup brewers flake yeast

Combine peanut butter and yeast. **Add** oil. **Mix** with fork until smooth. **Cover. Store** in cool, dark place. **Yield: 11 tablespoons. Yield: 16 servings.**

Burger Relish

1 cup almonds, raw $1/2$ teaspoon onion powder
1 cup cold water $1/4$ teaspoon garlic powder
2 tablespoons oil $1/2$ teaspoon sweet basil
$1/4$ cup lemon juice $1/4$ teaspoon sage
1 teaspoon sugar   turmeric
$3/4$ teaspoon salt

Blend almonds with water until very fine. **Add** oil gradually. **Add** enough lemon to make thick. **Add** seasonings and turmeric, enough to give a mustard-like color. **Chill. Yield: 16 servings.**

Savory Yeast Spread with Soy Milk

$1/2$ cup soy milk, cooked $1/4$ teaspoon salt, or to taste
  soybean concentrate (see   1 tablespoon soy sauce
  recipe), or evaporated milk $1 1/2$ cups flake yeast with B_{12}
2 tablespoons oil

Put milk into a pint-size bowl. **Add** soy sauce. **Beat** with a fork until oil is emulsified. **Continue** beating while adding yeast. **Yield: 16 tablespoons.**

Tartar Sauce

1 cup cooked soybean
  concentrate (see recipe)
1/4 teaspoon paprika, Spanish
1/4 teaspoon salt
1/4 teaspoon onion powder
1/8 teaspoon garlic powder

2 tablespoons oil
2-4 tablespoons lemon juice
1/4 cup chopped bread-and-
  butter pickles (see recipe)
1/4 cup chopped olives
1/4 cup chopped parsley

Put concentrate and seasonings into blender. **Blend** until well-mixed and very light. **Add** oil gradually. **Add** lemon juice until well-thickened.

Drain bread-and-butter pickles and olives. **Chop** medium-fine. **Add** with chopped parsley to whipped concentrate. **Yield: 24 servings.**

Variation
Chopped, hard-cooked egg may be added if desired.

Quick Tomato Catsup

1/2 cup onions, chopped
  (Spanish onions)
1 clove garlic
1/4 cup lemon juice
2 cups tomato purée
1 cup tomato paste

1 1/2 tablespoons brown sugar
1 teaspoon salt
1 teaspoon paprika, Spanish
1/4 teaspoon cumin
1/2 teaspoon sweet basil
1/4 cup water

Chop onion. **Peel** garlic clove and chop fine. **Blend** chopped onion and garlic with lemon juice and 1/2 cup tomato purée until very fine. **Combine** all ingredients.

Bring to boil. **Let simmer** a few minutes or until the desired consistency. **Seal** in sterilized half-pint jars. **Process** 20 minutes in boiling water bath. **Yield: 4 1/2-pint jars.**

Adequate fluid intake is absolutely essential to good health. The basic fluid, water, can be the vehicle for good taste and nutrition or for unhealthful sugars and additives – depending on your choice!

Beverages Without Sugar

"In health and in sickness, pure water is one of Heaven's choicest blessings. Its proper use promotes health. It is the beverage which God provided to quench the thirst of animals and man. Drunk freely, it helps to supply the necessities of the system, and assists nature to resist disease."[1]

Water, the liquid of life. "Water is truly the liquid of life. Nothing else can ever take its place. A safe water supply is essential to every home. Water enters into every reaction within the human body. More than two-thirds of your body is composed of water in some form. Every day your kidneys filter between fifteen and twenty gallons of water for you. Most of this fluid is taken back into the blood stream again. Only a small fraction passes out as urine. This excreted water carries away the waste chemicals your body no longer needs.

"The person who does not take enough water may soon have trouble with his internal organs. He may suffer from constipation and other digestive complaints. Stones may form in his kidneys and bladder, and severe infections may result. The lack of sufficient water may place an extra burden on his heart. Everyone who desires to remain strong and healthy should have an abundant supply of pure water each day, for water is truly the 'liquid of life.' "[2]

Drafts of clear, hot water taken before eating (half a quart, more or less) will be productive of good health.

Pre-breakfast bracer. Two glasses of very warm water drunk some little time before breakfast, gives a feeling of well-being, helps to cleanse the digestive system, and prepares it for the morning meal. It satisfies the thirst and makes undue drinking with the meal unnecessary. This does not apply to the glass of orange juice or milk (a solid in the stomach) which is a part of the meal. Do not serve ice-cold drinks; this delays digestion until the contents of the stomach can be warmed. Serve the oranges in slices or wedges often. When served as juice, include as much of the pulp as possible. The nutritive value of the entire orange is higher than strained orange juice.

Drink two or three full glasses of water — not too cold (or better, very warm) — between breakfast and noontime, and again during the afternoon.

A noncalorie, hot beverage served to guests upon arrival, to sip while visiting and awaiting the meal, has proved very acceptable. It savors of good fellowship, well-being, and relaxation.

The high-sugar, fruit-flavored cold drink should be replaced by one that is highly nutritious and not too cold, or should be dispensed with altogether.

1. Ellen G. White, *Counsels on Diet and Foods* (Washington, D.C.: Review and Herald Publishing Association, 1946), p. 419.

2. Clifford R. Anderson, *Modern Ways to Health* (Nashville, Tenn.: Southern Publishing Association, 1962), p. 253.

Apple Delight

2 cups pineapple juice
1 apple, cut in pieces

nut meats or meal, as desired
ice cubes

Combine and **blend** until apples are cut fine and fluffy. **Serve** at once. **Yield: 2 servings.**

Apricot Nectar

1 quart canned apricots

Blend, add water if necessary to thin. **Serve** at once. **Yield: 6 servings.**

Joyce's Frosty Fruit Drink

2 cups pineapple juice
1 6-oz. can orange
   concentrate

2 bananas
3 large ice cubes
1 cup water

Combine all ingredients in blender. Chop until ice cubes are broken into pieces. **Blend** until foamy. **Yield: 6 servings.**

Pineapple-Apricot Nectar

2 cups unsweetened
   pineapple juice

2 cups canned apricots

Combine. Blend. Serve at once. **Yield: 6 servings.**

Variations
1. Use 2 cups frozen apricots (frozen in pineapple juice).

2. Use 2 cups fresh apricots with 3 cups unsweetened pineapple juice.

3. Use 1 cup dried apricots soaked in 1 cup pineapple juice and ¼ cup chopped dates.

Pineapple-Mint Nectar

4 cups unsweetened
   pineapple juice
1 cup fresh mint leaves

other greens may be added
   as desired
ice cubes

Blend mint leaves with 1 cup juice until very fine. **Add** remaining juice and miniature ice cubes and **blend** briefly. **Serve** at once. **Yield: 4 servings.**

Vitamin Cocktail

discarded outer leaves,
   stems, peelings, tops,
   pea pods
1 cup boiling water, and
   ¼ teaspoon salt for each
   cup chopped vegetables

1 medium onion
1 tablespoon chopped
   tarragon or sweet basil
   leaves, or ½ teaspoon
   dried leaves, or chicken-
   like seasoning

Store carefully washed and dried vegetable parts in plastic bag or refrigerator tray until preparation of vegetable for meal is complete or until there is sufficient quantity for use. **Cut** chilled vegetables into medium pieces with a sharp knife or kitchen shears.

Add vegetables to rapidly boiling water using equal amounts of vegetables and water. **Add** salt. **Boil** gently for five minutes. **Blend. Strain** as much pulp through strainer as possible. **Chill. Combine** with equal parts of tomato juice. Or **serve** hot with a teaspoon of soy sauce or ½ teaspoon chicken-like seasoning per cup.

Crisp, sweet, dried sections of golden delicious apples make a snack that builds health and pleases the palate.

Food Preservation

Home Drying — A Lost Art? Drying is one of the earliest methods of food preservation, as well as one of the easiest and most practical. The finished product? You have some delectable surprises in store. Money cannot buy the delicious goodness of home-dried fruits and vegetables.

In our family, dried corn is a tradition — something very extra-special. It stems from early pioneer days in North Dakota and Minnesota. Canning vegetables was unheard of then and the only deep-freeze known was the whole out-of-doors during the long winter months but that was much too late to take care of the extra-sweet corn crop. Dried corn is just as delicious now as then and with modern appliances much easier and quicker to prepare.

Then, the wonderful variety of dried fruits! When care is taken to select the sweetest, ripest specimens you could hardly imagine how delightful dried fruits can be or how versatile. They are delicious served as dessert — really a conversation piece; and just the thing to take on a camping or backpacking trip. Also, in case of emergency they provide a ready supply of nutrition, packed with goodness.

And fresh-dried herbs that add so much in flavor to your favorite dish! Here is an adventure that will bring joy and lasting satisfaction to you and yours, and at so small a cost in money, time, or effort.

To Dry Apples

Apples dry very quickly and may be eaten as is, or may be used in cooking. Fully-ripe, sweet apples should be used. Gravensteins are especially suitable for drying.

Equipment needed:
1. Sharp paring knife
2. Apple corer
3. Bowl for apples
4. Colander for draining

Prepare a rinse water using 2 cups cold water, ¼ cup lemon juice or 1 teaspoon ascorbic acid. **Wash** apples carefully. **Remove** core with apple corer. **Peel. Slice** about ¼″ thick. **Place** in rinse water for a few minutes. **Drain** on white paper towels.

Arrange in a single layer on broiler pan or cookie sheet. **Place** in oven at 250°F, **reduce** heat at once to 140°F. **Prop** oven door open. When slices begin to dry on the top side, **turn** over carefully to avoid breaking. **Turn** occasionally. Drying time: 10 to 12 hours.

The finished product should be light in color and soft.

Apple slices strung on cord or dowel stick and suspended in a warm draft dry very quickly.

Extra-special: when Golden Delicious apples may be used, dry until crisp. Serve crisp.

Storage: dried apples may be stored in a cool, dry place in a covered jar.

Use: the slices may be eaten as they are, or they may be soaked or ground and used in cooking.

To Dry Apple Shreds

Wash apples. **Quarter,** cut out core, stem and blossom ends. **Do not peel. Drop** quarters into water containing ascorbic acid or lemon juice. **Remove** a few sections at a time. **Drain** off excess moisture on several thicknesses of paper towels. **Shred** on coarse shredder directly onto broiler pan. **Hold** cut surface down to remove skin.

Put under broiler 1 minute. **Dry** at 140°F (approximately), 6 to 8 hours. **Stir** occasionally to prevent sticking.

Banana Shreds

Peel bananas. **Shred** directly on broiler pan. **Use** coarse shredder. **Put** under broiler 1 minute. **Dry** at 140°F (approximately), 6 to 8 hours. **Stir** to prevent sticking.

To Dry Corn

Equipment needed:
1. Large trays (enamel broiler trays are excellent or a large cookie sheet may be used)
2. Sharp paring knife
3. Large kettle for cooking corn
4. Electric or gas oven

Gather corn that is just at right stage for eating. **Husk** and **silk.** (Brushing with a vegetable brush under running water is a very satisfactory method for removing silks.)

Place ears in a large kettle which has about an inch and a half of boiling water in bottom. **Crisscross** so steam can readily reach all parts. **Cover** and let steam 7 to 10 minutes. **Cool,** enough to handle. **Cut** rows of corn about half way down on kernels and **roll** cob slightly so that rows fall on pan with the cut side up.

Place rows of cut-off corn close together (do not overlap) and scrape part remaining on cob on top of them. (A scant amount of corn on tray will cause it to dry quickly and to be of excellent quality.)

Place trays in oven at 250°F for 15 minutes to heat through. (In electric oven, set heat about half way between "off" and 150°F — turned on far enough so that the light comes on. If using a gas oven, the pilot light may give enough heat. **Test** with oven thermometer. It should register about 90° - 140°F.)

Prop oven door open slightly with a small block of wood. (It is a good plan to start the drying process in the evening. There is no danger of scorching during the first 8 to 10 hours. After this the corn should be stirred occasionally with a fork. That on the outside has a tendency to dry first and should be moved to the center, and the corn that isn't so dry pushed to the outside. When the outside is quite dry the kernels can be separated by a few quick strokes with the fork, or broken with the fingers.)

As the corn gets nearly dry, **reduce** the heat a little. With occasional **stirring** there is little danger of browning.

(Time required is from 12 to 18 hours, depending on the amount of corn on the tray. A nicer product is obtained with quick drying. Finished product is a clear yellow with no browning. The kernels are brittle with no trace of moisture.)

Storage. Dried corn may be stored in covered glass jars, or in cloth bags It should be kept in a cool, dry place.

To prepare for serving. Soak corn in just enough cold

water to cover for several hours, or overnight. Boil gently and let simmer 30 minutes to 1 hour, or until tender and water is mostly absorbed. Season with salt, margarine, or butter, and add a little Soy Cream, half-and-half or evaporated milk. Serve piping hot.

To Dry Figs

Use large fully-ripe figs. **Wash** figs and dry on paper towels. **Cut off** stems and blossom ends with a sharp knife. **Place** close together on an enamel broiler pan.

Turn oven to about 140°F. **Prop** oven door open just a crack. **Take** pan out of oven occasionally and **turn** figs over. Time required for drying: approximately 1½ days.

Cool. Brush surface of dried figs very lightly with mild honey. **Pack** in plastic containers and store in refrigerator or freezer.

To Dry Herbs

Sage, summer savory, sweet basil, thyme, rosemary, oregano, mints, and others.

When growth is lush and just about ready to bloom, pick long branches. **Wash. Tie** in bunches and hang on clothesline in a shaded place in warm, drying weather. They will dry very quickly.

When leaves are crisp and brittle, pick them off and store in glass jars. **Crush** for use in palm of hand, or with mortar and pestle.

To Dry Pears

Select pears that are sweet and have a good flavor. Drying will not make delicious pears out of poor ones.

Equipment needed:
1. Large kettle for boiling water   2. Sharp paring knife
3. Enamel trays or cookie sheets for drying

Drop pears into rapidly boiling water until skins slip. **Cool** slightly. **Remove** skins as with peaches. **Cut** in halves. **Cut** out core with teaspoon. **Arrange sections** on tray in rows (alternate wide and narrow ends of sections for space saving).

Place pears under broiler for 3 minutes. **Turn** sections over and again place under broiler for 3 minutes. **Set heat** at approximately 140°F. **Prop** oven door open with a little 1/2" block. (As pears dry, some juice gathers in bottom of the pan. **Roll** pears in this juice to produce a glaze.)

Turn occasionally. (Should dry sufficiently in 8-10 hours, depending on size of pears and heat.)

The finished product. The sections shrink a great deal in drying, are leathery in texture but not hard or brittle. The color ranges from an off-white to a golden tan. The flavor is very sweet with a suggestion of tartness.

Note: The pears are very nice if taken out of oven when a little moist and stored in refrigerator or freezer.

To Dry Prunes

Select large, sweet, Italian prunes of the best quality, and fully ripe. Prunes that drop from the tree are usually sweeter than those that are picked.

Equipment needed:
1. Bowl or colander for washing
2. Trays with rim — enamel broiler tray exceptionally good

Wash prunes. **Place** close together on tray. **Place** in oven at 250°F for 15 minutes. **Turn** indicator to approximately 140°F. (Be sure oven light will come on.)

Let dry for 6 or 8 hours. **Roll** in juice. (Sometimes an extra quantity of juice accumulates. If so, drain into a dish and save.)

Turn occasionally. When prunes are nearly dry, **put** a little of the juice in pan and **roll** prunes in it to glaze. (It requires about 2 days to dry prunes.)

The finished product. Prunes should be well-dried but soft and moist. They may require refrigeration or freezing but are delicious to eat out of hand at this stage. Prunes that are to be used principally for cooking may be dried longer. Due to the high sugar content, some crystalization may occur on outside of the dried prunes. It has white sugary appearance. Do not mistake this for mold.

Salted Squash Seed

Wash squash seeds. **Drain. Sprinkle** lightly with salt. **Spread** on cookie sheet or other flat pan. **Place** in warm place until thoroughly dry. **Delicious.**

Other seeds: pumpkin seeds and watermelon seeds may be treated in the same manner.

Dried Apricot-Date Jam

¹/₂ cup dried apricots	1 cup pineapple juice
¹/₄ cup dates	

Soak apricots overnight or 4 to 6 hours in pineapple juice. **Combine** and blend until fruit is chopped fine. Very good on waffles. **Yield: 8 servings.**

Baked Figs

24 large figs   1 6-ounce can of apple juice
$1/8$ teaspoon salt   concentrate

Wash figs carefully. **Cut** off stem and blossom ends. **Arrange** in a flat, glass baking dish. **Pour** apple juice concentrate over figs.

Bake at 250°F, 30 to 40 minutes. **Stir** occasionally and **roll** figs over in juice. **Juice** should be thickened and mostly absorbed. **Serve** with Soy Cream (see recipe).

Variations

1. Candied Figs: Ingredients and method are the same as recipe above except reduce heat to 150°F and let dry an additional 30 minutes.

2. Dried Figs: Ingredients and method are the same as recipe above except reduce heat to 150°F and let dry. Turn occasionally.

3. Pickled Figs: Ingredients and method are the same as recipe above except add $1/4$ cup lemon juice and 1 tablespoon celery seed to apple juice concentrate and cook the same as for Candied Figs.

Preparing Vegetables for Freezing

Vegetables should be cooked considerably less for freezing than for serving. The freezing has an additional softening effect. When preparing food frozen in this manner for serving, additional cooking should be unnecessary — merely **heat** and serve at **once.**

The following table is suggestive. Experimental work may be necessary to determine the length of time for the variety and maturity of the vegetable selected.

Suggested Time for Steam Blanching

Broccoli, small pieces	4 - 5 minutes
Cauliflower, small pieces	4 - 5 minutes
Corn, cut off cob	4 minutes
Corn, on cob (to be cut off before freezing)	5 minutes
Corn, on cob	7 minutes
Peas	3 minutes
Shell beans	12 minutes
String beans	7 minutes

Squash and Pumpkin: Bake whole or in pieces until tender. Chill. Scrape out of shell. Sieve. Pack and freeze. Or wrap pieces in wax paper and seal with hot iron. Or place plastic bag or wrap with foil.

Corn on cob without blanching: Wrap corn in waxed paper or heavy paper without removing husks or silks immediately after gathering and put in freezer at once. Success of this method depends on getting corn into locker without delay after picking. Corn prepared in this way takes up considerable space and is not advisable if freezer space is limited.

The time suggested is based on small quantities prepared in a flat kettle with little head space. Large quantities would take longer to heat through and would have a tendency to overcook the bottom layer before the vegetables on top are sufficiently heated. A flat kettle with little head space is desirable in all vegetable cookery as it fills with steam quickly and shortens the **initial heating** period. It is during the period of initial heating that the greatest vitamin loss occurs.

To Freeze Peas

Assemble materials and supplies in five working areas:
Area I: Preparation
Bowl for peas, container for shells, peas to be shelled.

Area II: Cleaning
Colander, sink, running water.
Area III: Cooking
Heavy kettle with tight cover, $1/4$ to $1/2$ cup hot water.
Area IV: Cooling
Shallow tray — enamel or stainless steel, deep oblong pan for ice, ice cubes, slotted spoon **or** set kettle in cold water in sink to cool **or** let cool at room temperature.
Area V: Packaging
Cartons for peas, large spoon, waxed pencil for labels.

Order of Working
Keep extra peas in cold place until needed. Set up areas in consecutive order. Make sure that all equipment and supplies needed are ready for use and in place before beginning to work.

1. **Shell** peas in small lots, one to one-and-a-half quarts.
2. **Place** peas in colander and **wash** well under running water.
3. **Heat** $1/4$ to $1/2$ cup water in covered kettle. **Add** peas. **Cover** tightly. **Heat** through until kettle is well-filled with steam. **Reduce** heat. **Cook** 3 minutes. Use timer. (Length of time depends on tenderness of peas. Should be crisp-tender.) **Cool. Package, label, freeze.**

To Freeze Bell Peppers

Wash and **dry. Chop** red and green peppers and combine or freeze separately as desired. **Pack** loosely into small cartons. **Freeze.**

To Freeze Chives

Wash carefully, removing any dried ends or foreign particles. **Dry,** on absorbent towels. **Bunch** and **cut** with kitchen shears or with sharp knife on chopping board. **Pack** loosely in small cartons and freeze.

Use: May be used in salad, cottage cheese, or cooking.

To Freeze Parsley

Wash parsley carefully and dry on absorbent towels. **Remove** stems. **Pack** into freezing cartons. **Freeze.**

Use: May be used in cooking or salads. To use, shave off the amount desired and return the rest to the freezer to be used at a later time.

To Freeze Cherries

Wash and **stem** cherries.
1. **Pit** for salads or cooking.
2. **Do not pit** for fruit plates or eating "as is."
3. **Pit or not** as desired for sauce. **Cover** with unsweetened apple or pineapple juice.

Pack in freezer cartons. **Seal. Freeze.**

To Freeze Figs

Select fully-ripe, large figs. **Place** in plastic bags. **Freeze.**
To serve. Wash. Peel if desired. **Slice** in serving dishes. **Let stand** at room temperature until partly icy or completely defrosted as desired.

To Freeze Peaches I

Select fully-ripe, choice peaches. **Freeze** separately without removing skins. **Place** in plastic bags after frozen.

To serve. Hold under running water until skins slip. **Remove** skins. **Cut** in slices into serving dishes. **Let stand** at room temperature until partly icy or completely defrosted — according to preference. (Juice forms. No sugar is required.)

To Freeze Peaches II

Select fully-ripe, choice peaches. **Place** in boiling water **until** skin slips. **Remove** skins. Slice two or three peaches into bowl. **Sprinkle** lightly with sugar, perhaps brown, and ascorbic acid mixture. **Slice** another layer. **Sprinkle** with sugar mixture. **Continue** until bowl is full and juice comes up over peaches.

Place in freezing-cartons. **Press** down until juice covers slices. **Put** folded wax paper on top to fully cover peaches and **place** crumpled wad of paper on top to keep in place. **Freeze.**

To serve. Allow to partially or completely defrost as desired.

Sugar-ascorbic acid mixture: Add one teaspoon of powdered ascorbic acid to 1 cup sugar. **Mix.**

To Freeze Peaches III

Follow the method above except, instead of sugar, use unsweetened pineapple juice or apple juice concentrate with ascorbic acid.

Select fully-ripe, choice pears. **Place** in plastic cartons. **Freeze.**

To serve. Let water run over to loosen skins. **Slip** skins off. **Slice** into serving dishes. **Let stand** at room temperature to defrost as desired.

To Freeze Persimmons

Select fully-ripe, choice persimmons. **Freeze** separately. **Place** in plastic bag after frozen.

To serve. Hold under running water until skins slip. **Peel. Dice. Place** in serving dishes, and **let stand** at room temperature until partly icy or completely defrosted — according to preference; or, **pour** Soy Cream (see recipe) or "half-and-half" over frozen, diced fruit. (The cream freezes as the fruit thaws.)

Or, **scoop** pulp out of fully-ripe persimmons and **pack** in freezer cartons. May be diced and served as above.

To Freeze Plums

Select fully-ripe, large plums. **Place** in plastic bags. **Freeze.**

To serve. Wash. Slice into serving dishes. **Let stand** at room temperature until partly or completely defrosted as desired.

Strawberry Ice

Wash berries. **Stem. Chill. Force** berries through fruit press or strainer, or **mash** thoroughly. **Add** juice of one lemon to each quart of pulp, and **sweeten** to taste. Fill cartons to within an inch from the top. **Cover** tightly. **Freeze** at once.

To serve. Allow to thaw to the consistency of thick mush. **Serve** in sherbet glasses.

Mixed Berry Ice

Use equal parts of strawberries, loganberries, and boysenberries; or other assortment according to own choice.

Clean and prepare berries. **Chill. Force** berries through fruit press or strainer. **Sweeten** to taste. **Fill** cartons to within inch from top. **Cover** tightly. **Freeze** at once. **Serve** the same way as Strawberry Ice above.

Berries Without Sugar

Well-ripened, whole berries may be frozen without sugar. They do have a tendency to break down and deteriorate more quickly so should be used before completely thawed.

Select berries that have no green or soft spots. **Wash** carefully (cap strawberries). **Pack** without jamming. **Freeze** as quickly as possible after gathering.

Note: Pineapple juice, unsweetened, or concentrated apple juice may be used to sweeten berries.

Canned Pears Supreme
(without sugar)

Pears, ripe but firm
Pineapple juice, natural
    unsweetened

Pineapple, canned in
    unsweetened juice

Put pears into a kettle of boiling water, just a few moments — until skins slip. **Remove** the skins the same as for scalded peaches. **Cut** pears in half. **Remove** the core with the end of a teaspoon, and the stem section with a sharp knife.

Pack into jars, adding a few cubes of pineapple — 6 or 8 to the pint. **Fill** jar, about three-fourths an inch from top with pineapple juice. **Put** on scalded caps and rings and tighten.

Boil jars in hot-water bath 20 minutes. **Cool. Wipe** jars with damp cloth. **Remove** rings. **Store** in a dark cool place.

Note: Other fruits may be sweetened with pineapple or apple juice, or apple juice concentrate.

Rose hip purée in the making for use in fruit "butter" or other healthful preparations.

Apple-Quince-Rose Hip Butter

2 cups apple pulp
1 cup quince pulp
1 cup rose hip purée

1 6-ounce can apple juice concentrate
1/8 teaspoon salt

Wash apples and quinces thoroughly, discarding stem and blossom end. **Cut** in small pieces. **Cook** with small amount of water until tender. **Wash** rose hips. **Cut** open and scoop out seeds.

Cook until tender. **Blend. Strain** (or put through fruit press). **Combine** with apple juice concentrate.

Put in flat, pyrex baking dish. **Bake** uncovered at 250°F for 1 1/2 hours or until thick. **Stir** occasionally. **Fill** sterilized jars. **Seal.**

Crab Apple Pickles

4 quarts crab apples   4 cups water
1 12-ounce can apple juice   2 cups lemon juice
  concentrate   2 tablespoons celery seed

Wash crab apples thoroughly. **Leave** stems on. **Cut** out
blossom ends. **Combine** apple juice and water in large kettle.
Add crab apples.

Simmer until tender. **Add** lemon juice and celery seed.
Bring to boiling point. **Fill** jars. **Seal. Boil** in hot water bath
for 10 minutes.

Bread-and-Butter Pickles

4 quarts large cucumbers,   2 cups brown sugar,
  sliced   packed (or 2 cups apple
8 onions   juice concentrate)
2 green peppers   2 cups lemon juice
2 red peppers   2 cups water
1/4 cup salt   2 tablespoons celery seed

Slice unpeeled cucumbers (peel if extra-large cucumbers
are used and skins are rough), onions, and peppers. **Place** in
flat pan, sprinkle salt over layers as they are put into pan.
Place in refrigerator. **Let stand** for 3 hours.

Combine remaining ingredients and bring to boiling
point. **Add** sliced vegetables and bring to boiling point but
do not boil. Fill hot, sterilized jars. **Seal.**

Variation

Sliced, green tomatoes may be substituted for cucumbers.
Vegetables may be ground for a relish after removing from
refrigerator.

Dill Pickles

2 quarts water	16 grape leaves
1/3 cup salt	8 cloves of garlic
8 quarts cucumbers	16 stalks of dill or 4 table-
may be sliced or whole	spoons dill seed
(about four inches long)	

Wash grape leaves, cucumbers, dill, and garlic. **Place** grape leaf and part of dill in bottom of jar. **Pack** cucumbers into jar. **Put** rest of dill on top.

Cover with boiling brine to within 1/2 inch from top. **Cover** with grape leaf. **Seal** with enamel or glass-lined lids. **Boil** in hot-water bath 10 minutes.

Variation
Two cups lemon juice may replace 2 cups water in the above recipe.

Sauerkraut

freshly picked cabbage	sugar, 1/4 teaspoon to a
salt, 3/4 teaspoon to 1 pound	pound of cabbage
of cabbage	

Wash and shred cabbage fine on chopping board with a sharp knife. **Place** in crock and mash with wooden mallet. **Add** another layer, sprinkling lightly with salt and sugar. **Mash** thoroughly.

Repeat until crock is filled and juice covers top. (If there is not enough juice to cover well, add a little hot water.) **Cover** with two large cabbage leaves. **Place** a plate on top. **Weigh** down with a large, clean rock.

Let work 10 days. **Pack** in jars. **Seal. Process** 10 minutes in boiling-water bath.

The truly amazing nutritional values of dark-green, leafy vegetables should give them a central place in the diet of a every health-minded person.

A Green Garden

Amazing Nutritional Values of Raw Greens

The high values of the dark-green, leafy vegetables for the diet are little realized. Schuphann in 1948 stated that the protein of dark-green leaves has as high a biological value as muscle protein — rated as growth-promoting for children.[1]

Think of the value of leaf protein in combating a world protein shortage!

"The [leaf] protein is better nutritionally than most seed proteins, as good as many animal proteins, and can be presented at the table in platable forms. Leaf protein is probably one of the foodstuffs that will be used, especially in the wet tropics in ameliorating the protein shortage that now exists."[2]

The exceptional mineral and vitamin content of leaves was recognized as early as 1929:

"Milk and the leaves of plants occupy unique positions among available foodsuffs, in that they are constituted to correct, when suitable amounts are included in the diet, the defects of cereals, tubers, roots, and meats."[3]

The value of leafy vegetables as a source of riboflavin (vitamin B_2) and their use where animal food is restricted has been emphasized:

"Leafy vegetables . . . appear to be rich sources of riboflavin in spite of their high water content. . . . Except for cabbage, the riboflavin content of these vegetables is over 0.3 mg per 100 g.

"It thus appears . . . that for augmenting intake of riboflavin increased consumption of green leafy vegetables can be advocated. Although some foods of animal origin, for example milk, are rich in riboflavin, the limited availability and also the high cost of these foods preclude their intake in adequate amounts by a majority of people in the country. Green leafy vegetables, on the other hand, are relatively cheaper."[4]

1. Werner Schuphann, *Eiweiß Forschung* 1:32. January, 1948, p. 20.

2. N.W. Pirie, *Science* 152:1705. 1966.

3. E.V. McCollum and N. Simmonds, *The Newer Knowledge of Nutrition* (New York: Macmillan, 1929), pp. 438, 506.

4. P. Srinivasa Rao and B.V. Ramasastri, *Journals of Nutrition and Dietetics* 6:192. 1969.

Would you believe that dark-green, leafy vegetables equal or surpass whole milk in protein and other vital nutrients? It's the truth!

Green Winter Gardens

There are few ways in which a dollar will buy so much as when invested in vegetable seeds. A mini-garden in the backyard or the flower border of a city lot may supply a surprising amount of vegetables and greens for ones who do not have garden space. Even the garden dollar may be stretched through selection of vegetables which may be grown over a long period of time, and through successive plantings.

There are many hardy vegetables that will withstand temperatures as low as 10°F above zero, unprotected, and zero or even sub-zero weather if given a little protection. With a little care you may have the pleasure and healthful benefits of a variety of fresh vegetables all through the winter.

There are no general rules that can be given for the country as a whole, or even for some localities as a whole. Consider your fall and winter gardens an experiment. If you do not obtain the results you desire the first time, try to find the reason and try again with improved conditions.

The following will be of help:

1. Select a spot that is well-drained.
2. Choose a protected location. The southern exposure of a building is excellent.
3. Provide a place that will not interfere with a spring garden.
4. Protect with a mulch of straw or leaves if temperature is expected to drop below 10°F above zero. If covered by snow, hardy vegtables will survive sub-zero weather.
5. Transplant early enough to allow plants to become well-established before the cold weather sets in.
6. Use a cold frame for protection in case the winter may be severe. Such vegetables as celery, lettuce, parsley, chives, green onions and leeks may be planted in the cold

frame and provide a good supply of fresh vegetables through the winter.

7. Secure help from your county agricultural agent regarding planting dates and instructions for your locality. If information cannot be obtained, transplant and plant seeds for hardy varieties six weeks before the first killing frost to enable seedlings to become well-established.

8. Make ridges for plants (in areas of heavy rainfall), especially if the garden spot is not well-drained.

More value can be obtained from the garden than most people realize. The length of its productiveness may be greatly increased through successive plantings and late plantings of hardy vegetables.

Late plantings will yield corn, string beans, cucumbers, and other vegetables until frost. The hardy vegetables will continue much longer. Onion sets planted in September and later, in mild climates, may supply green onions all winter.

Hardy greens planted in the fall will grow rapidly with the first warm days of late winter. Spinach, mustard greens, and others that have lived through the winter may be among the earliest in the spring. Rutabagas, turnips, and kale will send up rapid growth during the first sunny days of late winter, and provide greens that are tender and delicious. The nutritive value of these quickly grown greens is high.

Proper care may improve not only the quantity but the quality as well of the vegetables we obtain from the garden. Tomatoes that are fully exposed to sunshine have been found to contain more ascorbic acid than those of the same variety, even on the same vine, that are partly shaded. To secure maximum values of the vitamin, plant tomatoes far enough apart to prevent shading; stake, and trim off large leaves as the tomatoes set on. Prepare a bed on the south side of a building; shelter during frosty nights to lengthen the season.

Broccoli
Broccoli, the green variety, is a vegetable of high quality that is rapidly growing in favor.

The first head should be cut out when tiny, to cause the plant to branch. Cut heads while the buds are still compact — do not allow blossoms to form. A second crop may be obtained.

One cup of cooked broccoli may supply as much calcium, riboflavin, and protein as two-thirds cup of milk, plus as much ascorbic acid as one orange, and as much provitamin A as one carrot. In addition, there are significant amounts of iron, thiamine and niacin.

Cabbage

The amount of cabbage received from each seed may be increased considerably through proper care.

Early cabbages are especially well adapted to use for repeated crops. Early Jersey Wakefield, Golden Acre, and Savoy have been used with good results.

Leave stalk in ground when harvesting cabbage. Split the stalk two ways about one and one-half inches in depth, dividing the stalk into four sections. Make sure that there is a leaf axil on each section.

The growth should be very rapid. Break off any extra sprouts, leaving only one on each section.

The heads formed are about the size of a man's fist; a good size for the average family, just right for a salad or for cooking without waste. From plants harvested in June or early July the second crop should be ready early in the fall. Two and one-half pounds of good solid heads were obtained from one plant, second harvest.

A third crop of cabbages may be obtained if the plant is left undisturbed until the following spring. Be sure to break off extra sprouts.

Quick-growing cabbage sprouts make good greens.

Savoy Cabbage

Savoy cabbage should be more generally known and used. The dark-green color penetrates deeply into the cabbage. This cabbage is crisp and tender even though the

Cabbage stalks split four ways produce four heads of cabbage – just right in size for the small family and full of nutrition.

heads may not be solid. Savoy cabbage is excellent for salads and is especially good for kraut.

Georgia Collards

Georgia collards have long been a favorite in the South, whereas in many other sections of the country they are practically unknown. This nutritious vegetable should have much wider use. It is hardy and well-adapted to colder climates. It is at its best after frost.

Collards are near the top of the list of protective foods. One cup cooked may contain enough calcium and riboflavin for the meal and more than the daily allowance of vitamins A and C. Collards require longer cooking than most other greens.

226

Brussels Sprouts

Brussels sprouts are very hardy; in fact, the flavor is improved by freezing. The plants are perennials and if planted where they need not be disturbed, may live from year to year where winters are not too severe, producing abundantly through the successive years.

Garden Cress

Garden cress is a quick-growing green of high nutritive value that is exceptionally good for salads or mixed greens.

One cup of cooked cress may furnish more than the requirement for the meal of calcium, iron, vitamin A and C, and a good amount of vitamins of the B complex, as well as a protein that will help improve the total protein of the meal. Cress is especially nice for salads and sandwiches. Its peppery, nasturtium-like flavor makes a very welcome addition.

Kale

Kale, for its beauty alone, merits a place in every garden. In addition, it is of high nutritive value. Even through the winter, with a little protection, it may be had fresh from the garden in areas where the climate is moderate. Kale is equally good used as greens or in salad. Blue kale is of superior quality, milder in flavor and is more tender than other varieties.

Kale is at its best when it puts forth rapid new growth in late winter and early spring. It is most tender and delicious.

One cup of cooked kale may provide more vitamin A and C than is needed for the entire day, together with high values for other vitamins and minerals.

Kale planted late in the flower border makes a beautiful showing long after the late flowers are gone. Use low-growing varieties. In planting for winter gardens, large quantities should be used, for there is little growth during the winter months. It may be budget-wise to furnish a good portion of the family allowance of ascorbic acid by the use of dark-green, leafy vegetables. Ten to twenty cents for kale seeds plus a minimum amout of effort may provide most of the yearly requirement of ascorbic acid for a family. In addition, these vegetables are rich in other vitamins and minerals as well, and have a protein that will help to improve the total protein of the meal.

Kohlrabi
Late plantings of kohlrabi will yield crisp, delicious vegetables until late fall and, where the climate is mild, sometimes all winter. This vegetable is especially nice in salads, cut in wedges for finger salads, or it may be cooked in a variety of ways.

Purple Kohlrabi
The beauty of this vegetable adds to the loveliness of the garden. I choose the purple variety for this reason. Kohlrabi is a good source of ascorbic acid.

Leeks
Leeks are hardy and will withstand quite severe weather. Leeks may be used in any place that calls for onions. Some who cannot tolerate onions may enjoy leeks.

Mustard Greens
Mustard greens grow very quickly. From seeds sown in late fall, very early growth may be obtained with the first warm days of late winter where the winters are not too severe. Successive plantings may provide greens through a long season.

One cup of cooked mustard greens may provide more vitamins A and C, calcium, and iron than is needed for the meal, as well as a good amount of vitamins of the B complex, together with a protein that will help to improve the total protein of the meal. Mustard greens when very young are not strong in flavor: for more mature ones, it is well to combine them with other greens that are more mild. Use small quantities at first until the family becomes accustomed to the flavor.

Green Onions
Green onions may be had throughout the year in many areas from sets put out in early fall.

Turnip Greens
Turnip greens are of excellent nutritive value. They grow quickly and withstand cold weather. Seeds sown in late summer will provide a crop for fall use, and if protected

Green gardens, winter or summer, are one of the most economical ways a family can supplement its own diet – and health!

with a mulch, may come on in the first sunny days of late winter, supplying very early greens. Where winters are mild a mulch is seldom necessary. Delicious greens may be had from rutabagas, cabbage, Brussels sprouts, and similar vegetables in the late winter and early spring. The rapid growth of the vegetables as they start to grow up to seed provides greens that are unexcelled. To lengthen the greens-producing season, place a shovel deep under the plant and lift the plant up three or four inches.

Turnip greens are strongly flavored and will have a more favorable reception with some people if they are mixed with greens of a milder flavor.

One cup cooked turnip greens may supply enough calcium and riboflavin for the meal, more vitamin A and C than are required for the entire day, vitamins of the B complex, and a protein of good quality. Although small in quantity this protein may go far toward improving the total protein of the meal.

Care in Harvesting

Vegetables should receive painstaking care from the time they are harvested until they are served on the table. Greens should not be bruised or crushed or allowed to wilt. Much value may be lost by leaving vegetables in the sunlight after they are harvested. When gathering quantities of vegetables, provide a cool place for them. Cover with damp burlap bags if there is no better way.

Nutritional Helps

Guides for Meal Planning

There are four basic food groups which must be represented in planning the daily dietary.

The Basic Four — Group I. The cereal group contains a wide variety of whole grains and products. This group is a very good source of calories, minerals, vitamins and proteins which supplement the proteins of legumes, nuts, and greens. Use at least four servings a day from this group.

The Basic Four — Group II. The protein group includes nuts, seeds, legumes — such as peanuts, beans, peas, lentils and meat analogs (vegetable proteins). These foods combined with the cereals provide an improved protein; in many cases equal in value to protein of animal origin. Choose two or more servings each day from this group.

The Basic Four — Group III. This group contains a wide variety of fruits and vegetables, some of which should be eaten raw. Use four or more servings per day — one high in vitamin C and one a yellow or dark-green, leafy vegetable for its vitamin A values.

The Basic Four — Group IV. The milk group serves as an excellent source of protein which supplements less effective proteins in other foods. In addition, milk assures an adequate intake of calcium, riboflavin, and vitamin B_{12}.

Fortified soy milk adequately serves as a milk alternate.

Dark-green, leafy vegetables compare favorably with milk in their content of calcium and riboflavin and provide an excellent source of vitamin A values. In addition, dark leaves are a good source of iron and ascorbic acid (vitamin C). When milk is not included in the diet one generous serving of dark-green, leafy vegetables should be eaten every day. Make sure that vitamin B_{12} is supplied in fortified soy milk, torula yeast, or taken orally. "It has been shown that milk and dark-green, leafy vegetables occupy a unique place among our ordinary foodstuffs in that they are the only foods regularly consumed in moderate quantities which are of a nature to correct the mineral deficiencies of cereals, legume seeds, tubers, and fleshy roots, or to adequately supplement them with respect to fat-soluble A." — McCollum, *Newer Knowledge of Nutrition,* p. 235.

Meal Pattern for a Day

Breakfast
    Cereals or bread, 1 or 2.
    Fruits, 2 or more, 1 raw.
    Milk or Soy Milk or other beverage.
    Special reinforcements for a heartier meal:
        1. Nuts — or peanut butter with fruit toast.
        2. Legumes — in waffles or cooked on toast or cereal for a farmer-style breakfast.
        3. Egg — not more than three a week.
        4. Breakfast cookie, oatmeal and fruit.

Dinner or Luncheon
    Cereal or bread, 1 piece.
    Vegetables, 2 or 3 — 1 raw, 1 dark-green, leafy
    Legumes, meat analogs (textured vegetable protein), cottage cheese or egg dish

Simple dessert, optional (hearty meals better without desserts).

Supper
Cereal or bread, 1 piece suggested: corn muffins, sandwiches, or zwieback as desired.
Fruit or simple fruit dessert.
Fruit plate.
Warm drink or soup: Postum made with milk; fruit soup, "chicken-style" noodle soup.

Some Healthful Menus
— Using Recipes in This Book

Breakfast

Orange Slices
(1 large orange)
Oats Special   Soy Cream or Non-Dairy Creamer
Whole Wheat Toast   Margarine
Milk, fortified soy or dairy

Dinner or Luncheon

Baked Potato
Margarine   Chives and Parsley
Soy-Oat Patty   Tomato Sauce
Zucchini
Swedish Limpa Bread   Margarine
Milk

Supper

Cream of Corn Soup   Crackers
Bread Pudding with Soy Cream
Apples, Pears, or other fresh fruit as desired.

Breakfast

Grapefruit — $1/2$

Soy-Oat Waffles, 2   Raisins   Applesauce, 1 cup
Almonds, 15   Margarine, 1 tablespoon
Milk, 1 glass, fortified soy, or dairy.

Dinner or Luncheon

Mashed Potatoes
Granddaughter's Favorite   Soy Sour Cream, with chives
Bean Patties   and parsley
Dilled String Beans   Sliced Tomatoes
Whole Wheat Rolls   Margarine
Carrot Cookies
Milk, soy or dairy

Supper

Fruit Soup
Zwieback   Margarine
Cottage Cheese or Creamed Soy Curd Cheese
Corn-Rice Muffins
Milk, Soy or Dairy

More Than Adequate Nutrients

A menu like those above can supply more than adequate nutrients as shown in the following analysis of one day's completely vegetarian diet compared (below) with the recommended daily dietary allowances:

	Cal.	CHO g.	FAT g.	PRO g.	CA mg.	P mg.	FE mg.	THI mg.	NIA mg.	RIB mg.	VIT A IU
	2578	404.1	88.9	76.9	1208	1721	30.5	2.7	20.1	1.9	25,034
Recommended allowances:											
Male											
22-35 yr	2700			56	800	800	10	1.4	18	1.6	5,000
Female											
22-35 yr	2000			46	800	800	18	1.0	13	1.2	4,000
Pregnancy	2300			76	1200	1200	36	1.3	15	1.5	5,000

The Packed Lunch

The packed lunch should be as carefully planned as other meals of the day and should furnish its full share of the required nutrients. It should be attractive, delicious, and substantial enough to satisfy the growing boy and girl or the workman; to carry them through without snacks, with a healthy appetite for an early supper.

First, plan the menu for the day with a substantial breakfast and midday meal and a light supper. In breakfast and midday menus provide protein and fat (polyunsaturated fatty acids) sufficient to furnish sustained energy and blood sugar to satisfy until the next meal. Remember that growing children have high requirements.

In planning the midday menu keep in mind the need of adapting the foods to the packed lunch. It is surprising how versatile some foods are. One well-planned meal prepared in quantity enough for the whole family is packed into the lunch boxes for the ones at school or at work and served at the table for the ones at home.

Adapting the Midday Menu to the Packed Lunch — an Example

Regular Midday Meal
Russian Mashed Potatoes.
Tomato Rosette Salad with
    cottage or creamed Soy
    Curd Cheese with Chives.
Garbanzo-Nut Burgers.
Whole Wheat Rolls.
Two Golden Macaroons.
Milk or Soy Milk.

School Lunch
Russian Mashed Potato Soup in
    thermos bottle. Hot or cold.
Tomato Rosette Salad with
    cottage or creamed Soy
    Curd Cheese.
Whole Wheat Burger Buns
    with Garbanzo-Nut Burger.
Two Golden Macaroons.
Milk or Soy Milk.

Improvement of Fractioned — Divided — Foods

A well-balanced diet may be obtained quite easily when *whole foods* are prepared simply with minimum loss of valuable nutrients. To try to restore the nutrients that have been removed by refining or by careless methods of preparation, storage, and cooking, is much more complicated and may result in less satisfactory results. Who could be sure of obtaining the original fine balance?

"All the king's horses and all the king's men couldn't put Humpty Dumpty together again!" — and so it is with fractioned foods. We can add minerals and vitamins and supplement the proteins but when it comes to restoring the fine balance of trace elements of the grain or other products we are helpless. Sometimes it is a lacking trace element which causes difficulty.

However, even though such foods may be second-best they are widely used. That is why this chapter is added — to help you to improve the nutritive value of some of the most widely-used fractioned foods by returning some of the parts that have been removed in refining.

The germ and bran of wheat and other grains are very concentrated in minerals and vitamins and may have a protein of excellent quality. They should not be used indiscriminately and in large quantities. They are most valuable as a supplement to the refined grain from which they are taken if used in proportions that approximate the original composition of the grain.

Gluten is much more refined than white flour. "Do pep" is the name for a gluten flour containing 75-80 percent protein, which has been used for many years by the baking industry to "pep up" bread dough.

The quality of protein is rated much the same as examination papers. In grading proteins, the "passing grade" is 70 for the growth of children; for adult maintenance it is 60.

Sixty-five is the rating for the protein of whole wheat; 52, the rating for refined white flour. And, though most people don't realize it, the rating for gluten is unfortunately only 40—30 points under the quality requirement for children and 20 points under the adult requirement! And, worst of all, gluten is almost totally lacking in minerals and vitamins.

The low quality of gluten as a protein is due to the limited amount of certain amino acids. It does have an abundance of other amino acids which can be used by the body if the missing ones are supplied; and it has other advantages many appreciate. Gluten has a desirable texture that makes it palatable. It is very versatile and can be used in many different forms and is a "timesaver" for the housewife on the move.

Because of its wide usage, it is very important to improve both the quality of its protein and its mineral and vitamin content; this is simple and inexpensive to do. All you have to do is to put back (as nearly as possible in proportion) the proteins, minerals, and vitamins that have been removed and further supplement the protein quality with soy, yeast, or other proteins.

The wheat kernel contains 1.5 to 2.5 percent germ and approximately 14 percent bran. These are excellent sources of minerals and vitamins — and superior protein. The wheat germ is added as such. The water-soluble nutrients of the bran are extracted by soaking, blending, and rinsing and added as bran water.

To restore, approximately, nutrients removed, use the following proportions:

Food	Amount	Wheat Germ	Bran
Refined Flour	1 cup	1/2 tablespoon	1/2 cup (only the part recovered in bran water)
Gluten	1 cup	2 1/2 tablespoons	2 1/2 cups

These amounts of wheat germ and bran have been used with the refined flour and gluten in some of the recipes in this book. The products are for the most part lacking in the cellulose of the bran and may be conducive to constipation in the same manner as refined foods.

Cooking Ideas: Using Herbs and Flavorings

Analogs: (see meat analogs).
Apple pie: fennel.
Asparagus: marjoram, savory, sesame seeds, sweet basil, tarragon, thyme.
Beans (dried): dill, garlic, mint, oregano, savory, sweet basil.
Beans (snap): dill, marjoram, oregano, savory, sweet basil, thyme.
Beets: bay leaves, dill, savory, sweet basil, tarragon, thyme.
Beverages (hot): apple mint, catnip, fennel, lemon balm, lemon verbena, mint, peppermint, rosemary, sage, spearmint, sweet basil.
Breads: caraway, coriander, fennel, garlic, marjoram, parsley, poppy seeds.
Broccoli: caraway, dill, marjoram, oregano, tarragon.
Brussels sprouts: caraway, dill, marjoram, sage, savory, sweet basil, thyme.
Butter (margarine): chervil, garlic, parsley.
Cabbage: caraway, celery seeds, dill, mustard seeds, sage, savory, tarragon.
Cakes: caraway, poppy seeds, saffron.
Carrots: bay leaves, caraway, chervil, dill, fennel, marjoram, mint, peppermint, sweet basil, thyme.
Cauliflower: caraway, celery seeds, dill, rosemary, savory, tarragon.
Cereals: apple mint, fennel.
Cheeses: caraway, celery seeds, chervil, chives, dill, fennel, paprika, sage, sesame seeds, thyme.
Cole slaw: caraway, dill, marjoram, mint, savory.
Cookies: caraway, fennel, sesame seeds.

Corn: bell peppers, savory, turmeric.

Cottage cheese: borage, chervil, chives, marjoram, parsley, sage, sweet basil.

Cream cheese: chives, onion salt, sage.

Cucumber: dill, savory, sweet basil, tarragon.

Curries: basil, chervil, coriander, sage, turmeric.

Dumplings: sage.

Eggplant: marjoram, oregano, rosemary, sage, sweet basil, thyme.

Eggs: chervil, chives, marjoram, paprika, rosemary, savory, sweet basil, tarragon.

Egg omelet: chives, marjoram.

Entrées (creamed): chives, marjoram.

Fruits: caraway, coriander, fennel, mint, rosemary, sesame seeds.

Fruit salad: marjoram, mint, rosemary, sweet basil, tarragon.

Green beans: celery salt, dill, marjoram, rosemary, sage, savory, sweet basil, tarragon, thyme.

Herb butter: chives, parsley.

Honey: cardamom.

Lima beans: chives, marjoram, oregano, sage, savory, sweet basil, thyme.

Mayonnaise: celery seeds, garlic powder, onion powder, thyme, turmeric.

Meat analogs: bay leaves, celery seeds, chervil, dill, garlic, marjoram, mushrooms, onions, oregano, paprika, parsley, rosemary, sage, savory, sesame seeds, thyme.

Noodles: poppy seeds.

Onions: caraway, celery seeds, oregano, sage, sweet basil, thyme.

Omelets: (see egg omelets).

Peas: borage, chervil, dill, marjoram, mint, oregano, poppy seeds, rosemary, sage, savory, sweet basil, thyme.

Pickles: dill, celery seeds.

Potatoes: bay leaves, caraway, celery seeds, chives, dill, marjoram, oregano, paprika, parsley, poppy seeds, rosemary, savory, sweet basil, thyme.

Rice: saffron, sesame seeds.
Salads: caraway, celery seeds, chervil, chives, coriander,
    cress (water and upland), dill, garlic, marjoram, mint,
    mushrooms, nasturtium, onion, oregano, parsley,
    sweet green and red peppers, poppy seeds, radishes,
    rosemary, savory, sesame seeds, shallots, sorrel,
    sweet basil, tarragon, thyme.
Salad dressings: dill, dried yeast, oregano, powdered kelp,
    sage, tarragon.
Sauces: bay leaves, chervil, chives, dill, fennel, garlic, mint,
    mushrooms, onion, paprika, parsley, rosemary, saffron,
    savory, sweet peppers, thyme, turmeric.
Soups: bay leaves, caraway, chervil, chives, coriander, dill,
    garlic, marjoram, mushrooms, onion, paprika, parsley,
    rosemary, savory, sesame seeds, shallots, thyme.
Spaghetti sauces: oregano, sweet basil.
Spinach: chervil, garlic, marjoram, oregano, rosemary,
    sweet basil, tarragon, thyme.
Spreads: celery seeds, parsley.

Measurements

Dry Ingredients
    All measurements are level. To level dry ingredients,
spoon lightly into dry cup or measuring spoon. Level with
the straight edge of a knife or spatula. For cups extending
above the cup mark, fill lightly with spoon and level as carefully as possible at the desired mark. Check at eye level.
    Flour. Stir with six strokes before measuring. Fill cup
lightly with a large spoon. Do not pack or shake. One cup
stirred flour approximates one cup of flour which has been
sifted once. The recipes in this book are based on stirred
flour.
    Note: The proportion of flour to water in breadmaking
varies with the protein content of the flour and possibly the
moisture content or other variables. For this reason the
measurement of flour is only approximate. One must learn

the "feel" of the bread to determine when the right amount of flour is incorporated. This is not difficult.

Brown sugar. Pack lightly into cup. If brown sugar becomes lumpy or hard, put a slice of raw apple into the cannister and put cover on tight. The sugar softens very soon.

Liquids

Using glass measuring cup, set on level surface. Check measurement at eye level. Using fractional measuring cups, fill to top.

When Measuring a Number of Ingredients:

Measure dry ingredients first.

Measure liquid and oil before measuring honey or molasses.

Table of Measurements
Liquid Measure
12 tablespoons = 1 cup
Dry Measure
16 tablespoons = 1 cup
4 tablespoons = $\frac{1}{4}$ cup
5 tablespoons plus 1 teaspoon = $\frac{1}{3}$ cup
3 tablespoons plus $\frac{1}{2}$ teaspoon = $\frac{1}{5}$ cup
2 tablespoons plus 2 teaspoons = $\frac{1}{6}$ cup
3 teaspoons = 1 tablespoon
2 cups = 1 pint
4 cups = 1 quart
4 quarts = 1 gallon

Approximate Weight
Liquids, unground grains, legumes = 1 pint approximates 1 pound

Your Health — Chance ... or Your Choice?
10 'Laws' That Will Help You To Choose Good Health

A wee girl puts the last pat on her pie and holds it up to me with a smile. "Grandmother, this one I made especially for you," she says with an air of satisfaction. A mud pie, with the fresh imprints of loving fingers!

While offering profuse thanks my mind takes a new train of thought. How much nourishment is in that little mud pie? Perhaps more than you think. Analysis would surely reveal minerals in abundance and hydrogen, oxygen, and perhaps nitrogen — the same elements that are found in our bodies. Someone has measured the chemicals that make up Us and has determined that they can be purchased, even in these times of high prices, for only a dollar or so per person.

We are earthborn children closely related to Mother Earth, the source of our nourishment. How grateful we are for the wonderful provisions that were made for our sustenance.

In the laboratory of nature, reactions are constantly taking place which our intellect cannot fathom. From the fertile soil — with sunshine, air, and water — living, growing plants of all varieties reassemble the life-giving elements of the mud pie into a bountiful array of nutritious, health-promoting foods.

In fruits, grains, nuts, and vegetables are found the elements that are needed for growth, maintenance, and well-being of the human family. In addition to this are the delightful flavors, aromas, textures, and exquisite beauty; all this "made especially for you."

Abundant health, with a clear mind, boundless energy, happiness, a lengthened prime of life, and the sheer joy of added years of useful achievement, is our potential; dependent, however, on strict adherence to right principles.

The human body is undoubtedly the master chemical laboratory of all our sphere. Through an understanding of the laws governing chemical reactions we may gain an understanding of the laws governing our bodies and may be enabled to obtain the highest possible benefits.

Law I: drink freely of fresh, pure water.

An abundant supply of clear, pure water, six to eight glasses per day, is a prime requisite for abundant health. Just as it is necessary to start with clean equipment in the laboratory, so it is in using our bodies. Warm water, two glasses or more at least half an hour before breakfast, cleanses and stimulates the digestive tract and prepares it for more efficient service. Drinking similar amounts of water from an hour after meals up to half an hour before meals is an excellent practice.

Warm water gives a distinct feeling of well-being. Tap water or bottled water at normal temperature are more desirable than ice water which draws fom the vital forces of the body to warm it to body temperature. Plenty of water between meals reduces the desire for drinking large amounts with meals.

If cold drinks or cold foods are served at a meal they should be small in quantity and should be consumed very slowly.

For the chemist to pour ice water into the beaker during a chemical reaction would be unthinkable. The dilution as well as the cold would greatly retard the process. Just as warmth and the correct concentration accelerates the chemical reaction in the laboratory, so warmth and the correct concentration facilitates efficient digestion, the very basis of abundant health.

Law II: eat wholesome foods.

Fruits, vegetables, and legumes (occasionally nuts) with whole grains, unrefined cereals or other whole-grain products are wholesome foods. They will insure an ample supply of energy, maintenance, and growth-promoting foods with the minerals and vitamins in the balance provided by an all-wise Creator.

Unfortunately, "empty calories" as found in refined sugar, fats and oils and in drinks, hard and soft, and in other sugary drinks provide up to 40 percent of the average American diet of today, with refined flour and refined cereal products providing an additional 20 percent.

"Empty calories" is really a misnomer. It is true that they are empty of the nutrients necessary for their use by the body but they are packed full of disaster healthwise. Cirrhosis of the liver has been found in teenagers who imbibe freely of soft drinks, just as it is found in the habitual drinker of alcohol. The great increase in the use of sugar parallels the increase in the incidence of diabetes, hypoglycemia, degenerative diseases of the heart and blood vessels, tooth decay, obesity, and many other ills that are responsible for much human suffering and early death.

More and more foods are being refined. Some of these are "enriched" by adding some of the nutrients which have been removed. Adding back only a part of the minerals and vitamins removed in refining does not make a good food out of a poor one. The milling industry is in a hard position to protect the health of the people who deliberately choose a devitalized food. They will gladly provide all of the entire wheat flour that is in demand.

Dr. Jean Mayer of Harvard University points out that "...it is risky to remove more and more minerals from a large fraction of the diet when only a fraction is restored; ... it may well be that some of the nutrients taken out are crucial from a health viewpoint."[1]

The wholesomeness of sweetened foods and their uitilzation by the system is largely a matter of quantity and concentration. Use only very small amounts of sugar — only enough to flavor, not to make excessively sweet: two teaspoons or less per serving in simple desserts and these only occasionally and with the well-balanced nutrients of unrefined foods. Often fruits, fresh or dried, and unsweetened fruit juices and concentrates may be used to provide the desired sweetening. Foods sweetened in this manner may sometimes be used by those who cannot tolerate sugar itself, refined or otherwise.

Fruits, either fresh or dried, are unexcelled for desserts. A lovely arrangement of fruits adds a note of elegance to grace any table, but even fruit should not be eaten following a full meal.

The chemist uses only the best quality ingredients. With your health at stake, will you settle for less?

Law III: eat simply.

Avoid too great a number of ingredients in a recipe or too great a variety of foods at one meal, which is conducive to overeating. But there should be a variety from meal to meal and from day to day to insure a supply of all the necessary nutrients.

Foods should be prepared simply, with little or no solid fat and a moderate amount of polyunsaturated oil, such as corn oil. Avoid grease-soaked foods: fried foods, rich gravies, sauces, and pastries. The digestion of the starch cells encased in fat is largely delayed until the food is emptied into the intestinal tract. The starches, which ordinarily would digest rapidly and with short gastric emptying time, are held in the stomach by the fats, which delay emptying time, resulting in fermentation, sourness, and distress.

What chemist would include in an experiment elements known to retard a desired chemical action and to produce inferior results?

Law IV: eat moderately.

Obtain an intelligent understanding of your requirements and keep within bounds — slightly under is better than slightly over.

Overeating is the cause of many ills, often bringing the action of the human stomach to an abrupt halt, just as a flooded carburetor will stall a car. A simple adjustment of the carburetor may right things for an automobile. Unfortunately it sometimes requires a longer time for the human organism to get back to normal operation. Continued overnutrition may result in debility not only of the stomach but also of other organs: liver, kidneys, cardiovascular system, these being associated with overweight and obesity.

It is a well-established fact that laboratory animals that are slightly underweight (having had an adequate diet; not an overabundance) live much longer than their fat, apparently healthy counterparts. The human likewise should leave the table feeling that he would enjoy eating more — a decision that is up to the individual himself. This is an act of will power.

Those who form the habit of eating slowly and thoroughly masticating food are less likely to overeat.

The chemist weighs with accuracy each ingredient he is using. To add an extra amount of any one of these just because of special preference is too ridiculous to even suppose. For the best health, similar consideration must be given to the amount of food one should eat. Appetite alone is not a safe guide.

Optimal health and added years of usefulness are rich rewards for self-control and moderation in eating.

Law V: eat regularly, and only at meal time.

Not one bite of solid food should be eaten between meals — not even fruit.

No chemist would introduce some unrelated substance into the test tube when the reaction is nearly complete. Between-meal snacks may be just as disastrous to the chemical reactions taking place in the digestive tract. The stomach normally may empty a simple meal in about four hours. A snack two hours after eating a regular meal has delayed the emptying time to *eight* or *nine* hours! Think of the sourness that develops in that mass of undigested food held twice as long as it should be in a warm, moist condition — just right for fermentation. A sour stomach will produce a sour, irritable disposition. If your children are irritable and quarrelsome check their eating habits and your own.

Law VI: eat slowly with thorough mastication of food.

Grinding material into very fine particles is a well-established laboratory technique which hastens chemical reaction.

Chewing not only grinds and softens the food but also allows thorough mixing with the first digestive juice, saliva; making possible a considerable amount of the digestion of the starch content of food before the action is checked by the acid of the gastric juice of the stomach. In our fast-moving modern life it is so easy to hurry through meals — but health is of first importance.

Law VII: eat when rested and relaxed.

Mealtime should be a happy occasion for all. Pleasant surroundings, the right environment are a boon to digestion and health, just as the right environment produces excellent results in the laboratory. Do not make it a time for disciplining the children! A good example set by parents in correct eating habits as well as a genuine liking for wholesome foods will be a positive influence that will prove a lifetime benefit to children.

Law VIII: provide fixed times of rest for the stomach.

Three meals a day are ample; sedentary workers often do better on two.

Unlike the test tube of the chemist's beaker the stomach is a living organism and in need of periods of rest. The heart rests between each beat. With some people the stomach rarely has a chance to rest.

The meals should be spaced, ideally, 5 or 6 hours apart to allow for complete digestion and an interval of rest before the next work assignment; then, with a good cleansing draft of water half an hour before the meal, the stomach should be ready to take up its duties with vigor.

Supper should be the lightest meal of the day. It should be of easily-digested foods: fruits, zwieback (zweibach — German) or whole-grain crackers, a warm drink or broth are suggestions. Supper should be served as early as possible for children, 5:00 to 5:30 P.M., to enable the stomach to be emptied before an early bedtime. Supper is the best meal to omit for weight-watchers. For these, particularly, two meals a day would solve many of their problems.

A burdened stomach causes inability to sleep and tiresome dreams; followed by a morning of sluggishness, a dull headache, a coated tongue, and a depressed appetite for breakfast.

For sound, undisturbed sleep make sure that the stomach is able to rest at the same time the body is resting.

Breakfast should furnish one-third of the nutrients for the day and possibly more. Carbohydrates for quick energy, protein for building and repair, and just a little fat to slow down emptying of stomach and for sustained energy. This will provide a sustained blood sugar that will carry one through to the next meal without a mid-morning slump. The abundant energy and the real joy of working is most rewarding.

It is as unthinkable to start the day with an empty stomach as it would be to start a trip in the car with an empty gas tank.

Lunch should be substantial; also planned to supply at least one-third of the calories for the day whether eaten at home or packed and carried off to work or school. With the thermos bottle and the modern lunch box this is accomplished with comparative ease.

Law IX: individual differences should be considered.

Differences make a difference. Just as there are no two snowflakes that are exactly alike, or no two leaves; so no two identical people can be found who do not have some variation in food needs. "What is food for one is poison for another," as the old saying goes.

The following individual differences are evident everywhere:

Child . . . Adult
Youth . . . Aged

Non-Allergic . . . Allergic
Hearty and healthy . . . Ill, convalescent
Quick digestion . . . Slow digestion
Strong digestive systems . . . Weak digestion
Manual laborer . . . Sedentary worker, scholar

Some are born with, or have a tendency to, metabolic disorders — such as the diabetic who may go through a period when he suffers from hypoglycemic episodes.

The manual laborer has more freedom in his eating habits than the sedentary worker.

The complexity of the situation is amplified by the gastric emptying time (the length of time the food is held in the stomach). The order of the normal length of time the food remains in the stomach, beginning with the shortest time, is: 1. sugars, fruits, starches; 2. proteins; 3. coarse vegetables; 4. fats.

Different types of food eaten together are held in the stomach as long as the one requiring the longest digestion time.

Sugars have the shortest gastric emptying time. The warm, moist contents of the stomach provide ideal media for fermentation when mixed with sugar; and the longer the time held, the greater the fermentation. Rich desserts after a hearty meal produce such results. Especially harmful are the rich pastries containing large amounts of fats and eggs.

Sweet jellies, jams, or desserts eaten with coarse vegetables will be held in the stomach and cause fermentation. Even the natural sweetness of fruit combined with coarse vegetables may cause distress for some.

Overcrowding the stomach, even with wholesome food, greatly retards digestion, causing fermentation, distress and debility of body and mind.

Fried foods, grease-soaked toast, rich sauces and gravies are held in the stomach by their fats, having the longest gastric emptying time. This is a matter of common experience and one is aware of the indigestion associated with these dietary insults.

When the stomach is overburdened, more blood is required to help take care of the load. This draws blood away from the brain, reducing its power of activity.

For sedentary workers and scholars a light meal of easily digested food is best when doing work requiring sustained mental energy and alertness. Fruits, or fruits with zwieback — without fat — is recommended at such times. Under extreme mental stress skipping a meal will prove beneficial.

The diet of children should be very simple and of the best quality.

Law X: do not eat when emotionally upset.

Emotions have a decided effect on digestion. Fear, for example, has been found to greatly delay the gastric emptying time.

Even overanxiety about food is not wholesome. Use your intelligence in gaining an understanding of your needs and in selecting moderate amounts of the best which is available to you at the time, without undue preoccupation. Do not *talk* food; *eat* it, *be thankful* for it, and *forget* it.

Calmness, trust, and gratefulness go far toward promoting good digestion. Good health, a clear mind, and a buoyant outlook on life are a natural consequence.

1. Jean Mayer, "How To Eat Better for Less Money," *U.S. News and World Report,* August 27, 1973, p. 23.

Nutritional
Evaluations

Recommended Daily Dietary Allowances,[1] Revised 1973

Food and Nutrition Board,

National Academy of Sciences — National Research Council

				Fat-Soluble Vitamins			Water-Soluble Vitamins								Minerals					
	(years)	Calories	Protein[2] (g)	Vita-min A (IU)	Vita-min D (IU)	Vita-min E[3] (IU)	Ascorbic Acid (mg)	Fola-cin (ug)	Nia-cin (mg)	Ribo-flavin (mg)	Thia-min (mg)	Vita-min B6 (mg)	Vita-min B12 (ug)	Cal-cium (mg)	Phos-phorus (mg)	Iodine (ug)	Iron (mg)	Mag-nesium (mg)	Zinc (mg)
Children	1-3	1300	23	2,000	400	7	40	100	9	0.8	0.7	0.6	1.0	800	800	60	15	150	10
	4-6	1800	30	2,500	400	9	40	100	12	1.1	0.9	0.9	1.5	800	800	80	10	200	10
	7-10	2400	36	3,300	400	10	40	300	16	1.2	1.2	1.2	2.0	800	800	110	10	250	10
Males	11-14	2800	44	5,000	400	12	45	400	18	1.5	1.4	1.6	3.0	1200	1200	130	18	350	15
	15-18	3000	54	5,000	400	15	45	400	20	1.8	1.5	1.8	3.0	1200	1200	150	18	400	15
	19-22	3000	52	5,000	400	15	45	400	20	1.8	1.5	2.0	3.0	800	800	140	10	350	15
	23-50	2700	56	5,000	400	15	45	400	18	1.6	1.4	2.0	3.0	800	800	130	10	350	15
	51+	2400	56	5,000		15	45	400	16	1.5	1.2	2.0	3.0	800	800	110	10	350	15
Females	11-14	2400	44	4,000	400	10	45	400	16	1.3	1.2	1.6	3.0	1200	1200	115	18	300	15
	15-18	2100	48	4,000	400	11	45	400	14	1.4	1.1	2.0	3.0	1200	1200	115	18	300	15
	19-22	2100	46	4,000	400	12	45	400	14	1.4	1.1	2.0	3.0	800	800	100	18	300	15
	23-50	2000	46	4,000		12	45	400	13	1.2	1.0	2.0	3.0	800	800	100	18	300	15
	51+	1800	46	4,000		12	45	400	12	1.1	1.0	2.0	3.0	800	800	80	10	300	15
Pregnant		+300	+30	5,000	400	15	60	800	+2	+0.3	+0.3	2.5	4.0	1200	1200	125	18+[4]	450	20
Lactating		+500	+20	6,000	400	15	60	600	+4	+0.5	+0.3	2.5	4.0	1200	1200	150	18	450	25

[1] The allowances are intended to provide for individual variations among most normal persons as they live in the United States under usual environmental stresses. Diets should be based on a variety of common foods in order to provide other nutrients for which human requirements have been less well defined.

[2] Approximately 17 per cent lower than previously recommended.

[3] Total vitamin E activity, estimated to be 80 per cent as α-tocopherol and 20 percent other tocopherols. See text for variation in allowances.

[4] This increased requirement cannot be met by ordinary diets; therefore, the use of supplemental iron is recommended.

Explanation of Tables
of Nutritional Evaluation

Almost all of the recipes in *The Oats, Peas, Beans & Barley Cookbook* are included in these tables. You can readily see how complete nutrition can be achieved in using nature's simple, basic foods.

You may also compare the values shown with those listed on Page 252 in the latest recommendations of the Food and Nutrition Board.

Please keep in mind that the values listed are approximate; that there are many variables; that the available data on food values is subject to change; that the weights and measures involved may be further refined; that the ability of the body to assimilate the nutrients varies from person to person; that even with the use of the computer and careful checking and rechecking some errors may be present. Even so, the tables provide helpful guides in checking on one's dietary intake.

The fatty acids contain wide gaps because of the large numbers of foods for which the values are presently unknown.

Bread. Variation of values for breads is due in part to size of slices. Bakers' bread varies from 23 grams to 46 grams or more per slice. A slice of homemade bread may weigh 60 or more grams. Size of servings causes variation for other foods as well.

Bran water. The amounts of the nutritive values present in the bran water as prepared here has not been determined. It is reasonable to assume that a high percentage of the water-soluble nutrients are extracted. One authority estimated that 75 to 80 percent may be reclaimed. Fifty percent would supply a good amount of valuable nutrients and even if the percentages were smaller the improvement obtained through the use of bran water would be well worth the effort.

Other fractions are in the same category. It is not possible to measure the minerals and vitamins rinsed from the whole wheat flour in making gluten, but we know that the major portion is in the rinse liquid and that it contains valuable proteins as well. Thus, its use in making burger buns, for example, will prove a valuable supplement to the gluten-burgers, or bread thus enriched would make a dressing of good supplementary value for gluten roast.

The protein value for whole wheat is rated at 65 (see Page 24) — adequate for adult maintenance. The nearer we come to using all the fractions of the wheat the nearer we approach its high rating, in protein and other nutrients as well.

Creamy curd cheese used at the same time as the liquid drained off in making it can be rated according to the original value of the soybeans.

Tofu. The ratings given for tofu in *U.S. Department of Agriculture Handbook 8* have been used for all recipes using tofu. However the calcium content of the tofu as given here would be higher. The combined tofu and whey will contain from 780 to 1560 mg of calcium. The whey may also contain as much as one-fourth of the nutrients of the soybeans used in making the tofu. This remains to be measured.

Values for raw vegetables have been used in the vegetable cookery section. With careful methods of preparation — small quantities of water used in cooking with all the water absorbed or used — there should be little loss of nutrients except for small amounts of thiamine and ascorbic acid.

The values given for raw vegetables are for those selected from the market two or three days after harvesting from the garden. Garden-fresh vegetables would have somewhat higher ratings.

Vitamin broth. The mineral and vitamin content of vitamin broth, asparagus soup, and peapod soup would be difficult to evaluate because of lack of information on nutritive values of discarded parts. For this reason there many valuable foods whose nutrient evaluations cannot be listed.

NUTRITIONAL EVALUATION

Entrées	Protein Quality Index (See p. 24)	Nutritional Evaluation based on one portion of recipe divided into this many portions	Food Energy Calories	Protein Gm.	Fat Gm.	Fatty Acids Saturated Fats Gm.	Oleic Acid Gm.	Linoleic Acid Gm.	Carbohydrate Gm.	Calcium Mg.	Phosphorus Mg.	Iron Mg.	Sodium Mg.	Potassium Mg.	Vitamin A value I.U.	Thiamine Mg.	Riboflavin Mg.	Niacin Mg.	Ascorbic Acid Mg.
Bulgar Chick Patties	72	6	157	5.1	5.7	1	2	3	22.3	35	102	1.9	158	197	14	.10	.04	1.0	1
Bulgar with Garbanzos and Mushroom Sauce		4	448	14.2	15.4	2	4	7	66.1	113	359	5.4	1295	580	78	.81	.34	4.3	4
Akara Balls with Brazil Nuts		14	74	3.6	3.7	1	2	1	7.7	24	125	1.2	231	163	2	.67	.18	1.7	0
Akara Balls with Sesame Seeds		14	71	3.8	3.0	0	1	1	8.1	59	122	1.4	233	163	3	.67	.18	1.8	0
Baked Beans		6	455	19.1	6.3	1	1	3	84.7	188	381	9.0	813	1587	1825	.61	.25	3.4	35
Beans		7	137	8.9	.5	-	-	-	25.2	57	178	2.5	311	393	5	.32	.09	.9	1
Beans and Bread		6	326	13.5	9.9	1	2	2	98.2	101	306	3.6	793	522	231	.47	.14	2.3	1
Bean-Oat Patties (Granddaughter's Favorite)	79	8	135	6.9	4.4	1	2	2	18.6	52	205	2.3	3	299	4	.73	.23	2.1	1
Burritos	78	6	303	14.4	6.0	1	1	3	51.1	69	301	4.2	84	588	11	.31	.12	2.2	3
Chili	78	10	262	14.4	1.2	-	-	-	51.3	85	310	4.1	656	732	687	.54	.15	2.5	15
Cuban Black Beans with Rice	80	4	413	16.4	8.8	1	2	4	69.5	119	398	5.6	1258	831	646	.46	.18	3.2	47
Garbanzos		7	139	6.8	3.6	0	1	2	20.8	53	111	2.3	271	276	21	.10	.05	.7	1
Garbanzos Burgers large		4	351	24.4	9.5	1	3	5	46.1	175	398	7.2	565	1116	64	.59	.22	1.9	2
Garbanzos Burgers small		8	176	12.2	4.8	1	1	2	23.1	88	199	3.6	283	558	32	.30	.11	1.0	1
Garbanzo-Herb Cheese	80	14	93	4.3	5.3	1	3	1	8.5	45	133	1.6	134	207	337	.49	.17	1.6	5
Garbanzo-Pimiento Cheese	80	16	82	3.7	4.7	1	2	1	7.6	36	115	1.4	117	168	168	.43	.15	1.4	8
Falafels (Complete)		8	366	14.1	15.1	2	5	7	48.3	249	380	5.7	753	664	867	.93	.47	5.3	17
Garbanzo Chicken-like Loaf	68	9	239	12.5	9.3	1	3	5	25.6	49	138	1.9	282	202	8	.50	.17	1.7	0
Garbanzo-Gluten Roast		8	290	19.2	10.2	2	5	3	32.4	87	223	2.5	513	392	50	.21	.07	.8	3
Garbanzo-Gluten Roast with Dressing		16	230	12.3	7.3	2	2	2	31.0	71	188	2.0	540	285	88	.19	.07	1.2	3
Garbanzo-Gluten Roast with Vegetables		4	471	21.2	18.5	2	7	7	59.7	173	387	5.6	1439	1311	11031	.48	.28	4.1	37
Garbanzo Patties or Loaf		8	185	8.9	5.4	1	2	3	26.4	66	196	3.1	326	327	13	.94	.30	2.9	0
Garbanzo-Rice Patties	75	4	323	11.9	18.3	3	9	5	31.7	104	375	3.7	595	508	13	1.10	.28	3.3	0
Garbanzo-Soy Patties		10	122	7.4	3.0	0	1	1	17.4	49	134	2.2	187	308	15	.20	.06	.6	0
Garbanzo-Soy Patties with Brazil Nuts	79	10	170	8.7	9.0	1	3	4	15.6	68	171	2.5	463	394	19	.25	.07	.7	0

Entrées	Protein Quality Index (See p. 24)	Nutritional Evaluation based on one portion of recipe divided into this many portions	Food Energy Calories	Protein Gm.	Fat Gm.	Saturated Fats Gm.	Oleic Acid Gm.	Linoleic Acid Gm.	Carbohydrate Gm.	Calcium Mg.	Phosphorus Mg.	Iron Mg.	Sodium Mg.	Potassium Mg.	Vitamin A value I.U.	Thiamine Mg.	Riboflavin Mg.	Niacin Mg.	Ascorbic Acid Mg.
Garbanzo-Soy-Oat Patties		10	135	7.4	4.4	1	1	2	17.4	49	134	2.2	187	308	15	.20	.06	.6	0
Garbanzo-Soy-Oat Patties with Brazil Nuts	78	10	167	8.1	7.8	1	3	3	17.9	58	169	2.3	188	343	15	.25	.07	.7	0
Garbanzo-Wheat Patties		8	167	8.9	3.3	0	1	1	27.2	55	219	3.0	470	339	12	.87	.25	2.9	0
Garbanzos with Mushroom Sauce		4	265	10.5	11.2	1	3	6	32.4	99	224	3.4	1067	469	78	.68	.29	2.6	4
Garbanzos with Mushroom Sauce, Rice		4	443	14.3	12.1	1	3	6	70.6	117	333	4.2	1489	574	78	.82	.32	4.7	4
Garbanzos with Mushroom Sauce, Noodles		4	451	16.6	13.5	1	3	6	67.0	114	312	4.8	1070	535	182	.89	.41	4.4	4
Garbanzos with Mushroom Sauce II		4	218	12.5	6.6	0	2	3	29.6	93	250	4.0	575	457	67	.75	.31	2.8	4
Garbanzos with Mushroom Sauce II, Noodles		4	404	18.6	8.8	0	2	3	64.2	108	338	5.4	578	523	171	.95	.43	4.6	4
Garbanzos with Mushroom Sauce II, Rice		4	397	16.2	7.5	0	2	3	67.8	111	359	4.8	997	562	67	.88	.34	4.9	4
Garbanzos with Onions	76	6	98	4.6	3.2	0	1	2	13.7	39	96	1.6	315	216	22	.32	.11	1.0	3
Garbanzos with Onion and Bulgar Wheat	71	12	223	7.1	6.0	1	2	3	36.8	49	189	3.0	467	293	22	.41	.14	2.3	3
Garbanzos with Onions and Rice	77	6	199	6.2	6.0	1	2	3	30.8	49	145	2.0	622	264	22	.40	.12	2.1	3
Garbanzos with Onions and Whole Wheat Noodles	69	6	252	11.8	9.3	1	3	5	32.6	60	203	2.6	468	361	26	.47	.15	2.0	3
Beef-less Burgers large		6	288	15.7	9.6	1	3	5	37.5	90	335	4.2	290	504	49	1.49	.48	5.0	5
Beef-less Burgers small		12	144	7.9	4.8	1	2	2	18.8	45	168	2.1	145	252	25	.75	.24	2.5	3
Savory Pepper Steaklets		6	190	10.3	8.5	1	2	4	19.9	46	190	2.2	562	268	432	1.06	.34	3.0	30
Savory Steaks		12	100	8.4	1.5	0	0	1	13.8	34	137	1.4	455	191	27	.69	.22	1.9	2
Vegeburgers		6	142	11.7	4.5	0	1	2	16.2	52	190	2.7	316	240	12	.18	.12	2.2	1
Lentils		7	132	8.2	2.4	0	1	1	20.5	31	126	2.3	273	274	24	.12	.08	.7	1
Lentil Roast	74	6	246	11.3	8.6	2	4	1	33.0	69	255	3.2	415	413	21	.38	.14	1.9	0
Mary Lou's Lentil Tostados		6	213	11.7	4.4	1	1	1	34.7	79	218	3.7	185	557	1161	.28	.15	2.0	27
Quick Lentil Roast	72	6	149	3.3	5.7	1	3	1	22.0	32	118	.8	224	172	35	.17	.03	1.4	2
Stew with Lentils		4	193	8.6	4.0	0	1	2	32.4	69	161	2.6	978	674	5334	.19	.13	1.7	20
Macaroni and "Cheese" with Almonds		4	314	9.6	17.6	2	9	6	31.9	84	232	3.0	731	324	329	1.00	.55	4.8	20
Macaroni and "Cheese" with Cashews		4	282	8.5	15.5	2	8	4	29.4	43	199	2.7	920	257	346	1.02	.41	4.2	20

NUTRITIONAL EVALUATION

Entrées	Protein Quality Index (See p. 24)	Nutritional Evaluation based on one portion of recipe divided into this many portions	Food Energy Calories	Protein Gm.	Fat Gm.	Fatty Acids Saturated Fats Gm.	Oleic Acid Gm.	Linoleic Acid Gm.	Carbohydrate Gm.	Calcium Mg.	Phosphorus Mg.	Iron Mg.	Sodium Mg.	Potassium Mg.	Vitamin A value I.U.	Thiamine Mg.	Riboflavin Mg.	Niacin Mg.	Ascorbic Acid Mg.
Macaroni and "Cheese" with Peanut Butter		4	311	11.3	16.7	2	7	6	31.5	53	215	2.6	839	305	329	.98	.40	7.0	20
Macaroni and "Cheese" with Peanuts		4	309	11.0	16.6	3	6	6	31.6	53	215	2.6	731	306	329	1.14	.40	7.0	20
Macaroni and "Cheese" with Soy Beans		4	307	14.8	12.2	2	3	6	36.8	98	280	4.3	731	603	349	1.23	.46	4.7	20
Macaroni and "Cheese" with Soy Flour		4	277	12.4	11.2	1	3	6	33.5	75	235	3.6	730	463	347	1.10	.43	4.5	20
Breaded Nuteena		4	266	15.1	16.5	1	2	2	17.5	67	321	3.1	603	409	159	1.53	.58	5.0	0
Breaded Nuteena with Garbanzo		4	289	15.9	15.6	1	2	2	25.0	80	335	3.7	229	491	6	1.56	.56	5.2	0
Onion Pie with Cashews		6	295	8.0	19.1	3	10	5	25.8	46	174	1.9	531	309	54	.23	.11	1.4	5
Onion Pie with Garbanzos		6	283	10.7	10.0	1	3	5	39.2	87	196	3.3	536	466	48	.23	.10	1.6	5
Onion Pie with Chicken-Style Textured Protein		6	207	7.4	11.6	1	2	4	19.4	47	86	1.6	720	201	31	.13	.05	1.0	5
Onion Pie II		6	209	5.6	8.9	1	2	4	27.7	44	102	1.5	996	232	22	.11	.05	1.1	4
Peanut-Carrot Roast		12	179	8.1	9.3	2	4	3	18.0	41	136	1.5	982	302	2023	.27	.06	3.7	1
Peanut Butter Loaf or Patties		5	224	9.0	10.4	2	5	3	26.5	32	185	2.4	671	422	798	.21	.08	3.6	16
Peanut Butter Carrot Loaf		8	145	6.0	6.1	1	3	2	19.1	44	113	1.3	740	320	3454	.11	.07	2.8	9
Garden of Rice		6	154	5.4	.8	-	-	1	32.7	34	123	1.6	718	358	874	.18	.09	2.1	44
Garden of Rice with Chick		10	142	11.3	2.2	0	0	1	21.2	38	151	1.1	255	275	378	.12	.06	1.2	24
Green Rice	76	6	147	4.7	6.6	1	2	3	18.4	56	96	1.8	553	296	1575	.16	.08	1.1	30
Esau's Pottage	68	6	122	3.3	5.1	1	1	3	16.3	19	67	.9	311	132	16	.08	.03	.8	3
Golden Nuggets	79	6	213	12.5	3.4	0	1	1	34.2	44	227	3.4	282	446	40	1.32	.43	4.0	0
Hearty Hash		4	336	11.5	13.4	1	4	7	46.8	87	373	3.8	719	890	48	1.75	.53	6.5	28
Hearty Hash with Rice		4	407	11.5	20.4	3	8	7	48.5	92	433	3.7	734	946	46	1.86	.52	6.8	28
Hurry-up Hearty Hash		4	217	7.3	9.3	1	2	5	28.1	44	240	2.6	349	577	32	1.18	.35	3.8	19
Savory Roll'ems		6	411	10.8	22.4	3	8	9	45.8	69	350	3.0	649	503	31	.92	.28	3.9	8
Tamale Pie		12	193	5.5	6.1	1	3	2	32.3	41	127	1.8	863	330	819	.15	.09	1.5	24
Soybeans		7	131	11.0	5.7	1	1	3	10.9	74	179	2.7	132	543	26	.36	.10	.7	0
Baked Soybeans		8	282	17.9	12.7	2	3	7	26.6	131	297	4.8	530	1011	500	.59	.18	1.5	14

NUTRITIONAL EVALUATION

Entrées

	Protein Quality Index (See p. 24) Nutritional Evaluation based on one portion of recipe divided into this many portions	Food Energy Calories	Protein Gm.	Fat Gm.	Fatty Acids Saturated Fats Gm.	Oleic Acid Gm.	Linoleic Acid Gm.	Carbohydrate Gm.	Calcium Mg.	Phosphorus Mg.	Iron Mg.	Sodium Mg.	Potassium Mg.	Vitamin A value I.U.	Thiamine Mg.	Riboflavin Mg.	Niacin Mg.	Ascorbic Acid Mg.
Soy-Oat Patties	8 → 80	142	7.5	7.4	1	2	4	12.8	48	139	2.0	360	334	14	.25	.07	.5	0
Breaded Fried Chicken Style with Egg	5	196	13.3	10.4	1	2	2	12.9	56	169	2.8	585	172	127	1.22	.39	3.2	0
Breaded Fried Chicken Style with Garbanzo	5	214	13.9	9.6	0	1	2	18.9	65	179	3.3	575	238	5	1.24	.37	3.4	0
Stew with Beef-style Soyameat and Gravy	6	130	7.4	5.6	0	1	1	13.2	39	45	1.4	545	328	2671	.07	.05	.9	14
Stroganoff	4	302	13.3	14.3	1	2	4	30.7	55	132	2.2	955	193	33	.14	.17	2.3	3
Creamed Curd Cheese	8	190	13.4	10.5	2	3	5	13.2	90	218	3.3	174	660	31	.43	.12	.9	0
Scrambled Tofu	8	124	8.7	8.2	1	2	4	5.7	101	141	2.2	176	243	11	.18	.06	.4	0
Rice with Tofu	8	179	8.0	4.9	1	1	2	26.7	92	184	2.1	280	141	0	.57	.17	2.5	0

Breads

	Protein Quality Index (See p. 24) Nutritional Evaluation based on one portion of recipe divided into this many portions	Food Energy Calories	Protein Gm.	Fat Gm.	Fatty Acids Saturated Fats Gm.	Oleic Acid Gm.	Linoleic Acid Gm.	Carbohydrate Gm.	Calcium Mg.	Phosphorus Mg.	Iron Mg.	Sodium Mg.	Potassium Mg.	Vitamin A value I.U.	Thiamine Mg.	Riboflavin Mg.	Niacin Mg.	Ascorbic Acid Mg.
Barley Bread	30 → 66	70	2.3	.9	-	-	-	13.5	3	16	.2	123	56	25	.03	.05	.4	0
Date-Pecan Rolls	36	144	3.5	5.0	0	2	1	24.0	19	99	1.2	1	187	12	.17	.06	1.3	0
Pita Buns	20	155	5.3	3.6	0	1	2	27.6	17	152	1.4	185	162	0	.23	.12	2.1	0
Modified Pioneer Bread	30	98	4.4	2.1	0	0	1	16.8	14	107	1.1	185	136	1	.16	.13	1.6	0
Oatmeal Bread	30	97	3.9	2.2	0	1	1	17.0	14	113	.9	140	113	1	.14	.06	1.0	0
Orange-Date Bread	15	204	6.0	5.4	0	1	3	37.2	33	148	1.9	3	286	22	.21	.16	2.2	4
Pioneer Bread	30	104	4.0	1.4	0	0	1	20.0	10	100	.8	124	100	0	.14	.08	1.4	0
Potato Bread	60	86	2.8	1.3	0	0	1	16.0	7	45	.6	136	86	1	.10	.07	1.0	2
Potato Rolls	24	180	4.3	1.8	0	1	1	38.1	10	81	.9	176	89	1	.14	.10	1.5	0
Refrigerator Rolls	24	139	5.5	3.1	0	1	1	22.8	13	82	1.0	154	103	17	.15	.08	1.2	0
Sandwich Buns	16	230	7.5	7.4	1	2	3	34.3	30	148	2.1	245	138	138	.27	.16	1.6	0
Swedish Limpa Bread	45	73	3.1	1.8	0	0	1	12.5	11	77	.7	122	99	63	.10	.04	.8	0
Wheat-Soy Bread	50	101	4.5	2.2	0	1	1	16.8	18	91	.9	166	132	3	.14	.05	.9	0
Whole Wheat Bread	45	139	5.1	1.7	0	0	1	27.9	17	145	1.4	124	150	0	.21	.05	1.8	0

NUTRITIONAL EVALUATION

Quick Breads

	Protein Quality Index (See p. 24)	Nutritional Evaluation based on one portion of recipe divided into this many portions	Food Energy Calories	Protein Gm.	Fat Gm.	Saturated Fats Gm.	Oleic Acid Gm.	Linoleic Acid Gm.	Carbohydrate Gm.	Calcium Mg.	Phosphorus Mg.	Iron Mg.	Sodium Mg.	Potassium Mg.	Vitamin A value I.U.	Thiamine Mg.	Riboflavin Mg.	Niacin Mg.	Ascorbic Acid Mg.
Apple-Oatmeal Muffins	8	8	216	3.6	13.4	1	3	7	22.8	24	104	1.3	118	192	14	.13	.04	.3	1
Barley-Oat Muffins	70	8	194	3.1	8.2	1	2	4	28.8	14	53	.9	118	161	12	.08	.03	.2	1
Cornbread	86	12	115	3.3	6.2	1	2	3	11.7	32	70	.5	174	71	156	.07	.08	.3	0
Cornmeal-Rice Muffins	75	8	166	3.5	8.6	1	2	5	19.6	14	81	.8	167	125	99	.12	.04	.7	0
Corn Muffins	76	6	194	4.2	11.4	1	3	6	20.2	20	94	1.1	306	166	131	.16	.04	.6	1
Date-Bran Muffins		8	187	3.3	11.0	1	3	6	23.1	26	143	1.9	116	223	17	.13	.06	1.7	1
Hoe Cake	87	6	191	4.1	12.3	2	4	6	16.8	18	88	1.0	328	87	314	.09	.08	.4	0
Oat Cake	76	8	196	5.6	13.0	1	3	7	15.8	29	130	1.5	115	96	24	.18	.05	.4	0
Oat Cake with Sesame Seeds		6	173	6.1	11.2	2	4	5	13.7	165	161	2.4	161	232	8	.26	.07	.9	1
Oat Cake with Walnuts		6	137	4.6	8.5	1	2	5	11.9	26	105	1.2	153	165	6	.16	.04	.3	1
Barley Sticks	68	14	123	2.1	8.0	3	2	2	11.8	5	17	.3	131	72	1	.01	.01	.1	0
Crackers	69	60	59	1.6	3.1	0	1	2	6.7	5	52	.5	46	44	0	.08	.02	.3	0
Flat Bread	73	12	157	5.6	6.8	1	2	3	20.3	26	134	1.5	154	225	7	.19	.06	.8	0
Sesame Seed-Oatmeal Crackers		60	54	1.6	3.2	0	1	2	5.1	19	40	.5	47	51	2	.06	.02	.1	0
Wheat Lefse		12	142	4.0	5.3	1	1	3	21.3	13	112	1.0	77	111	0	.17	.04	1.3	0

Waffles

	Protein Quality Index (See p. 24)	Nutritional Evaluation based on one portion of recipe divided into this many portions	Food Energy Calories	Protein Gm.	Fat Gm.	Saturated Fats Gm.	Oleic Acid Gm.	Linoleic Acid Gm.	Carbohydrate Gm.	Calcium Mg.	Phosphorus Mg.	Iron Mg.	Sodium Mg.	Potassium Mg.	Vitamin A value I.U.	Thiamine Mg.	Riboflavin Mg.	Niacin Mg.	Ascorbic Acid Mg.
Almond-Oat	67	4	237	6.6	12.5	1	6	4	26.4	47	184	1.9	230	202	16	.21	.16	.7	0
Barley-Soy	75	4	201	9.4	7.5	1	2	4	25.9	47	111	1.7	231	375	16	.22	.06	.4	0
Buckwheat-Oat		4	223	7.4	7.0	1	2	3	34.3	31	190	2.1	230	181	5	.29	.07	.8	0
Cashew-Oat	74	4	226	6.2	11.0	2	6	3	27.3	22	164	1.8	231	158	11	.23	.07	.5	0
Cornmeal-Cashew Nut	77	4	248	5.6	10.7	1	5	3	34.8	14	142	1.4	231	164	203	.20	.07	1.0	0
Cornmeal-Soy	79	4	245	10.2	8.5	1	2	4	34.3	54	206	2.6	230	441	207	.36	.10	1.2	0
Filbert-Oat	69	4	241	5.8	13.5	1	6	4	26.0	43	163	1.8	230	193	0	.24	.04	.4	0
Garbanzo-Oat	74	4	234	8.3	6.7	1	2	3	36.1	47	187	2.7	235	265	10	.24	.07	.7	0

Waffles

	Protein Quality Index (See p. 24)	Nutritional Evaluation based on one portion of recipe divided into this many portions	Food Energy Calories	Protein Gm.	Fat Gm.	Saturated Fats Gm.	Oleic Acid Gm.	Linoleic Acid Gm.	Carbo-hydrate Gm.	Calcium Mg.	Phos-phorus Mg.	Iron Mg.	Sodium Mg.	Potas-sium Mg.	Vitamin A value I.U.	Thiamine Mg.	Ribo-flavin Mg.	Niacin Mg.	Ascorbic Acid Mg.
Lentil-Oat	4	70	230	9.2	6.0	1	2	3	35.9	33	196	2.7	236	263	12	.25	.09	.7	0
Millet-Soy	4	78	193	9.3	7.8	1	2	4	24.9	52	188	3.4	230	442	16	.40	.16	1.0	0
Multi-Grain	4	73	199	8.7	6.7	1	2	3	28.7	37	213	2.3	230	347	10	.29	.09	1.3	0
Peanut-Oat	4	68	219	7.5	11.8	2	4	5	22.6	25	172	1.6	230	189	0	.30	.06	2.3	0
Pecan-Oat	4	71	247	5.4	14.6	1	8	5	25.8	26	157	1.7	230	181	16	.29	.06	.4	0
Pinto Bean-Oat	4	77	232	8.8	6.0	1	2	3	36.7	44	212	2.6	232	302	0	.35	.08	.7	0
Pinto Bean-Wheat	4	78	218	9.4	4.4	0	1	2	37.3	48	215	2.5	233	354	0	.36	.08	1.7	0
Rice-Soy	4	77	393	12.7	8.6	1	2	4	67.2	72	283	2.9	237	502	16	.49	.10	4.1	0
Soy-Oat	4	77	229	11.1	9.3	1	3	6	27.2	63	232	3.1	231	441	16	.40	.11	.8	0
Sunflower Seed-Oat	4	69	232	7.2	11.7	1	3	7	26.4	32	226	2.2	233	220	6	.42	.07	1.0	0

Breakfast Foods

	Protein Quality Index (See p. 24)	Nutritional Evaluation based on one portion of recipe divided into this many portions	Food Energy Calories	Protein Gm.	Fat Gm.	Saturated Fats Gm.	Oleic Acid Gm.	Linoleic Acid Gm.	Carbo-hydrate Gm.	Calcium Mg.	Phos-phorus Mg.	Iron Mg.	Sodium Mg.	Potas-sium Mg.	Vitamin A value I.U.	Thiamine Mg.	Ribo-flavin Mg.	Niacin Mg.	Ascorbic Acid Mg.
Cooked Wheat Cereal	4		115	4.9	.8	-	-	-	24.1	14	134	1.1	230	129	0	.20	.04	1.5	0
Cooked Wheat Cereal with Soy Cream	4		165	6.8	5.2	0	1	2	25.4	26	161	1.5	230	129	23	.24	.06	1.6	0
Corn Granola or Corn Crisps	8		217	6.0	9.6	1	3	5	28.0	24	175	1.6	345	208	80	.29	.08	1.4	0
Cornmeal Slices with Savory Crumbs	8		92	3.7	3.0	0	1	2	13.2	22	98	1.2	274	137	52	.52	.16	1.5	0
Cornmeal with Soy Grits	6		64	2.7	1.3	0	0	1	10.9	14	56	.7	458	104	71	.08	.03	.3	0
Granola	8		256	6.2	11.4	1	4	5	35.8	38	193	2.1	230	312	6	.22	.12	1.4	0
Oats Special with Dates	4		189	7.0	3.1	1	1	1	36.4	35	248	2.9	230	329	11	.42	.14	1.3	0
Oats Special with Raisins	4		185	7.0	3.0	1	1	1	35.5	34	254	2.9	235	336	4	.42	.14	.9	0
Fruit Toast	4		302	10.1	9.3	1	4	2	49.5	69	188	1.8	339	537	2277	.17	.10	4.3	5
French Toast with Soybean Concentrate	8	74	138	5.4	7.5	1	2	4	13.9	43	101	1.3	236	209	7	.16	.05	.8	0
Garbanzo French Toast	6	71	115	4.5	6.1	1	2	3	11.6	35	74	1.3	348	114	21	.09	.04	.5	0
Soya French Toast	6		190	9.7	9.2	1	3	5	20.0	72	156	2.0	286	349	14	.26	.08	1.1	1

NUTRITIONAL EVALUATION

Protein Quality Index (See p. 24)

Desserts	Nutritional evaluation based on one portion of recipe divided into this many portions	Food Energy Calories	Protein Gm.	Fat Gm.	Fatty Acids — Saturated Fats Gm.	Oleic Acid Gm.	Linoleic Acid Gm.	Carbohydrate Gm.	Calcium Mg.	Phosphorus Mg.	Iron Mg.	Sodium Mg.	Potassium Mg.	Vitamin A value I.U.	Thiamine Mg.	Riboflavin Mg.	Niacin Mg.	Ascorbic Acid Mg.
	128	15	.1	1.0	1	0	0	1.6	3	3	.1	3	18	4	0.00	0.00	0.0	0
Coconut Candy	36	59	.8	3.2	1	0	1	7.9	10	24	.5	14	90	4	.02	.01	.2	0
Fruit Candy	64	37	1.9	2.4	0	1	1	2.9	9	17	.1	25	38	0	.01	.01	.6	0
Peanut Butter Fudge	16	191	3.9	10.2	2	4	3	22.9	30	93	1.3	81	165	921	.12	.07	.7	2
Carrot Cake with Glaze	48	111	1.3	3.1	0	1	1	21.3	18	38	.8	22	147	74	.05	.03	.3	2
Mini-Fruit Cakes	24	103	1.7	5.4	1	1	3	13.4	12	46	.7	39	132	133	.06	.03	.3	2
Banana-Date Cookies	24	146	1.5	9.3	1	3	5	16.3	23	42	.7	41	73	4	.05	.02	.1	0
Carob-Apple Brownies	36	57	.6	3.9	1	1	2	5.1	7	16	.3	29	52	694	.02	.01	.1	1
Carrot-Oatmeal Cookies	36	99	1.4	6.4	1	2	3	10.1	9	38	.6	26	78	6	.05	.02	.2	0
Date-Apple Cookies	16	181	3.5	8.6	1	2	5	24.9	25	97	1.4	146	203	8	.13	.04	.6	1
Fruit Bars	16	146	2.6	7.1	1	2	4	20.2	20	75	1.0	60	144	25	.11	.03	.2	4
Fruit Squares	24	95	.8	7.6	3	2	3	6.6	9	20	.4	42	72	504	.02	.01	.1	0
Golden Macaroons	24	69	1.3	4.9	2	1	1	5.5	7	28	.4	38	30	8	.04	.01	.1	0
Macaroons with Soy Cream	24	57	.8	4.7	3	1	1	3.5	5	16	.3	38	49	1	.02	.01	.1	0
Macaroons with Soy Concentrate	24 ('73)	111	2.1	7.2	1	2	4	10.6	13	53	.7	39	101	5	.08	.02	.3	0
Yummie Oatmeal Cookies	24	160	4.5	11.7	2	4	5	10.9	15	83	.7	40	128	0	.17	.03	2.2	0
Brittle Peanut Cookies	24	96	4.0	5.4	1	2	2	9.3	15	74	.7	69	124	2	.08	.03	1.5	0
Peanut Butter Cookies	24																	
Almond-Banana Cream Pie	6	510	9.8	29.1	2	13	10	60.3	97	250	3.4	195	646	126	.25	.32	2.8	5
Apple Pie	6	384	5.5	21.8	2	6	11	45.4	25	161	1.9	178	277	97	.24	.07	1.8	2
Apple-Date Pie	6	376	5.5	19.2	2	5	10	50.7	47	136	2.0	118	384	89	.23	.09	1.5	8
Orchard Apple Pie	6	300	4.4	15.6	1	4	8	38.8	32	106	1.4	118	262	80	.20	.06	1.2	8
Cranberry Delight Pie	8	261	3.0	10.3	1	2	5	42.5	28	94	1.9	60	317	33	.13	.07	.9	6
Date-Pumpkin Pie	6	342	9.8	18.0	2	5	9	40.6	79	203	3.0	156	679	4863	.34	.14	2.1	5
Lemon Pie with Coconut	6	273	3.2	12.8	2	4	6	38.9	22	86	1.0	101	215	118	.15	.04	1.0	13
Lemon Pie DeLuxe or Lemon Cream Pie	6	333	4.3	17.3	2	5	8	42.9	30	101	1.2	141	206	134	.18	.05	1.1	13

NUTRITIONAL EVALUATION

Desserts	Protein Quality Index (See p. 24)	Nutritional Evaluation based on one portion of recipe divided into this many portions	Food Energy Calories	Protein Gm.	Fat Gm.	Fatty Acids Saturated Fats Gm.	Oleic Acid Gm.	Linoleic Acid Gm.	Carbohydrate Gm.	Calcium Mg.	Phosphorus Mg.	Iron Mg.	Sodium Mg.	Potassium Mg.	Vitamin A value I.U.	Thiamine Mg.	Riboflavin Mg.	Niacin Mg.	Ascorbic Acid Mg.
Prune Pie	6		307	4.7	15.5	1	4	8	41.8	35	118	2.2	195	306	399	.17	.09	1.5	3
Raisin Pie--large	6		477	6.9	21.7	2	6	11	71.3	54	205	3.2	192	567	96	.29	.10	2.0	5
Raisin Pie--small	8		358	5.1	16.3	2	5	8	53.5	40	154	2.4	144	425	72	.22	.07	1.5	4
Strawberry Pie	6		299	4.7	15.8	1	4	8	37.7	39	114	2.0	157	246	76	.17	.11	1.5	61
Pie Pastry	6		150	2.7	9.9	1	3	5	14.2	9	75	.7	77	74	0	.11	.02	.9	0
Pie Pastry--Variation 1	6		174	3.3	13.5	1	4	7	11.5	12	96	.9	77	108	2	.15	.04	.7	0
Pie Pastry--Variation 2	6		176	3.0	13.4	1	4	7	11.4	9	58	.8	77	71	2	.14	.06	.6	0
Barley Pie Pastry	6		122	2.9	7.8	1	2	4	10.9	8	49	.5	92	84	3	.08	.03	.2	0
Garbanzo-Rice Pie Pastry	6	75	143	3.6	5.6	1	2	3	19.8	24	75	1.1	220	128	6	.08	.03	.9	0
Almond-Banana Cream Pudding	6		290	5.9	13.8	1	9	3	41.7	80	157	2.4	78	571	111	.11	.29	1.9	5
Apple-Date Pudding	6		157	1.6	3.8	0	1	2	32.1	30	44	1.1	2	310	74	.09	.05	.6	8
Golden Apple Dessert	6		80	.4	.3	0	0	0	20.2	15	14	.4	1	187	65	.06	.03	.2	8
Dutch Barley-Fruit Pudding	6		186	3.6	.6	0	0	0	44.3	24	116	1.6	157	266	3	.09	.05	1.4	1
Grandmother's Old-Fashioned Bread Pudding	6	75	239	8.3	8.3	1	3	4	36.4	75	171	2.7	215	476	16	.27	.09	1.1	1
Lemon Pudding	6		114	.4	2.0	1	1	1	24.3	13	9	.3	24	132	118	.04	.02	.2	13
Lemon-Coconut Pudding	6		123	.5	2.9	1	1	1	24.6	13	11	.3	24	140	118	.04	.02	.2	13
Prune Pudding	6		87	.7	.2	0	0	0	23.2	18	25	1.2	78	232	384	.03	.05	.6	3
Prune Pudding or Prune Whip	6		157	2.0	5.7	1	1	3	27.5	27	43	1.5	118	232	399	.06	.06	.7	3
Creamy Rice Pudding	4		405	16.1	14.7	2	4	7	57.4	118	303	4.8	239	950	43	.56	.16	2.4	4
Strawberry Glaze Dessert	6		79	.7	.5	0	0	0	19.1	22	22	1.0	41	172	61	.03	.07	.6	61
Empanadas with Filling 1	6		267	5.9	8.9	1	2	5	45.8	37	167	2.2	196	348	12	.23	.07	1.9	1
Empanadas with Filling 2	6		215	4.9	5.6	1	1	3	40.4	29	141	1.7	194	281	45	.22	.06	1.7	8
Empanadas with Filling 3	6		263	5.4	9.0	1	2	5	43.9	29	158	2.0	193	304	28	.23	.08	1.6	2
Fruit Plate Deluxe	1		218	5.0	1.8	0	0	1	50.7	71	69	2.0	28	835	7289	.15	.16	2.2	125
Peach Sherbet	8		71	2.3	1.1	0	0	1	14.2	16	7	.3	1	70	369	.01	.02	.4	23

NUTRITIONAL EVALUATION

Vegetables	Nutritional Evaluation based on one portion of recipe divided into this many portions	Food Energy Calories	Protein Gm.	Fat Gm.	Fatty Acids Saturated Fats Gm.	Oleic Acid Gm.	Linoleic Acid Gm.	Carbo-hydrate Gm.	Calcium Mg.	Phos-phorus Mg.	Iron Mg.	Sodium Mg.	Potas-sium Mg.	Vitamin A value I.U.	Thiamine Mg.	Ribo-flavin Mg.	Niacin Mg.	Ascorbic Acid Mg.
Asparagus Tips on Toast with Evaporated Milk.	4	324	13.1	10.5	3	5	2	48.9	172	298	3.0	729	577	1225	.42	.40	3.9	33
Asparagus Tips on Toast with Soy Cream.	4	369	13.1	16.5	3	6	6	47.4	112	267	3.4	755	491	1157	.45	.33	4.0	33
Asparagus Tips on Toast with Evaporated Milk, Parsley.	4	327	14.4	10.5	3	5	2	49.5	186	303	3.4	732	628	1827	.43	.42	4.0	45
Asparagus Tips on Toast with Soy Cream, Parsley.	4	372	14.3	16.5	3	6	6	48.0	127	272	3.8	758	542	1759	.46	.34	4.0	45
Dilled Green Beans.	4	62	2.2	3.1	1	1	1	8.1	64	50	.9	43	276	797	.09	.12	.6	22
Beets with Greens.	4	28	1.4	.2	0	0	0	6.4	58	24	1.2	512	290	2556	.06	.10	.2	24
Harvard Beets.	6	60	1.5	.1	0	0	0	14.7	19	30	.7	288	322	22	.03	.04	.4	21
Just Plain Cabbage.	4	49	1.3	3.1	1	1	4	5.4	54	30	.4	742	233	247	.05	.05	.3	47
Cabbage Baked in Soy Cream.	4	108	3.2	8.4	1	2	1	6.6	64	56	.9	478	233	152	.10	.07	.4	47
Cabbage Greens.	4	41	1.6	3.1	1	1	1	2.4	166	44	.8	105	306	3210	.05	.10	.8	25
Panned Cabbage and Celery.	4	60	1.5	3.8	0	1	2	6.4	60	36	.5	280	318	190	.06	.06	.4	49
Carrots with Crumbs.	4	91	3.6	2.3	0	1	1	15.1	53	126	1.7	320	417	10230	.82	.27	2.6	7
Creamed Carrots with Evaporated Milk.	4	116	3.5	5.4	2	2	1	14.4	111	99	.7	570	407	10438	.08	.15	.7	8
Creamed Carrots with Soy Cream.	4	89	2.9	4.6	0	1	2	10.3	48	61	1.1	273	316	10250	.10	.07	.7	7
Parsleyed Carrots.	4	60	1.1	3.1	1	1	1	8.0	44	32	1.0	303	309	9053	.05	.06	.5	18
Cauliflower Baked in Soy Cream.	4	77	4.6	4.6	0	1	2	6.4	38	83	1.6	239	295	83	.16	.12	.8	78
Cauliflower with Crumbs.	4	78	5.3	2.3	0	1	1	11.2	43	148	2.1	289	394	60	.87	.32	2.7	78
Celery and Green Beans with Margarine.	4	50	1.4	3.0	1	1	1	5.6	51	37	.6	560	292	536	.05	.07	.4	14
Celery and Green Beans Creamed with Evaporated Milk.	4	95	3.5	6.0	2	2	2	8.3	122	94	.6	558	373	508	.07	.17	.5	14
Celery and Green Beans Creamed with Soy Cream.	4	75	3.3	4.6	0	1	2	6.7	62	63	1.0	524	292	442	.10	.09	.6	14
Corn on the Cob.	6	182	6.6	2.0	-	-	-	42.0	6	178	1.2	Trace	392	800	.24	.20	2.8	18
Creamed Corn.	4	203	10.3	3.7	-	-	-	40.1	33	232	2.1	458	330	845	.31	.23	2.8	14
Corn Custard.	4	173	7.2	4.5	2	2	0	30.5	95	187	1.1	693	260	1283	.08	.24	1.6	48
Escalloped Corn with Tomatoes.	8	166	5.7	4.2	1	2	1	29.7	37	124	1.6	569	286	789	.12	.09	1.7	12
Corn Fritters with Soy Concentrate.	4	144	5.0	6.6	1	2	3	19.2	24	100	1.0	380	210	230	.12	.06	1.0	4

NUTRITIONAL EVALUATION

Vegetables

Vegetables	Nutritional Evaluation based on one portion of recipe divided into this many portions	Food Energy Calories	Protein Gm.	Fat Gm.	Saturated Fats Gm.	Oleic Acid Gm.	Linoleic Acid Gm.	Carbohydrate Gm.	Calcium Mg.	Phosphorus Mg.	Iron Mg.	Sodium Mg.	Potassium Mg.	Vitamin A value I.U.	Thiamine Mg.	Riboflavin Mg.	Niacin Mg.	Ascorbic Acid Mg.
Corn with Green and Red Peppers	4	136	4.4	2.9	0	1	1	27.9	14	112	1.0	528	149	1059	.08	.10	1.6	48
Succotash with Evaporated Milk	8	102	5.2	3.0	1	1	1	14.9	59	108	1.3	264	344	319	.13	.12	.9	13
Succotash with Soy Milk	8	87	4.6	2.1	0	1	1	13.8	26	86	1.4	247	301	280	.13	.08	.9	13
Eggplant	4	19	1.0	.2	0	0	0	4.1	17	21	.6	917	150	10	.05	.04	.5	3
Eggplant with Egg and Crumbs	4	140	5.9	7.1	1	2	3	14.3	45	144	2.1	675	260	171	.80	.31	2.6	3
Eggplant with Garbanzos	4	119	4.8	4.6	0	1	2	16.2	40	84	1.9	235	353	19	.10	.08	.9	5
Eggplant with Garbanzos and Crumbs	4	194	9.5	6.3	1	2	3	26.5	74	254	3.8	668	478	18	1.54	.48	4.7	3
Eggplant with Margarine	4	53	1.0	4.0	1	2	1	4.1	15	22	.6	505	151	166	.05	.04	.5	3
Eggplant with Tomato Sauce	4	66	2.0	2.1	0	1	1	11.4	19	41	1.1	184	359	505	.09	.08	1.0	27
Okra	4	9	.6	.1	0	0	0	1.9	25	13	.2	230	62	130	.04	.05	.3	8
Parsleyed Parsnips	4	72	1.1	3.8	0	1	2	9.3	41	43	.8	238	321	613	.05	.06	.2	20
Parsnip Patties	6	102	3.3	3.2	0	1	2	16.0	45	78	1.2	314	367	21	.08	.06	.3	8
Parsnip Patties with Egg	6	74	2.0	3.7	1	1	1	8.9	32	57	.6	322	286	121	.05	.07	.1	8
Green Peas	4	61	4.2	3.2	1	1	1	9.6	20	78	1.3	265	112	544	.23	.09	1.9	18
Creamed Peas	4	83	6.3	4.0	1	1	1	11.6	32	106	1.8	265	113	567	.28	.11	2.1	18
Creamed Peas in Toasted Shells	4	222	11.4	5.7	1	1	2	39.5	49	251	3.2	389	263	567	.49	.16	3.9	18
Creamed Peas with Potatoes	4	153	8.2	4.1	1	1	1	27.3	38	155	2.3	268	486	567	.38	.15	3.4	36
Mashed Potatoes with Evaporated Milk	4	166	4.4	7.0	2	3	2	22.2	108	119	.7	530	548	208	.13	.14	1.8	23
Mashed Potatoes with Soy Cream	4	137	3.4	5.2	1	2	2	20.0	18	74	.9	496	462	128	.14	.05	1.8	23
Russian Mashed Potatoes	4	162	3.7	7.0	1	2	3	22.2	24	83	1.0	499	502	138	.14	.06	1.8	25
Steam Boiled Potatoes	4	86	2.4	.1	0	0	0	19.4	11	60	.7	461	462	0	.11	.05	1.7	23
Parsleyed Potatoes	4	108	2.6	3.1	1	1	1	18.3	38	62	1.5	273	510	1322	.11	.08	1.7	45
Rutabagas	4	46	1.1	.1	0	0	0	11.0	66	39	.4	234	239	580	.07	.07	1.1	43
Mashed Rutabagas	4	72	1.1	3.0	1	1	1	11.0	68	40	.4	269	240	700	.07	.07	1.1	43
Zucchini	4	19	1.4	.1	0	0	0	4.1	33	33	.5	230	229	363	.06	.10	1.1	22

NUTRITIONAL EVALUATION

Soups	Protein Quality Index (See p. 24)	Nutritional Evaluation based on one portion of recipe divided into this many portions	Food Energy Calories	Protein Gm.	Fat Gm.	Saturated Fats Gm.	Oleic Acid Gm.	Linoleic Acid Gm.	Carbohydrate Gm.	Calcium Mg.	Phosphorus Mg.	Iron Mg.	Sodium Mg.	Potassium Mg.	Vitamin A value I.U.	Thiamine Mg.	Riboflavin Mg.	Niacin Mg.	Ascorbic Acid Mg.
Creamy Bean Soup with Evaporated Milk	83	5	160	9.6	3.9	2	1	0	22.2	154	221	1.8	423	412	145	.25	.21	.7	0
Creamy Bean Soup with Soy Milk	81	5	133	8.0	3.3	1	1	1	18.8	50	150	2.2	397	276	112	.27	.07	.7	0
Creamy Bean Soup with Soy Concentrate	79	5	200	11.4	5.4	1	1	3	27.8	70	219	3.1	187	507	6	.41	.10	1.0	1
Old Homestead Bean Soup		4	244	12.7	6.6	1	2	2	34.8	86	242	4.4	539	680	234	.37	.12	1.4	0
Ye Olde Time Soup		6	194	9.6	2.5	1	1	1	35.2	22	144	2.2	697	325	125	.29	.12	1.7	2
Borsch		4	194	7.8	10.2	1	3	5	20.1	69	143	2.1	485	650	65	.26	.11	1.3	29
Ketty's Borsch		4	181	7.5	10.2	1	3	5	17.3	65	131	2.2	514	588	50	.23	.11	.8	13
Corn Chowder with Evaporated Milk		8	96	3.7	2.5	1	1	0	16.2	86	106	.5	584	306	237	.06	.14	.9	10
Corn Chowder with Soy Concentrate		8	95	3.2	3.3	0	1	2	14.9	24	71	.8	551	291	150	.09	.05	1.0	11
Cream of Corn Soup		4	193	7.7	6.4	1	2	3	31.8	36	167	1.8	304	358	463	.18	.12	1.7	9
Kale Soup		4	78	2.5	3.8	0	2	2	9.7	74	49	1.0	480	260	2505	.08	.09	1.0	55
Split Peas--Plain		7	113	7.8	.3	0	0	0	20.3	14	87	1.7	536	290	39	.24	.09	1.0	0
Split Peas Soup.	79	4	233	13.9	4.1	0	1	2	36.6	28	156	3.0	940	527	73	.42	.17	1.7	1
Split Pea Chowder I.	79	6	334	18.1	3.4	0	1	1	59.5	48	235	3.9	658	753	1394	.57	.22	3.0	5
Split Pea Chowder II with Soy Milk		6	178	10.3	2.9	1	1	1	29.0	26	131	2.3	348	483	143	.32	.13	1.7	9
Split Pea Chowder II with Evaporated Milk		6	217	11.6	5.3	2	2	1	31.9	113	190	2.0	393	598	249	.30	.24	1.7	9
Potato Soup with Soybean Concentrate		8	68	2.4	3.2	0	1	2	8.4	23	48	.6	476	260	38	.08	.03	.6	9
Potato Soup with Soy Concentrate, 1		8	111	5.5	3.3	0	2	2	15.9	33	95	1.5	480	359	46	.13	.06	.9	9
Potato Soup with Soy Concentrate, 2		8	74	2.6	3.2	0	1	2	9.5	24	52	.8	508	314	263	.10	.04	.8	13
Potato Soup with Soy Concentrate, 3		8	116	5.7	3.3	0	1	2	17.0	34	99	1.6	512	413	270	.14	.07	1.0	13
Potato Soup with Evaporated Milk.		8	69	2.9	2.3	1	1	0	9.7	85	83	.3	509	275	126	.05	.12	.6	9
Potato Soup with Evaporated Milk, 1		8	112	6.0	2.4	1	1	0	17.2	95	130	1.2	513	374	133	.10	.15	.8	9
Potato Soup with Evaporated Milk, 2		8	75	3.2	2.3	1	1	0	10.7	86	87	.4	542	329	350	.06	.13	.8	13
Potatoe Soup with Evaporated Milk, 3		8	117	6.3	2.5	1	1	0	18.2	96	134	1.3	545	428	358	.11	.15	1.0	13
Russian Mashed Potato Soup		8	83	2.5	4.3	1	1	2	9.3	22	49	.7	462	243	14	.09	.04	.6	10

Soups

Soups	Nutritional Evaluation based on one portion of recipe divided into this many portions	Food Energy Calories	Protein Gm.	Fat Gm.	Fatty Acids Saturated Fats Gm.	Oleic Acid Gm.	Linoleic Acid Gm.	Carbohydrate Gm.	Calcium Mg.	Phosphorus Mg.	Iron Mg.	Sodium Mg.	Potassium Mg.	Vitamin A value I.U.	Thiamine Mg.	Riboflavin Mg.	Niacin Mg.	Ascorbic Acid Mg.
Cream of Tomato Soup	4	171	6.4	9.5	1	3	5	17.6	47	112	3.2	956	741	2006	.25	.10	2.0	41
Hearty Vegetable Soup	12	53	3.1	1.3	-	-	-	7.8	27	27	.7	561	130	1364	.03	.03	.4	12
Washington Chowder with Evaporated Milk	8	156	5.5	6.9	3	3	1	19.8	132	153	.7	482	427	868	.08	.21	1.3	17
Washington Chowder with Soy Cream	8	125	4.1	5.8	1	2	2	16.5	25	83	1.1	427	284	739	.11	.07	1.3	17
Washington Chowder with Soy Concentrate	8	129	3.6	6.3	1	2	3	16.7	23	79	1.0	427	355	720	.11	.07	1.3	17

Salads

Salads	Nutritional Evaluation based on one portion of recipe divided into this many portions	Food Energy Calories	Protein Gm.	Fat Gm.	Fatty Acids Saturated Fats Gm.	Oleic Acid Gm.	Linoleic Acid Gm.	Carbohydrate Gm.	Calcium Mg.	Phosphorus Mg.	Iron Mg.	Sodium Mg.	Potassium Mg.	Vitamin A value I.U.	Thiamine Mg.	Riboflavin Mg.	Niacin Mg.	Ascorbic Acid Mg.
Carrot Salad	4	193	3.5	16.2	8	3	4	11.2	38	71	1.3	369	271	6074	.09	.05	.5	8
Carrot Salad with Peanuts	4	216	7.3	17.0	3	6	6	11.7	48	120	1.2	445	319	6074	.14	.07	3.6	8
Cole Slaw	4	131	3.3	8.4	1	2	4	12.8	62	57	.9	20	248	155	.10	.07	.4	52
Combination Bean Salad with Piquant Dressing	4	228	10.8	7.8	1	2	4	31.0	89	194	3.7	216	610	950	.30	.13	1.4	19
Green Beans with Piquant Dressing	4	108	3.2	6.9	1	2	4	10.1	60	57	1.9	318	308	1156	.10	.08	.7	21
Lettuce Wedges with Piquant Dressing--1/2 cup	8	48	1.3	3.4	0	1	2	3.8	13	24	.5	87	141	288	.05	.03	.3	9
Lettuce Wedges with Piquant Dressing--1 cup	4	96	2.5	6.8	1	2	4	7.6	27	47	.9	174	282	576	.11	.07	.6	18
Loose Leaf Lettuce with Piquant Dressing--1/2 cup	8	49	1.4	3.4	0	1	2	4.0	27	25	.7	87	166	733	.05	.04	.3	12
Loose Leaf Lettuce with Piquant Dressing--1 cup	4	99	2.7	6.9	1	2	4	8.0	54	49	1.4	174	333	1466	.10	.08	.6	24
Eggplant Caviar (Lebanese)	8	87	1.2	7.3	1	2	4	5.6	19	25	.8	233	185	913	.06	.06	.5	54
Winter Garden Salad	4	289	2.3	28.7	3	8	15	8.4	92	41	1.5	281	250	3707	.07	.10	.8	74
Lemon-Honey French Dressing	8	132	.1	14.2	1	4	8	1.8	1	2	.1	15	23	58	.01	.01	.1	4
Piquant Tomato Dressing	4	267	6.0	20.2	2	6	11	18.0	46	105	1.9	506	548	1166	.22	.10	1.2	42
Sour Cream Garlic Dressing	8	51	2.0	4.4	0	1	2	1.7	13	28	.5	57	8	24	.05	.02	.1	3
Soy Mayonnaise	24	30	.7	2.7	0	1	1	1.2	4	9	.2	38	3	8	.02	.01	0.0	1

NUTRITIONAL EVALUATION

Spreads etc.	Nutritional evaluation based on one portion of recipe divided into this many portions	Food Energy Calories	Protein Gm.	Fat Gm.	Saturated Fats Gm.	Oleic Acid Gm.	Linoleic Acid Gm.	Carbo-hydrate Gm.	Calcium Mg.	Phos-phorus Mg.	Iron Mg.	Sodium Mg.	Potas-sium Mg.	Vitamin A value I.U.	Thiamine Mg.	Ribo-flavin Mg.	Niacin Mg.	Ascorbic Acid Mg.
Bran--2 cups	--	170	12.8	3.7	--	--	--	49.4	95	1019	11.9	7	895	0	.57	.28	16.8	0
Dried Apricot-Date Jam	14	67	.9	.1	0	0	0	17.1	17	20	1.0	4	208	1326	.02	.03	.6	4
Cranberry Sauce	24	37	.1	.1	0	0	0	10.1	5	3	.2	20	23	12	.01	.01	.1	4
Orange-Honey-Whipped Margarine	32	67	.1	5.7	1	2	2	5.0	6	2	0.0	70	10	244	0.00	0.00	0.0	3
Soybean Concentrate	--	302	11.3	24.7	3	7	13	11.8	75	184	2.8	2	569	28	.37	.10	.7	4
Soybean Concentrate with Added Calcium	--	302	11.3	24.7	3	7	13	11.8	180	184	2.8	2	569	28	.37	.10	.7	4
Whipped Topping from Powdered Soy Milk--large	6	274	18.6	18.5	2	4	10	12.4	122	0	0.0	0	0	0	0.00	0.00	0.0	0
Whipped Topping from Powdered Soy Milk--small	8	206	13.9	13.9	2	3	7	9.3	92	0	0.0	0	0	0	0.00	0.00	0.0	0
Soy Cream	8	275	15.4	21.0	1	4	8	10.0	95	218	3.6	0	0	181	.36	.14	.9	0
Soy Sour Cream	8	51	1.9	4.5	0	1	2	1.2	12	27	.5	30	0	23	.05	.02	.1	0
Soy Sour Cream with Parsley and Chives	8	56	2.2	4.6	0	1	2	2.1	26	34	.8	31	49	879	.06	.04	.2	11
Burger Relish with Almonds	16	70	1.7	6.5	1	4	2	2.3	21	45	.4	86	73	1	.02	.08	.3	2
Burger Relish with Soybeans	24	20	.7	1.6	0	0	1	1.1	5	12	.2	57	39	2	.02	.01	0.0	1
Peanut Butter-Yeast Spread	11	198	11.9	14.3	2	6	5	9.4	44	339	2.9	159	420	0	2.20	.63	8.9	0
Savory Yeast Spread Evaporated Milk	16	66	6.0	2.5	1	1	1	6.2	48	264	2.5	90	293	23	2.22	.63	5.4	0
Savory Yeast Spread Soy Milk	16	59	5.8	2.0	0	1	1	5.7	32	253	2.6	147	272	3	2.22	.61	5.4	0
Tahini Sauce	8	128	3.2	11.8	2	4	5	4.2	197	104	1.8	125	132	6	.17	.04	.9	3
Tartar Sauce	24	19	.5	1.7	0	1	1	.7	6	9	.2	30	30	84	.02	.01	0.0	3
Tomato Ketchup	8	45	.9	1.9	0	1	1	6.6	8	17	.4	195	165	577	.04	.03	.5	20

Index

Entrées

Homemade Gluten and Other Wheat Recipes

Breads

Quick Breads

Crackers and Flat Breads

Waffles and Other Breakfast Foods

Soybean Magic

Desserts

Vegetables

Soups

Salads

Spreads, Relishes, etc.

Beverages

Preserving Foods and Preserved Foods Recipes

Photography, Elwyn Spaulding,
Edyth Young Cottrell, Howard E. McClure,
James Fisher, *Loma Linda, California*

Typography, Friedrich Typography
Santa Barbara, California

Printing and Binding
Publishers Press and Mountain States Bindery
Salt Lake City, Utah